Understanding
Trauma-Related
Disorders from
a Mind-Body
Perspective

DOES
STRESS
DAMAGE
THE BRAIN?

DOES STRESS DAMAGE THE BRAIN?

Understanding Trauma-Related Disorders from a Mind-Body Perspective

J. Douglas Bremner

W. W. Norton & Company

New York   London

For information about permission to reproduce selections
from this book, write to Permissions, W. W. Norton & Company, Inc.,
500 Fifth Avenue, New York, NY 10110

Composition by Bytheway Publishing Services
Manufacturing by Haddon
Book design by Charlotte Staub
Production manager: Leeann Graham

The Library of Congress has cataloged the hardcover edition as follows:

Bremner, J. Douglas, 1961–
Does stress damage the brain? : understanding trauma-related
disorders from a mind-body perspective / J. Douglas Bremner
p   cm.
Includes bibliographical references and index.
ISBN 0-393-70474-2
1. Post-traumatic stress disorder.   2. Traumatism.   3. Stress
(Psychology).   4. Stress (Physiology).   5. Neuropsychiatry.
I.   Title.

RC552.P67 B735 2002
616.85′21—dc21   2002070265

ISBN 0-393-70474-2 (pbk.)

W. W. Norton & Company, Inc., 500 Fifth Avenue,
New York, N.Y. 10110
www.wwnorton.com

W. W. Norton & Company, Ltd., Castle House, 75/76 Wells Street,
London W1T 3QT

1   2   3   4   5   6   7   8   9   0

DEDICATED TO

my wife Viola

and children

Dylan & Sabina

CONTENTS

PREFACE

This book represents the synthesis of more than 10 years of research, reflection, and observations as a clinical psychiatrist on the effects of stress on the individual. As a researcher in the field of clinical psychiatry, I have long been fascinated by the possibility that experience can have lasting effects on the individual, and have wondered whether experience can even change how the brain works. This has led me to wonder whether what we see, hear, and feel can lead to changes in the brain or, phrased more simply in a single provocative question, can stress damage the brain? If stress-related psychiatric symptoms have their basis in the brain, can stress-induced changes in brain structure and function lead to psychiatric disorders such as post-traumatic stress disorder (PTSD) and depression?

The idea that stress damages the brain could have important implications for mental health. A group of psychiatric disorders related to stress, what I call *trauma-spectrum disorders*, could share in common a basis in brain abnormalities that are caused by stress. Trauma-spectrum disorders are those that are known to be linked to stress, including PTSD, dissociative disorders, borderline personality disorder, adjustment disorder, depression, and anxiety. This view of trauma-spectrum disorders may be different than the commonly accepted view in psychiatry that psychiatric disorders are completely different from one another, and have different causes. It would mean that our current methods for diagnosing psychiatric disorders are incorrect, being based on the faulty logic that these are truly discrete disorders. The idea of trauma-spectrum disorders would help to explain why there is so much overlap in biological findings and bases in the brain between the different psychiatric disorders that are related to stress. It would also explain why if you have one of the trauma-related disorders, you are much more likely to have another one of the disorders.

The idea of a trauma-spectrum group of disorders came out of research conducted by colleagues and myself, and by groups at other institutions, on the effects of traumatic stress on the brain. As a young psychiatry doctor in training, I noticed that many of my patients with PTSD from the Vietnam War had trouble remembering their appointments, or remembering what they had for breakfast that morning. However, when they showed me pictures from their scrapbooks of Vietnam, they could remember events from 30 years before as if they had happened the day before.

During that period of my training, a combat veteran called me in the middle of the night, trapped in the midst of a flashback. He kept saying over and over, "Got to get them out, got to get them out" for 20 minutes before he was able to slow down and have a regular conversation with me. During those 20 minutes, when he was not aware of what I was saying and was lost in his own world, it occurred to me that this patient was like others I had seen who were having seizures. It turned out that he had been a fireman in Vietnam and had to go into burning helicopters and pull soldiers out. Sometimes he was able to save people, but at other times he was unable to get the soldiers out in time, and all that he pulled out were charred bodies. The night he phoned me he had rushed into a burning house and pulled out two small children. He had, in fact, been a hero. However, this event had triggered a flashback that took him back to Vietnam. Flashbacks are a symptom of PTSD that represent playing out a traumatic event in an altered state, something we call *dissociation*, which is discussed in more detail later in this book. Patients often describe flashbacks as if a movie were playing in front of their eyes, complete with a visual image, sounds, and smells. When patients are having flashbacks, as my veteran was here, they are unaware of what is going on in the present. When I experienced my first patient having a flashback, I was impressed at the automatic and uncontrollable nature of the symptoms, which were similar to those in patients I had seen who were having seizures. I wondered if, like seizures, they represented a neurological rather than a psychological condition, as they were considered to be at that time. If so, flashbacks should involve the same brain areas that are most affected by seizures, specifically the hippocampus (which is affected in 80% of patients with epilepsy).

At this time we became aware of research in animals showing that stress has long-term effects on the brain. Studies in humans exposed to extreme stress showed similar results, including the effects of stress on the brain, to those found in animal studies. The idea that stress causes neurological damage has natural implications for diagnosis and treatment of trauma-related disorders. If a single type of neurological insult follows exposure to stress, then it makes sense that all psychiatric disorders related to stress have in common one type of neurological deficit.

A correlate of the theme that stress has effects on the brain and neurological function is that stress has effects on all parts of the body, including the heart, immune systems, digestion, immunity, and could even be related to cancer. This leads us to the natural conclusion that distinctions between mind and brain, body and spirit, and psychology and biology are artificial, and that doctors do a disservice to their patients, and patients do a disservice to themselves, by perpetuating this false dichotomy. If doctors start listening to their patients and patients listen to their own hearts, minds, and bodies, we may go a long way toward alleviating the debilitating effects of stress on our lives.

During the course of my career working with trauma survivors it has become increasingly clear that a large portion of the general population of our country is suffering from PTSD from a variety of causes. At the time of this writing, the scope of trauma has expanded to include our entire society in the aftermath of the terrorist attacks on New York and Washington. There are many patterns of response to the current tragedy that are similar to other traumatic events from prior history; however, in many respects this particular event was unprecedented in world history. One thing I can say from my experience is that our country will be sorting out our responses to this tragic event for many years to come. If knowledge is power, then our citizens will benefit from a greater knowledge of the potential effects of traumatic stress on mind, brain, body, and spirit.

PREFACE TO

PAPERBACK

EDITION

It is two years since the initial publication of *Does Stress Damage the Brain?* The publication of this book has been an eye-opening experience for me. What was originally designed to be a technical book for mental health professionals has been eagerly grabbed up by a wide range of individuals, including mental health professionals, patients, family members, and other interested individuals. The title has attracted many to its central question. Does stress really damage the brain? This is the question that we all would really like answered.

A fundamental premise of *Does Stress Damage the Brain?* is that the physiological stress reaction is an adaptive response to challenges in the environment. Our stress response (release of neurohormones like cortisol and adrenaline) help us to think fast, run hard, and fight back. Brain areas like the hippocampus, amygdala, and frontal cortex help us to remember threatening situations, respond quickly, and not over-react when there is no true threat. In crucial life-threatening situations these responses can be life-saving. Stress response systems were designed for survival. However, nature was not prepared for childhood abuse, rape, crime, random violence, and technology, which developed automobiles that can become death traps. Chronic exposure to these stressors from which there is no escape can lead to imbalances in the neurohormonal systems and changes in the structure and function of parts of the brain involved in memory and emotion. This doesn't happen to everyone, but a fundamental premise of *Does Stress Damage the Brain?* is that these changes in physiology and the brain lead to symptoms of posttraumatic stress disorder (PTSD), including nightmares, avoidance, flashbacks, feeling cut off from others, hyperarousal, memory and concentration problems, increased startle, and sleep disturbance. *Does Stress Damage the Brain?* introduces the concept of *trauma spectrum disorders*, or the idea that several disorders and symptom complexes, including PTSD, anxiety, depression, substance abuse, dissociation, somatic complaints, and eating disorders, are overlapping and have a common root in psychological trauma. The book also describes how psychological trauma can actually lead to changes in your body, resulting in physical disorders like heart disease, cancer, asthma, ulcers, memory loss, and thinning of the bones. But *Does Stress Damage the Brain?* also offers hope for the trauma survivor. It describes late-breaking research that has found that specific treatments lead to a reversal of the effects of stress on the brain and the body's physiology.

This book is designed to provide all of the information needed to understand the science behind the effects of stress on the brain and the body. After a general overview, the first few chapters describe the details of brain imaging and neuroscience that enhance the reader's understanding of the science that has led to such exciting discoveries in the field of psychological trauma. Readers more interested in the effects of traumatic stress on one's psyche can focus on Part II, where a history of the development of the traumatic stress concept is described, as well as a range of examples of the effects of stress on the individual, causes and risk factors for trauma-related disorders, and important research results. Finally, the book concludes with treatment options for PTSD and other trauma-related disorders, with descriptions of how these treatments actually work, and how they change brain and biology.

In my years as a psychiatrist and a researcher focusing on the field of PTSD I have found that education is what helps trauma survivors and PTSD patients the most. You have to take responsibility for teaching yourself as much as possible about stress and stress responses. Education actually helps in the recovery process. If you are a trauma survivor and have been affected by your traumatic experiences, I hope this book will be the first step in your recovery. If you know someone who is a trauma survivor, reading this book will help you understand them so that you can assist in their healing process.

Understanding
Trauma-Related
Disorders from
a Mind-Body
Perspective

DOES
STRESS
DAMAGE
THE BRAIN?

part one   MIND & BRAIN FROM A TRAUMA-CENTRIC PERSPECTIVE

CHAPTER ONE — The Lasting Effects of Stress on Mind and Brain

It seemed that out of battle I escaped
Down some profound dull tunnel, long since scooped
Through granites which titanic wars had groined.
Yet also there encumbered sleepers groaned,
Too fast in thought or death to be bestirred. . . .
Then, as I probed them, one sprang up, and stared
With piteous recognition in fixed eyes,
Lifting distressful hands as if to bless.
And by his smile, I knew that sullen hall,
By his dead smile, I knew we stood in Hell, . . .
And no guns thumped, or down the flues made moan.
"Strange friend," I said "here is no cause to mourn"
"None," said that other, "save the undone years, . . .
I am the enemy you killed, my friend.
I knew you in this dark: for you so frowned
Yesterday through me as you jabbed and killed,
I parried; but my hands were loath and cold,
Let us sleep now" . . .

—From "Strange Meeting,"
by Wilfred Owen

Stress Affects the Entire Body

We carry our stress with us for a lifetime. Our bodies have biological systems that respond to life-threatening danger, acting like fear alarm systems that are critical for survival. When faced with a threatening situation, such as being attacked by a tiger, a flood of hormones and chemical messengers is released into our brains and bloodstream almost instantly. These hormones rapidly shift our energy resources away from noncritical tasks, and toward more critical tasks that are required for survival. Energy is shunted to the brain and the muscles to help us think fast and run quick, and away from the stomach and digestive track as well as the reproductive system, since we are not now under a time pressure to eat lunch or reproduce. This stress-responsive activation of biological systems helps us to shift our priorities in use of resources and energy, and to focus the body in a variety of ways on doing whatever it takes to survive. If we later encounter a similar threatening situation, specific fear-related areas in the brain turn on more quickly and activate the fear areas with greater efficiency, because the stress hormones more strongly engrave the circumstances surrounding the life-threatening event in memory, by acting on brain areas that are involved in memory.

The short-term survival response can be at the expense of long-term function. For instance, release of stress hormones can cause thinning of the bones, ulcers, and damage to a part of the brain involved in memory. Surprisingly, the same biological systems that help us survive life threats can also damage the brain and body.

A central thesis of this book is the development of the idea that stress-induced brain damage underlies and is responsible for the development of a spectrum of trauma-related psychiatric disorders, making these psychiatric disorders, in effect, the result of neurological damage. Another primary thesis of this book is that there is no true separation between what happens in the brain and what goes on elsewhere in the body. Our old distinctions— between mind and brain, psychology and biology, mental and physical—increasingly appear to have no meaning as science deepens our understanding of how the mind and body function in health and disease. This leads us to the final thought that stressors, acting through a depression or disruption of mental processes, can translate directly into an increased risk for poor health outcomes, including heart disease, cancer, and infectious disease, in addition to the increased risk for psychiatric disorders. Brain areas responsible for memory play an important role in the stress response. It makes sense that a good memory and quick thinking would be important for survival. If a large and scary animal jumps out at you when you are strolling through the jungle, you need to know whether that is your playful but loyal dog Spot who is returning from a run, or whether it is that human-eating tiger that almost had you for lunch last summer. If you react like your life is going to come to an end every time Spot jumps out of the bushes, you won't be very happy in the great outdoors. Ironically, you also may not be as likely to survive. If you have an all-out fear reaction every time you hear "Boo," you may not be able to respond as efficiently as you should when a real threat appears. Like Peter who cried "Wolf" too often, your body's defense systems may become depleted by repeated responses to nonthreatening events, so that when a truly threatening event comes along they are not able to respond in the way that they should. In a similar way, traumatized individuals who have excessive fear reactions for even the most trivial events are ironically in greater danger than most people, because when they encounter a truly dangerous situation they are already depleted and not able to mount as good a defense as they otherwise would have been able to do.

This is why having a good memory can really help you out in a jam. It shouldn't be surprising that the same parts of our brains that play a role in memory and quick thinking also play an important role in the stress response. Hormones such as cortisol and adrenaline, which are released during stress, bathe these brain areas and change their function, bringing them back to a similar state as during prior dangers when there was also a stress induced outpouring of the stress hormones cortisol and adrenaline. These hormones help us check our mental notes for the current event against past dangers, and think quickly about what is the right thing to do, be it to run away or stay and fight. The stress response mobilizes brain systems and brain areas that mediate memory and responses to stress that are critical for survival. However, with excessive or repetitive stress, some individuals can develop long-term changes in these same brain systems that mediate memory and the stress response. Like a car engine that burns out on the excessive speeds of the Autobahn (the German freeway where there are no speed limits), our bodies can become irreversibly damaged by our own stress responses. Our stress response systems are fine-tuned to adapt to changes in our environment. However, like a thermometer that is exposed to a really hot summer, after awhile it can no longer respond to excessive increases in the heat, and doesn't turn the temperature down. In the same way, individuals exposed to repeated stress develop dysfunction in their stress response systems, and can no longer properly adapt to new stressors. Stress responses that are useful for short-term survival can be at the expense of long-term function.

The stress hormones cortisol and adrenaline mediate many of the negative long-term consequences of stress on the body. Although cortisol released during the time of the life-threatening danger is one of the most important factors that help us to survive, it may have long-term negative effects on several organ systems. The parts of the body that are most sensitive to the "wear and tear" effects of stress over time are (logically enough) those areas that are mobilized during the stress response (McEwen & Stellar, 1993; Seeman, Singer, Rowe, Horwitz, & McEwen, 1997). Many of these effects are mediated by increased release of the body's hormonal systems—including cortisol—that act like fire alarms to mobilize the resources of the body in life-threatening situations. The hormones cortisol and adrenaline travel throughout the body and brain and have a number of actions that are critical for survival during life-threatening danger. Adrenaline has a number of actions in the body, including stimulation of the heart to beat more rapidly and squeeze harder with each contraction, whereas norepinephrine acting in the brain helps to sharpen focus and stimulate memory. Blood pressure increases to increase blood flow and delivery of oxygen and glucose (necessary energy stores for the cells of the body to cope with the increased demand). There is a shunting of blood flow away from the gut (digestion of the pasta salad you had for lunch can wait for awhile) and toward the brain and the muscles of the arms and legs (you need to think fast and/or run hard to get away from the threat). The spleen increases the release of red blood cells, which allows the body to send more oxygen to the muscles. The liver converts glycogen to glucose, the type of sugar that can be immediately used. Breathing becomes heavy, so that extra oxygen can get to the lungs, and the pupils dilate for better vision. Release of endogenous opiates acts on the brain to dull our sense of pain, so that the pain of a physical injury incurred during an attack does not impair our ability to escape from the situation. More delayed stress responses include release of cortisol, which dampens the immune system (we are less likely to die immediately from an infection than from our attacker), and conversion of fat to glucose in the liver (Figure 1.1).

These stress hormones can have more insidious, detrimental long-term effects. For instance, excessive levels of cortisol result in a thinning of the lining of the stomach, which increases the risk for gastric ulcers. Cortisol also results in a thinning of the bones, which increases the risk of osteoporosis or bone fractures in older people, or impairment in reproduction (which can play havoc with the desire of stressed-out young professionals to start a family). Other diseases that have been linked to stress include heart disease, diabetes, and asthma. Stress also impairs the immune system, which can lead to an increase in infections and possibly even increased rates of cancer. Chronic stress with decreased blood flow to the intestines can result in chronic ulcers.

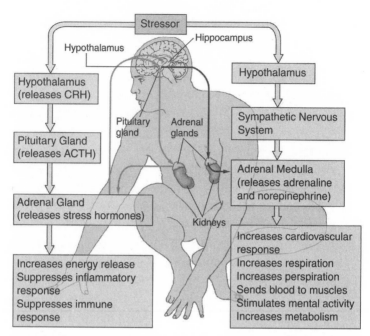

Figure 1.1 When the body experiences stress, a series of biological changes occurs. There is activation of the sympathetic nervous system, which in turn activates the adrenal medulla, which secretes adrenaline and noradrenaline, leading to increased psychological arousal. There is also activation of the HPA (hypothalamic-pituitary-adrenal) axis. Activation of the hypothalamus leads to the release of hormones that travel through the bloodstream to the pituitary gland, which in turn secretes other hormones and activates the adrenal gland, which releases the stress hormone, cortisol.

Public wisdom emphasizes the relationship between stress and heart disease; however, there has been surprisingly little research actually conducted in this area. The studies that have been conducted do support such a connection, and in fact suggest that stress-related hormonal release may represent the mechanism of increased risk for heart disease. Cortisol released during stress acts to increase blood pressure, heart rate, and cholesterol, and raises blood levels of adrenaline (norepinephrine and epinephrine; McEwen & Stellar, 1993).

All of these factors can lead to an acceleration of atherosclerosis. Studies in animals in fact have found direct evidence for the damaging effects of stress on blood vessels in the heart (Rozanski, Blumenthal, & Kaplan, 1999). Studies in monkeys undergoing chronic social stress, related to changes in their hierarchies of which monkey is dominant at any one particular time, found a relationship between stress and accelerated cardiovascular disease (Kaplan, Manuck, Adams, Weingand, & Clarkson, 1987; Kaplan, Manuck, Clarkson, Lusso, & Taub, 1982). Monkeys undergoing stressors had increased activation of cortisol and norepinephrine systems, which led to the accelerated development of arteriosclerosis. Stressed monkeys had increased injury to the inner lining of the blood vessels in the heart, which led to greater clumping of platelets and the forming of blood clots, increasing the risk for heart attack (Kaplan et al., 1982, 1987). These studies showed that there is a direct link between stress and the development of heart disease, and in fact the body's hormonal response to stress is involved in the mechanism for the development of heart disease.

Stress-related release of cortisol and other metabolic and endocrine stress-related changes may also increase susceptibility to stroke. For instance, prisoners of war from WWII were found to be seven times more likely to have had a stroke at some time in their lives than were non-POWS (Brass & Page, 1996).

Stress interacts with other aspects of behavior to increase the risk for poor physical health. For instance, women who were sexually abused in childhood, even those without any psychiatric disorders, were found to be twice as likely to smoke as were nonabused women. Having the diagnosis of posttraumatic stress disorder (PTSD) increased the risk for smoking even more. Experiments showed that exposure to reminders of their trauma increased the craving for cigarettes, as well as PTSD symptoms, in patients with PTSD. Administration of nicotine reduced both craving and anxiety and PTSD symptoms. Cigarettes actually act on the brain to release a neurotransmitter called dopamine, which has a beneficial effect on reward centers in the brain. Thus, both stress and PTSD can increase the risk of heart disease and cancer, acting through an increase in risky behaviors like cigarette smoking.

Effects of Stress on Mental Health

Stress has been associated with a number of mental disorders including posttraumatic stress disorder (PTSD), depression, substance abuse, somatic disorders, dissociation, and anxiety. PTSD by definition requires exposure to a threat to life for its diagnosis. PTSD symptoms include nightmares, flashbacks, feeling worse with reminders of the event, intrusive memories of the event, avoidance of reminders, problems with concentration, gaps in memory, feeling like there is no future, problems relating to others or feeling loving feelings for others, guilt for surviving the event, hyperarousal, hypervigilance, sleep disturbance, and startle responses.

With the recent attack on the World Trade Center and the Pentagon, our country has thousands of individuals who are coping with their responses to the trauma at the time of this writing (Figure 1.2). The images are everywhere in the nation's media and are helping to keep fresh the memory of the trauma itself (Figure 1.3).

Psychiatric disorders related to stress, including both PTSD and depression, may confer their own additional risk for poor physical health. Patients with both depression (which is related to stress in many cases) and heart disease are about five times as likely to die suddenly in the aftermath of a heart attack than are patients with heart disease but not depression. Stress has been closely linked with the onset of depression, and it is not known

Figure 1.2 The reality of the possibility of unpredictable threats to our lives has entered into the national consciousness (© AFP/Corbis).

whether stress has a direct effect on cardiovascular disease in patients who also develop depression, or whether the effects are mediated directly through the depressive disorder. For example, there are several findings in depression that may influence cardiovascular function. Patients with depression have increased levels of cortisol and adrenaline. As mentioned earlier, increased levels of cortisol and adrenaline/norepinephrine can affect cardiovascular function in several ways, including increasing heart rate and blood pressure, damaging the inner surface or causing constriction of the blood vessels in the heart, or affecting the function of platelets that are involved in forming blood clots. Both stress and depression may also decrease the variability of the heart's rhythm, which is known to be associated with an increased risk for sudden death.

PTSD has also been associated with an increased risk for several physical disorders. PTSD patients are at increased risk for heart disease, above and beyond the risk associated with expo-

Figure 1.3 Images that would have been inconceivable before September 11, 2001, are now part of the images of the United States (© AFP/Corbis).

DOES STRESS DAMAGE THE BRAIN?

sure to stress. New evidence suggests that PTSD, apart from the influence of stress per se, may increase the risk of several other physical disorders, including diabetes, ulcers, asthma, and possibly cancer. As mentioned earlier, PTSD is associated with an increased risk for smoking, which may lead to increased risk for heart disease and cancer. Treating PTSD may therefore improve more than just the misery associated with living with this disorder—it may also lead to an improvement in physical health symptoms.

The effects of stress on physical health appear to be caused by a disruption of the balance between different organs of the body, or homeostasis. According to this model, stress results in long-term wear and tear, which leads to poor health and an increased risk for mortality.

A number of research studies are also consistent with the idea that stress can also have detrimental effects on brain structure and function. Stress has detrimental effects on memory and cognition that can lead to long-term dysfunction. This is at least partially mediated through the effects of stress on a brain area involved in learning and memory called the hippocampus. Elevated levels of the stress hormone cortisol during stress can bring about damage to this brain area. Therefore, stress is often associated with deficits in memory, specifically the ability to learn new information. Chronically elevated levels of cortisol may also affect mood, leading to depression and feelings of fatigue.

It may seem paradoxical that the stress response systems responsible for the survival of the individual may actually have damaging effects. This paradox makes more sense when considered in the light of evolution. Surviving long enough to pass on your genes is the only concern from the standpoint of human evolution. Once you have performed this task, and have survived long enough for your offspring to become self-sufficient, from the standpoint of evolution it doesn't matter whether or not you live to a ripe old age. Therefore, more chronic and nonacute ailments, such as memory problems or gastric ulcers, are not as important as whether you released enough adrenaline and cortisol to escape the acute life-threatening situation. In prehistoric times, most people didn't live very long beyond the time it took to reproduce and raise their offspring, so the effects of stress didn't really matter anyway. It is only now that we are faced with the prospect of vast legions of the elderly who have sacrificed their minds to a stressful life devoted to building careers, and now are spending their well-earned retirement years wandering around a Walgreen's Pharmacy in South Florida, trying to remember which medication they need to buy for their gastric ulcers.

Behind the idea that stress can cause changes in physical health, and also result in neurological changes that underlie psychiatric disorders, is a seemingly radical idea that what you see, hear, smell, and feel—what comes in through the eyes, ears, nose, and fingertips—can cause lasting changes in physical health. This is a notion that crosses conventional thinking. Such conventional thinking is based on the false dichotomy between mind and brain/body that dates back to a French philosopher of the 18th Century, René Descartes. However, scientific discoveries of the past few decades are not consistent with the false dichotomy of Descartes. What we are learning is that events in the environment—including stressful experiences, education, and family events—can affect our physiology, even acting to modify our genetic material.

Overcoming the False Dichotomy of Biology and Psychology

The current false dichotomy between psychology and biology has not always existed. In fact, the word *psychology* derives from the word *psyche*, the Greek word for the soul or the spirit, and literally means "butterfly." For the Greeks, the psyche was an actual physical entity, although invisible, and would inhabit the body until the time of death, at which point it would travel to the

Underworld of Hades. The Greeks had other words for physical parts of the body that also had carried emotional meaning. For instance, the Greek word *thumos* represented a part of the body that was thought to be somewhere in the region of what we now know is the stomach. *Thumos* represented several qualities, including strength of will and character. Another organ, called *phrenos*, was located roughly in the area of the liver, which is the source of our word *diaphragm*. This word refers to psychological qualities and can be translated as mind or spirit. In fact, a number of psychological, spiritual, or emotional qualities were ascribed to physical organs whose function today we would assign to the brain. The Greeks did not separate mind or spirit from body. They were eminently practical people and it would not have occurred to them that any part of a human being would not have a physical substance or substrate. Even their gods were considered in a very concrete and physical manner, as living their lives in a sort of superhuman way on top of Mount Olympus. It was with the origin of Christianity that humans developed the idea of pure spirit or mind as being separate from any aspect of our physical body. This led to the absurd practices of fasting, self-flagellating the body, or retreating to live in isolation on top of a pillar—practices of Christianity that were designed to punish or diminish the body in order to amplify the spirit, practices performed by early Christians that were considered insane by the ancient "pagan" Greeks. The dualistic way of thinking engendered by Christianity underlies our current false dichotomy between mind and brain—psychology and biology—that led to its absurd climax in the philosophical thinking of Descartes, who searched for a source of the soul somewhere in the brain, and ultimately decided that it lay in the pineal gland.

The false dichotomy between mind and brain led to the basis of the 20th-century view of psychology that was dominated by the thinking of Sigmund Freud. Under the influence of Freud and psychoanalysis, psychology was completely divorced from medicine and the physical sciences. This led to the absurd situation where, in my father's generation, young doctors spent 10 years studying medicine and basic sciences, only to "unlearn" the scientific principles and way of evaluating information in their subsequent psychiatric education and "training psychoanalyses." However, the knowledge that strong emotions or things that happen to you can affect your physical health has continued to be preserved in folk wisdom, like some long-lost harbinger from the ancients, in the popular knowledge that extreme emotions can influence function of the heart, stomach, and other physical organs. Over the past two decades, there has been an explosion of research and scientific knowledge establishing that what you experience and what you think and feel can have profound effects on your body's physiology and on your brain. This has led us to the point where we are now ready to reintegrate mind and brain, body and spirit.

This new way of thinking about the effects of stress on the individual has important implications for mental health. Mental disorders were previously felt to have no basis in the body or the brain. Gradually, scientists came to realize that many mental disorders may have their basis in stress-induced alterations in brain function and structure. Even more recently we started to realize that not only the brain, but other organ systems as well, may mediate so-called mental disorders. We may be moving back to the old Greek concepts of *thumos* and *phrenos*, examining the effects of stress on a range of "physical" and "mental" outcomes, including heart function, digestion, metabolism, immunity, and brain function. The concepts of *thumos* and *phrenos* may be particularly applicable for those mental disorders that have long been recognized as being associated with stress exposure, such as PTSD, anxiety, and depression, as opposed to other mental disorders, like schizophrenia, that have not been associated specifically with stress and were long believed to be have their basis in the brain, genetics, and abnormal brain development. This new way of thinking about the effects of stress and other environmental factors on the individual will be beneficial for everyone in our society, not just for those who are diagnosed with mental disorders. In an increasingly stressful society, it will be useful to think about the effects of stress on the entire individual, in the brain, the heart, and other physical systems. This reversal of the false dichotomy of mind and brain established by the philosophy of Descartes will have beneficial effects for promoting health and happiness in everyone.

A central theme of this book is that stress can have lasting effects on the individual, leading to changes in function of the brain as well as other physical systems. An important point to be made in the ensuing chapters is that these changes in the brain underlie many of the symptoms of mental disorders related to stress, including PTSD and depression, as well as other disorders whose basis is probably at least in part due to exposure to stress, including alcohol and substance abuse, eating disorders, borderline personality disorders, somatization disorders, and anxiety disorders.

The Creeping Epidemic of Abuse and Other Traumas

In recent years, there has been a rapid change in thinking about the effects of stress on the individual. This can be seen in the increased number of reports in the media and our legal system of childhood abuse. Could it be that we have a new epidemic of childhood abuse? Or has there been a change in people's attitudes about whether or not to keep these terrible secrets within the family or to bring them out into public view? Likewise, there has been an incredible expansion in our direct exposure to traumatic stressors on a daily basis. You only have to turn on the television to see a shooting at a public school taking place in front of our very eyes in real time, or to see round-the-clock coverage of a hostage standoff. The rapid expansion of technology has made it possible for us to see all the terrible things that are happening everywhere in the world at any time. This has been both a blessing and a curse. If it weren't for the media, people in Atlanta and Omaha would have no knowledge—or fears—related to anthrax exposure or to terrorists flying airplanes into buildings. The fact is that Atlanta and Omaha have no real threat, and nothing significant to worry about. However, since we see what is happening in other places as it is occurring, and we feel that what happens anywhere in our country is affecting us equally, our sense of danger and fear is heightened. Our constant exposure to traumatic events has created the feeling that we are in an increasingly unsafe world. This goes against our natural need to feel safe, to work and take care of our families, and to not become distracted by the possibility that a traumatic event could intrude into our lives at any moment.

Nevertheless, in our society we are exposed to surprisingly high rates of traumatic stress in our daily lives. For instance, epidemiologic studies have shown that 25% to 50% of Americans are exposed to a psychological trauma at some time in their lives (Acierno, Kilpatrick, & Resnick, 1999), and the magnitude of psychological trauma in our society is much greater than most people think. There are about one million veterans of the Vietnam War who experienced the stress of combat between 1963 and 1971, which included seeing others killed or wounded, and being exposed to artillery or gunfire. Several hundred thousand veterans of the Gulf War experienced the stress of being in the Gulf War theater in 1990 and 1991. These soldiers were exposed to the constant stress of missile attacks, air raid alarms, participation in the assault on Kuwait that involved bulldozing Iraqi soldiers into their trenches, or passing hundreds of charred bodies that had been torched by the air strikes that preceded the land assault. Add to this the stress of exposure to burning oil wells and the possibility (or reality) of chemical attack, and this was not a happy time for many veterans. Equal numbers of veterans, or even greater, participated in combat in our previous wars, including Korea, World War I, and World War II.

Far greater, however, is the invisible epidemic of civilian traumas, which represents a major public health problem in our society today. Childhood abuse, car accidents, combat, rape, assault, and a wide variety of other severe traumas can all be associated with lasting effects on the individual. The American Psychiatric Association defines a traumatic event as something that is threatening to the self or someone close to you, accompanied by intense fear, horror, or helplessness. The definition of a traumatic event is outlined in the *Diagnostic and Statistical Manual* (the bible of the American Psychiatric Association). Exposure to a traumatic event, defined in this way, is required for the diagnosis of posttraumatic stress disorder. Researchers make a distinction between traumatic stressors such as these and what we call minor stressors, such as stress on the job or getting a divorce. We are not arguing that getting a divorce is not upsetting, but in order to study this area we need to have a definition of a severe stress that is clearly beyond the range of human experience. Nevertheless, as mentioned earlier, about half of the general population will experience a traumatic stress at some time in their lives. Of these, about 15% will develop chronic symptoms of posttraumatic stress disorder (Kulka et al., 1990). PTSD affects 8% of the population at some time in their lives, making it eight times more common than cancer or schizophrenia. PTSD is twice as common in women as it is in men (Kessler, Sonnega, Bromet, Hughes, & Nelson, 1995), which may be at least partially related to higher rates of abuse to women than of abuse to men.

Traumatic stress has a particularly dramatic toll on our littlest citizens, who are not able to protect themselves physically or verbally, and who lack the large and well-financed lobbying and advocacy groups that support people who own handguns or want to sell cigarettes. Studies using large samples of the national population showed that 16% of women were sexually abused at some time before their 18th birthday (McCauley et al., 1997), where sexual abuse was defined as rape, attempted rape, or sexual molestation. These figures add up to the startling fact that about 25 million women were sexually assaulted in childhood in this country, and probably about half as many men. There is documented evidence that one million children are abused in this country every year. In addition to PTSD, trauma survivors are at increased risk for other mental disorders, including depression, alcohol and substance abuse, anxiety disorders, somatic disorders, and dissociative disorders, as well as physical problems including heart disease, cancer, increased infections, gastric ulcers, and cognitive disorders. PTSD is 10 times more common than cancer, but our society spends one tenth as much for research on this disorder as for cancer research. This discrepancy is growing as our senators have recently urged a greater expenditure for cancer research, whereas no one is piping up on behalf of victims of childhood abuse and other traumas.

Posttraumatic stress disorder is an important possible outcome of exposure to traumatic stress. The symptoms of PTSD encompass a broad range of effects on memory, thinking, and behavior (Saigh & Bremner, 1999b). First and foremost is the requirement for a psychological trauma, currently defined as a threat to one's life or that of someone close. The diagnosis also requires one symptom in an intrusive memories category, including intrusive memories of the event, nightmares, feeling worse or increased physiological reactivity with reminders of the trauma, and flashbacks. Three symptoms are required from the avoidant category, including avoiding thinking of the event or reminders of the event, amnesia for the event, decreased interest in things, feeling cut off from others, feeling emotionally numb, or sense of foreshortened future. Two symptoms are also required from a hyperarousal category, including increased startle, hypervigilance, irritability, decreased concentration, and decreased sleep. These symptoms must last a month or longer and are associated with significant disturbance or distress in work, family, or social functioning.

Psychological trauma can result in other mental disorders besides PTSD. These include depression, substance and alcohol abuse, anxiety disorders, eating disorders, borderline personality disorder, and somatic disorders (Kulka et al., 1990). Why some individuals will develop PTSD following a psychological trauma and others will develop depression is not well understood. There is a complex interplay among environment, genetics, and other factors that determines what type of psychiatric disorders an individual will develop. However, we do know that there is a great deal of overlap, so that a traumatized individual is most likely to have several disorders, be they PTSD and depression, or PTSD and alcoholism, eating disorder and substance abuse, and so on. This suggests that there is a central "core" disorder (which we will argue has its basis in a stress-induced neurological deficit) that underlies all of these disorders. According to this argument, there are not separate distinct disorders, but instead a single spectrum of disorders that have been improperly categorized as distinct disorders by our current diagnostic schema (Figure 1.4).

Psychological trauma can lead to more than the development of specific psychiatric disorders: it can have a major impact on our total way of viewing the world and ourselves that transcends a specific disorder. We all have an illusion that the world is a safe and just place that we cherish. That's because we need such an illusion in order to survive. The world would be a terrible place if we could foresee the future, if we knew everything that was going to happen to us. We wouldn't be able to survive, we would become trembling and terrified infants who were afraid to take a single step on our own. It is our ignorance of the true nature of the world that keeps us sane. Traumatized patients with the diagnosis of PTSD often do not see the world as a safe place. A woman who has a child snatched from her arms by a

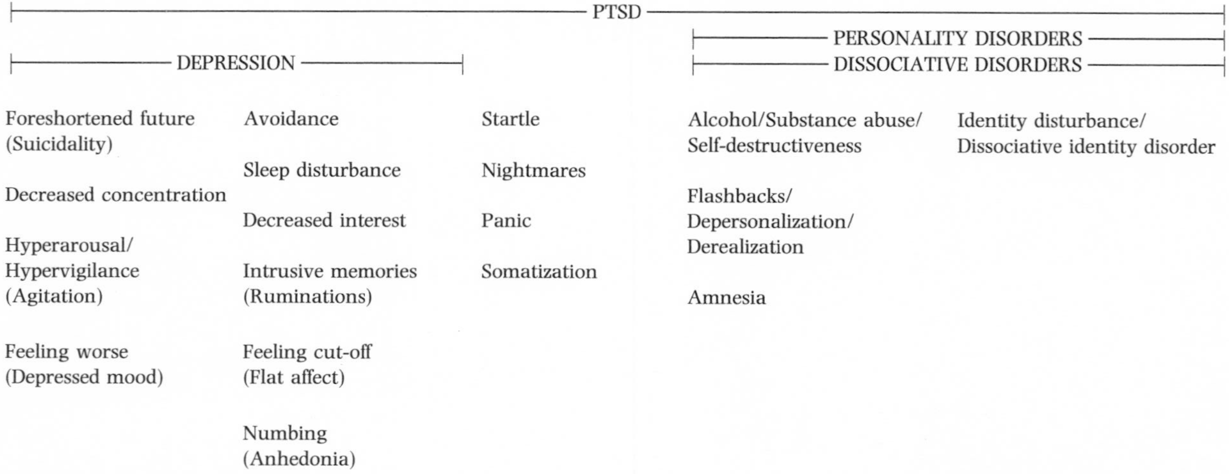

| | PTSD | | | PERSONALITY DISORDERS |
DEPRESSION				DISSOCIATIVE DISORDERS
Foreshortened future (Suicidality)	Avoidance	Startle	Alcohol/Substance abuse/Self-destructiveness	Identity disturbance/Dissociative identity disorder
Decreased concentration	Sleep disturbance	Nightmares		
Decreased interest			Flashbacks/	
Hyperarousal/Hypervigilance (Agitation)	Intrusive memories (Ruminations)	Panic	Depersonalization/Derealization	
		Somatization		
Feeling worse (Depressed mood)	Feeling cut-off (Flat affect)		Amnesia	
Numbing (Anhedonia)				

Figure 1.4 Trauma is associated with a range of psychiatric disorders, including PTSD, depression, personality disorders, and dissociative disorders. For example, hyperarousal in PTSD may be thought of as the agitation in depression, or feeling cut off from others in PTSD may be similar to the flat affect in depression. Many of the symptoms of these disorders are overlapping, suggesting that they have a common origin in trauma, hence the term *trauma-spectrum disorders*.

DOES STRESS DAMAGE THE BRAIN?

kidnapper will forever after live with the knowledge that anyone at any time could suddenly take another of her children from her. Someone who was taken hostage will never feel safe walking down a city street. In a sense it is as if such people are the ones who see things clearly, who know the truth, and yet knowing the truth makes it impossible for them to live in the world.

Not only individuals but entire nations and cultures can be traumatized as well. I was putting the finishing touches on this book when a group of terrorists hijacked four jetliners and crashed into the World Trade Center and the Pentagon, taking roughly 5,000 lives. The scenes of devastation and sad images such as firefighters rushing to certain death and families searching hospitals for survivors will stay in the national consciousness of the United States for as long as this generation is alive. This event surely had a traumatic effect on the nation. I saw one survey that said that 30% of Americans had trouble sleeping soon after the attack. In a way typical of stress responses, this figure had dropped to half of that amount one month later.

In addition, we now have the ongoing stress of terrorists sending anthrax in the mail to our leaders in the media and public sectors. Terrorists try to target aspects of life that we take for granted, such as the public mail system, in an effort to jolt us out of a sense of safety and security. By sending anthrax in the mail, these terrorists have created a sense of national fear, where every one is hanging on every piece of news, trying to understand what is happening and to protect themselves. The anthrax scare has effectively created a traumatic event for the entire nation, since every one feels the potential threat of receiving infected mail, to varying degrees.

Ten Thousand Years of Trauma

It hasn't only been in the 20th and 21st centuries that humankind has experienced psychological trauma. In many ways we are safer now than we have ever been in human history. In ancient times, it was not unusual when a city was conquered by a neighboring city, all of the buildings were razed to the ground, the men were slaughtered, the women were raped, and they and their children were sold into slavery (if they were lucky). We take for granted the fact that an enemy will not suddenly ride into our towns, burn down our houses, and kill our family. The security we have from such things happening is only a recent thing, and represents a small portion of the whole of human history. This has been recently highlighted by the fact that our sense of security in the mail system has been compromised by the anthrax scare.

In fact, psychological trauma has been with us for as long as we have existed as a species. Of course, our first experience of psychological trauma was our vulnerability to predators, the natural elements, and our marginal ability to obtain enough food to stay alive and provide a rudimentary shelter. It was not until humans learned how to cultivate the ground and raise food for their own consumption that acts of violence began to be perpetrated by one human being against another. Not until 10,000 years before Christ did humans develop agriculture, which made possible the collection of food stores in advance, which in turn made possible the stockpiling of food and other material goods that could potentially be stolen and plundered from other, weaker groups. It is no accident that the rise of socialized humans living in organized towns and cities and working together in a collective way to ensure the production of food occurred in parallel with the advent of warfare and the wholesale slaughter of peoples. In the beginnings of agricultural society lie the rudimentary elements of what one would call civilization. Agriculture first began in ancient Sumeria in the old cities that emerged between the Tigris and Euphrates rivers. One of the earliest activities in these ancient states was the development of irrigation, which permitted much larger areas of land to be cultivated over time. When one group of people began to acquire more wealth than their neighbors, this led the neighbors to want to take what wasn't theirs, with continuous efforts to attack cities, slaughter the men, and take into captivity the women and children. In fact, most of our history over the last few years has been characterized by this continuous effort to destroy other cities and collect the spoils of war. In the ancient world, there were sedentary cities with more established cultures living in the flat and fertile valleys adjacent to rivers, such as Mesopotamia or the Nile Delta, that were conquered periodically by more primitive nomadic groups of hunter warriors who descended from the North to plunder these cities.

The continued stress of warfare, rape, and plunder, and the continuous uncertainty associated with this pattern of living, must have taken a terrible toll on the people who lived in these cities and in these times. However, one of the most interesting aspects of the literature of these times is that there are few descriptions of the psychological impact of the experience of combat or other stressors. Most of the emphasis was on the actions of the individual in combat scenarios, stressing aspects such as courage and agility, with a view of the warrior as a hero whose honor came from performing great deeds in battle, and whose desire was to die gloriously in battle rather than to survive and continue living without land or city. The warrior hero actually relied on a continuous state of warfare in order to provide the opportunity to perform great deeds of combat, which helped to further his name as a warrior. Descriptions of the details of combat rarely took the point of view of women and children, other than to summarize details of their invariably dismal fate, which were presented without any emotional or psychological commentary.

Any descriptions that had to do with the mental life of the warrior focused on aspects of mental state that were relevant to whether or not the hero would perform acts on the battlefield that would increase his reputation, such as courage or bravery. The literature of warrior as hero dealt with mental phenomena such as matters of character that may have affected whether or not the warrior hero was able to endure severe hardship during individual combat or tests of endurance. Inherent in this outlook was, of course, the assumption that members of the warrior class would be able to show the necessary strength of character and endurance that was required to prevail in combat or triumph over adverse conditions. It was assumed that members of the lower classes did not have such strength of character or courage.

In spite of the emphasis on the warrior, there still are some hints in ancient literature of the negative effects of traumatic stress on the individual. Jonathan Shay (1994) wrote about similarities between descriptions of the effects of combat on Achilles in the *Iliad* and the effects of combat that he saw in veterans of the Vietnam War. Warriors across the centuries had in common a loss of the sense of meaning or order in the universe. The stress of combat and the loss of his friend led Achilles to go beserk in battle and no longer care about his own survival. Achilles was alienated from those around him, and felt like he had lost the sense of meaning in the battle between the Achaeans and Troy.

An emphasis on the warrior hero had a beneficial effect for primitive societies. The strong individual who placed greatest emphasis on success in combat was more useful than someone who focused on internal reflection and self-examination. In fact, excessive reflection or sensitivity to others could have been detrimental, in that it inhibited decisive action and the resolution to commit bold and destructive acts of war. It was only in the relative security of 5th-century Athens that self-reflection could take place to such a degree as to allow the development of philosophers such as Socrates. And this was only a temporary phenomenon that was quickly snuffed out in the ensuing advance of chaos and anarchy that swept up the ancient world and that lasted until relatively recent times.

It was only with the advent of the 20th century that we were able to develop more fully the concept of the life of the mind.

This was originally based in the Age of Reason during the 18th century, which saw the development of scientific thinking in our modern era, stemming from the thinking of the French philosophers Rousseau and Voltaire. Perhaps Rousseau could be thought of as the first psychologist, for in his work *Confessions* he was unique in devoting an entire book to an honest description of his mental state and his thoughts, fears, and motivations, both good and bad. This was the harbinger of an increased emphasis on self-reflection, and led to an expansion of interest in mental life that ultimately in the late 19th century resulted in an examination of mental disorders in the field of medicine.

An important crossroads between mind and brain, psychology and biology lies in the mental health consequences of stress. For the past two centuries, scientists and clinicians have been struggling with the potential consequences on mind, brain, and body of things that we see, hear, feel, and experience. An important clinical area related to stress is the effects of extreme stressors, such as war, on the individual. During the American Civil War, DaCosta (1871) first described a syndrome involving symptoms of exhaustion and increased physiological responsivity ("Soldier's Heart" or "DaCosta's Syndrome") seen in soldiers exposed to the stress of war. DaCosta felt that this syndrome was a physical disorder, involving the cardiovascular system, that was caused by the extreme stress of war. DaCosta's approach was similar to theories of the time later advanced by Kraepelin (1919), a Swiss psychiatrist from the late 19th century, who also believed that schizophrenia had its basis in the constitution, leading to abnormalities in the brain and physiology. Brain-based explanations of psychiatric disorders were discarded at the turn of the 20th century with the development of psychoanalysis.

The crossroads between the mind and medicine in the late 19th century lay in a disease called hysteria. The French physician Charcot brought the description, study, and treatment of hysteria into the medical mainstream. Charcot described hysteria as a condition involving symptoms of a loss of feeling and function in a particular part of the body not due to a definable neurological condition, which affected women more often than men. Charcot and his colleagues treated hysteria with a new technique called hypnosis. Following up the work of Charcot was a young Viennese neurologist named Sigmund Freud, who felt that mental disorders such as hysteria could be described using the new physical sciences such as physics, which he believed might represent a model for understanding the basis of these disorders in the brain. Much of the physics-based language of what was essentially a pseudoscience would become incorporated into the new discipline of psychoanalysis that was advanced by Freud. The study and treatment of hysteria similarly represented an important foundation for the development of the new science of the mind, which galvanized a new interest in the psychological content of the patients under the treatment of the proponent of this new science. This science of the mind led to the development of what would be called the talking cure, which we know today as psychotherapy.

Modern Psychiatry's Approach to Traumatic Stress

Working with Breuer, Freud looked for the causes of hysteria in childhood sexuality (Breuer & Freud, 1955). In Freud's first book, he described the famous case study of Anna O., who was suffering from hysterical symptoms that appeared to be related to witnessing sexual events during childhood. Freud originally believed that Anna O. was a victim of exposure to traumatic sexual experiences in childhood. Following this initial observation, he noticed an increasing number of women in his practice who reported exposure to sexual events in childhood. Could it be that Vienna was suffering from an epidemic of childhood sexual abuse? At the time, childhood sexual abuse was considered to be a rare phenomenon. Freud changed his views into the theory that *fantasies* of childhood sexuality were leading to neurotic behavior in his patients, rather than the *reality* of childhood sexual abuse (Freud, 1962). His final formulation of psychodynamic theory did not incorporate environmental events such as traumatic stress in the development of mental disorders.

In retrospect, we now know that much of this was probably wrong—that it is highly probable that many of these patients actually were sexually abused, perhaps including Freud's most famous patient, Anna O. However, this is not to detract from the unique contributions that Freud made. His greatest contribution was opening up our awareness of the life of the mind, and making us cognizant of the fact that many of the most important events of mental life take place below the surface of the water, in the domain of the unconscious, which is not readily available to conscious reflection. Modern science has, in fact, proven that the unconscious mind exists and plays a very important and perhaps dominant role in mental life, thus validating Freud's idea of the unconscious mind.

Freud's other major contribution was to solidify the importance of mental life or psychology as a suitable object of discussion or scientific investigation. Up until that time, we were largely operating according to the principles of the warrior class, in which action was paramount and the reflections of the individual were never really part of the common discussion of the culture. Because of this, there had been no framework for discussing the relationship between mental life and the functions of the brain. This view of psychological life as being essentially separated from the brain and the body dominated American psychiatry for the greater part of the 20th century. In many ways, psychoanalysis became like a religion that was not challenged by the usual methods of scientific practice, including the requirement to obtain empirical data to support or refute hypotheses. Psychoanalysis was more like a belief system than a scientific theory. In order to be able to provide an authoritative opinion about psychoanalysis, it was necessary to become properly trained in this area, which included long years of scientific training: completion of medical school, psychiatric residency training, followed by psychoanalytic training with a training analysis. Much of the latter part of this training was ostensibly outside of the usual pattern of scientific training, so that trainees were no longer able to reenter the mainstream of scientific dialogue. As one of my colleagues once told me, "Psychiatric training ruins the capacity for logical thought." Freud the neuroscientist would surely have flipped over in his grave.

Freud's era of psychoanalysis ushered in a new development in human culture that I call the advent of the postwarrior man. Most of 20th-century psychiatry was dominated by the emphasis of psychoanalytic theory on the workings of the mind, to the exclusion of an individual's actions, even to the perverse extreme of subverting an individual's actions to a reductionistic analysis based on speculations related to psychological life, encompassed by the term *acting out*. This term came from psychiatry and referred to the acting out of mental events in behavior, implying that actions had no real meaning in themselves. Perhaps the supreme embodiment of this figure would be the French philosopher John Pierce Sartre, author of *Being and Nothingness* and other works. For Sartre and other existentialist philosophers, the life of the mind was the only object of serious inquiry, and the life of action was not even worthy of discussion. However, civilization never really makes a clear transition from one era to the next. Our current society is not a discrete reflection of either the warrior man or the postwarrior man. One only has to turn on the television to see a quick example of the warrior man in action. He does not pause to reflect, nor is he troubled by self-doubts or criticisms that could get in the way of doing what is required. We also have examples of the postwarrior man, who is reflected in theater, novels, and other "higher" forms of our culture. It is safe to say that our current society is a mixture of the two—postwarrior man and warrior man—in the same way that many people still believe that the earth is flat, or that the sun revolves around the earth, several centuries after we were supposedly enlightened on these issues by Galileo and Copernicus.

It was only when we began to think about the life of the mind and psychology that we could accept the idea that stress could have a detrimental effect on mental life. However, even with the advent of Freudian psychoanalysis, the field of psychological trauma continued to emphasize the mental over environmental events, which were still relegated to the back seat of the field of psychiatry. With the advent of World War I, the large number of psychiatric casualties of combat temporally forced attention on the effects of war stress and led to the description of "combat fatigue" (Mott, 1919; Saigh & Bremner, 1999a). Psychiatrists described phenomena such as amnesia on the battlefield, where soldiers forgot their name or who they were. After the war, however, the effects of combat stress on the mind were soon forgotten. With World War II, interest in the mental health effects of war stress was revived. Again, psychiatrists described amnesia and other dissociative responses to trauma (Sargent & Slater, 1941; Torrie, 1944). It was also found that internment in concentration camps resulted in a number of symptoms that we would today attribute to traumatic stress, including feelings of detachment and estrangement from others, sleep disturbance and hyperarousal, as well as problems with memory and concentration.

The first edition of the *Diagnostic and Statistical Manual (DSM–I)* was published in 1952. In *DSM–I*, the first attempt to formulate a psychiatric diagnosis related to traumatic stress aided in adding *gross stress reaction* to our psychiatric nomenclature. Gross stress reaction described a series of stress-related symptoms in response to an extreme stressor that would be traumatic for almost anyone. This may have stemmed from the experience of military psychiatrists in WWII, who observed during the war that many normal men were having mental breakdowns in the face of combat. However, gross stress reaction specified that the individual must have a normal prestressor personality, and that the symptoms should naturally resolve with time. Gross stress reaction was dropped from the *DSM-II* in 1968. It wasn't until another major conflict, the Vietnam War, that the lasting effects of traumatic stress on the mind were fully recognized. This led to the inclusion of PTSD (with both acute and chronic types) as a disorder in the *DSM-III* in 1980. With *DSM-III*-based PTSD, we finally had a diagnosis that recognized the lasting pathological effects of traumatic stress. Because of the specific way in which PTSD develops, it is unique among psychiatric disorders in requiring exposure to an extreme stressor.

The dominance of American psychiatry by Freud's theories lasted until the advance of biological approaches to psychiatry, which have become increasingly prominent over the past 30 years. Biological psychiatrists placed great emphasis on genetic abnormalities leading to physiological changes, with their phenomenological expression in psychiatric disorders, and little emphasis on the role of environment in the genesis of psychopathology.

The biological psychiatrists who used this model, however, were really not much different from the psychoanalysts who preceded them. Both groups gave little or no credence to the role that *environment* could play in the development of psychiatric illness. It is clear that genetic factors do play an important role in psychiatric disorders. Most likely, a *combination* of genetic and environmental factors, of nature and nurture, is involved in the development of psychopathology. In terms of possible environmental causes of psychopathology, stress is a good candidate.

Neurological Consequences of Stress as a Biological Basis for a Common Spectrum of Psychiatric Disorders

One of the most important brain areas that mediates, and in turn is affected by, the stress response is the *hippocampus*. The hippocampus plays an important role in new learning and memory

(Zola-Morgan & Squire, 1990). This function is critical to the stress response; for example, in assessing potential threats during a life-threatening situation, as occurs with exposure to a predator. Alterations in memory form an important part of the clinical presentation of patients with stress-related psychopathology. PTSD patients demonstrate a variety of memory problems, including deficits in declarative memory (remembering facts or lists, as reviewed below), and fragmentation of memories (both autobiographical and trauma related). PTSD is also associated with alterations in nondeclarative memory (i.e., types of memory that cannot be willfully brought up into the conscious mind, including motor memory such as how to ride a bicycle). These types of nondeclarative memories include conditioned responses and abnormal reliving of traumatic memories following exposure to situationally appropriate cues (Brewin, Dalgleish, & Joseph, 1996).

Recent findings that environmental events, such as stress, can lead to long-term changes in brain areas, such as the hippocampus, have potentially radical implications for how we think about mind, brain, and mental health. The concept that what you see, think, and feel may change your brain function and even its structure could force us to rethink many issues of mental health. Perhaps it is time to think of victims of psychological trauma not as people with bad characters or bad luck, or as subjects of our pity or charity, but rather as individuals with neurological disorders that have been caused by their life experiences, in much the same way that, for example, many people with epilepsy have brain lesions that cause their disease. In fact, using the example of epilepsy, in the 19th century this disorder was felt to be related to bad spirits, and it was only with advances in medicine and neuroscience that we were able to find the cause. We may be at a similar threshold with regard to mental disorders, in the initial stages of identifying a neurological basis for disorders we previously thought of as purely "psychological." Recognizing that environmental events can lead to neurological disorders is in many ways a return to the original ideas of Freud. As Freud started out doing, I now propose to describe mental disorders as alterations in physical phenomena (which he described using the terms of 19th-century physics, and we now describe with neuroscience and neuroanatomy). As Freud believed originally, in this book I propose that early childhood trauma is an important determinant of many mental disorders. I also propose that dynamic mental life plays a role in "real" mental disorders (thoughts, feelings, and meaning of events) as opposed to mental disorders being primarily fixed predetermined conditions.

The requirement of exposure to a traumatic stressor for the diagnosis has led to an odd dichotomy over the years between PTSD and other psychiatric disorders. There are other disorders that are strongly linked to trauma, most notably dissociative disorders, borderline personality disorder, alcoholism and substance abuse, somatic disorders, eating disorders, anxiety, and depression. However, the relationship between trauma (especially in early childhood) and development of these disorders has been repeatedly documented. There is also considerable overlap in symptoms and so-called comorbidity (e.g., between PTSD and dissociative disorders, or between PTSD and alcohol/substance dependence and depression). These findings raise the question of whether they are in fact separate disorders, or whether they are part of a spectrum of psychiatric disorders.

In fact, in this book I argue that these disorders are part of a trauma-spectrum group of disorders that all have a relationship to a common stress-induced neurological deficit. This idea is based on several pieces of evidence. For instance, all of these disorders mentioned above that I include as "trauma spectrum" have in common a high association with exposure to traumatic stress, especially childhood abuse. PTSD requires for its diagnosis exposure to traumatic stress, and essentially all patients with severe dissociative disorders such as dissociative identity disorder have been abused in childhood. Eighty percent of patients with borderline personality disorder have a history of childhood abuse, and other studies have found elevated rates of childhood abuse in patients with alcohol or substance abuse or dependence, or panic disorder and depression.

There also is considerable overlap in the actual symptoms listed under the trauma spectrum disorders (Figure 1.4). For instance, many symptoms of depression are equivalent to symptoms of PTSD. Psychomotor agitation can be rephrased as hyperarousal, and hopelessness as a sense of foreshortened future. Other symptoms that are identical in the criteria for depression and PTSD include decreased sleep, decreased concentration, and feelings of being cut off from others. In fact, the only symptom of depression that is not included in the criteria for PTSD is depressed mood, and on a clinical basis feelings of depression are common in patients with PTSD. The only symptoms of PTSD that are not part of depression are increased startle, feeling on guard, flashbacks, and amnesia. There are also important overlaps between PTSD and other disorders. For example, flashbacks and amnesia are essentially dissociative phenomena. Dissociative responses to trauma have been linked to both long-term dissociative disorders as well as to PTSD. Some studies have shown that flashbacks in almost all cases meet criteria for a panic attack, and depersonalization and derealization (dissociative symptoms) are in fact listed in the criteria for a panic attack. Disturbances of identity are relevant to borderline personality disorder, and dissociative responses are common in patients with this disorder, often leading to self-injurious behavior, which patients claim "breaks" dissociative states.

Another disorder that should definitely be included in the trauma-spectrum disorders is acute stress disorder (ASD). The development of ASD in the *DSM* has an odd history of its own, which is partially related to the abandonment in earlier versions of *DSM* of a diagnosis to capture the acute trauma response. I would propose that ASD and PTSD should be considered to be closely related, if not identical, disorders. Their criteria should therefore be made to be consistent with one another. Considering the important role of dissociation in the acute stress response, and the relationship between ASD (as currently configured) and PTSD, inclusion of dissociative symptoms in the diagnosis of PTSD should be considered. In addition, based on the propensity of PTSD patients to have dissociative responses to subsequent traumas and even minor stressors (i.e., amnesia, depersonalization, and derealization), it makes sense to create a similar dissociative cluster for chronic PTSD. This cluster would also include symptoms such as emotional numbing. With incorporation of amnesia, depersonalization, and derealization into chronic PTSD, these could be dropped as separate diagnoses in the dissociative disorders that are theoretically unconnected to trauma. Dissociative identity disorder, a more extreme response to stress, could be maintained as a separate disorder.

An accurate description of psychiatric responses to trauma might be served by the development of a new category of trauma-spectrum disorders. This would include both acute PTSD (the current ASD) and chronic PTSD (using revised criteria to be in line with ASD), dissociative identity disorder, conversion disorder, adjustment disorders, and possibly borderline personality disorder or other proposed disorders such as traumatic grief. Other disorders linked to stress—such as depression, panic disorder, eating disorders, anxiety, and alcohol/substance abuse—may not fit as neatly into the trauma-spectrum disorders, because there are obviously some patients with these disorders who do not have a history of trauma.

The development of a trauma-spectrum–disorder approach would represent an obvious divergence from the thrust of psychiatric diagnosis, at least in the United States, over the past 20 years. Much of the recent history of psychiatry has represented an emphasis on the evaluation of psychiatric diagnosis, with the assumption that psychiatric diagnoses represent discrete entities, much as medical disorders represent discrete disorders. If there is an increased overlap among different psychiatric disorders, it is assumed that patients have comorbidity rather than that the diagnostic schema are not adequate to describe the phenomena. However, the absurd rates of comorbidity force us to the realization that many psychiatric disorders, especially the trauma-spectrum disorders, may not represent discrete disorders, but rather are aspects of an array of psychiatric outcomes that have historically been artificially divided into discrete disorders.

Stress-induced neurological disorders may underlie trauma-spectrum disorders. A common neurological deficit may be the cause of the considerable overlap between these supposedly discreet disorders. According to this idea, stress-induced deficits in specific brain areas, such as the hippocampus and possibly the prefrontal cortex, are the neurological basis of the disorder. Why some individuals develop depression and others PTSD may be related to severity of the injury, interaction with genetically determined personality traits, developmental epoch when the trauma occurred, or some combination of all of the above. In this book, I explore the critical question of whether stress damages the brain. Additionally, I outline the possible implications a stress-induced neurological deficit may have for psychiatric diagnosis and treatment, most notably the idea of a unifying group of psychiatric disorders under the umbrella of the trauma-spectrum disorders. But before I go further on this topic I lay the groundwork for a discussion of the idea that stress can cause brain damage. I do this by reviewing the background behind the incredible revolution that has taken place in the science of the brain over the past two decades. In particular, I highlight two important areas, genetics and brain imaging, that have provided important tools that have greatly expanded our knowledge of psychiatric disorders.

CHAPTER TWO **The Working Mind: What It Does and Why**

Dopo di allora, ad ora incerta,
Quella pena ritorna,
E se non trova chi lo ascolti
Gli brucia in petto il cuore.
Rivede I visi dei suoi compagni
Lividi nella prima luce,
Grigi di polvere di cemento,
Indistinti per nebbia,
Tinti di morte nei sonni inquieti

[Since then at an uncertain hour,
This pain returns,
And even if no one can hear it
It burns in the depths of one's heart.
And brings back the images of one's companions
Glowing in the first light,
Gray with the dust of cement,
Hard to make out because of the fog and mist,
With shades of death and restless dreams]
(translation by the author)

—From "Ad Ora Incerta" ("At This Uncertain Hour"),
by Primo Levi

A Brief History of the Brain

As we enter the 21st century, we leave behind us the "Decade of the Brain" from the 1990s. This has an inherent logic, because the explosion of understanding about the intricacies of neuroscience, and new discoveries about how the brain works, have led to a sea change not only in our understanding of neurological and psychiatric diseases, but also in our general outlook on the world. Our society, blunted in its ambitions to reach into the stars in the 1980s, burrowed into the depths of the individual brain in the 1990s, with perhaps a greater payoff in knowledge and enlightenment.

It was only a century ago that the basic fundamentals for understanding how the brain works were laid down. At that time, the basic building blocks or cells of the brain, neurons, were first discovered. As discussed in the previous chapter, before that time we had an unclear idea about how thoughts and emotions were generated, and it was not generally appreciated that cognition occurs in the brain. Also discussed in the previous chapter were the various ideas about where thoughts, memories, and emotions occur within the physical makeup of humans. Thinking among the early Greeks was that emotions and mental forces took place in the region of the liver or the heart. Much of the content of emotional life was held to be part of what we would translate as the soul or spirit, or *psyche*, which had no definite location within the physical being. The *psyche* has found its way of course into the English words *psyche* and *psychiatry*, which have been appropriated by the fields of psychiatry and psychology. Another idea related to emotion and individual motivation among the ancient Greeks was that of *daimon*, which they conceived of as a spirit assigned to the individual person. The word *daimon* has taken on a somewhat sinister transformation into English as the word *demon*, which is a deviation from the original meaning of the word. Yet another concept developed by the Greeks and adopted in the Middle Ages was that of the four elements of earth, wind, fire, and air. All matter was considered to be composed of these four elements, and an unbalance of the elements led to ill health, including insanity. In the Middle Ages, this idea of a natural balance of elements was translated into the idea of "bodily humors," which were required to be in balance for good health. An excess of one of the bodily humors, "black bile," was felt to cause mental disorders such as depression. The idea of bile being involved in mental disorders harkens back to the ancient Greeks' notion of the liver representing a seat of the emotions and character.

It took the advance of the Scientific Age for the realization that thoughts and emotions are located within the brain. With the development of the microscope it was possible to visualize the cell, the basic building block of the body. The cells of the brain are called *neurons* (Figure 2.1a). These basic building blocks have a "cell body," which contains branches called *dendrites* (the Greek word for "tree") that communicate with other neurons, as well as long processes called *axons* that reach out to other neurons. At the end of the axons, chemicals called *neurotransmitters* are released and travel into the space between neurons, called *synapses*, until they reach the adjacent neurons. There the neurotransmitters attach to sites on the other neuron called *receptors*, where they transmit information to the adjacent cell. Some of the neurochemicals (also known as *neurotransmitters*) in the brain

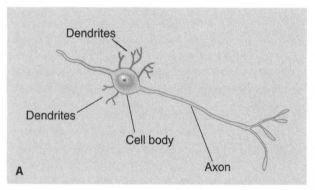

Figure 2.1a. A diagram of a human neuron, the basic cell of the brain. The neuron is composed of a long axon, a cell body, and dendrites. Neurotransmitters are released from the dendrites, the branching ends of the neuron, into the space between neurons, called the synapse. Neurotransmitters travel through the synapse, then attach to an adjacent neuron's dendrites, which receive signals from adjacent neurons. Reuptake sites (where medications like Prozac work) suck the neurotransmitters up into the neuron.

DOES STRESS DAMAGE THE BRAIN?

include serotonin, norepinephrine, and dopamine. These neurotransmitters have their cell bodies in the brainstem (the primitive part of the brain, located in the neck, that controls basic processes such as hunger, thirst, sleep, and temperature regulation), and long axons that extend to all parts of the brain and modulate emotions like fear or sadness. At the end of the axons there are also reuptake sites that take back the neurotransmitters from the synapse (Figure 2.1b). Modern antidepressant medications like Prozac or Paxil block the serotonin reuptake sites, effectively in-

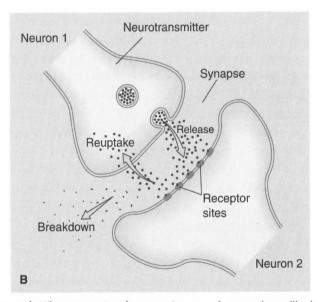

Figure 2.1b When a nerve impulse occurs in neuron 1, a neurotransmitter is discharged into the synapse (the gap between neuron 1 and neuron 2). This stimulates neuron 2 to fire when the neurotransmitter makes contact with the receptors on the membrane of neuron 2. The neurotransmitter is now sitting in the synapse and on the membrane of neuron 2. Neuron 2 will continue to fire until the neurotransmitter is inactivated. There are several ways that decreased availability might occur. One way is by reuptake, in which neuron 1 reabsorbs the neurotransmitter, thereby inactivating the neurotransmitter at the receptors. A second way is by breakdown, in which the neurotransmitter is broken down chemically and rendered inactive. In addition, there might be decreased synthesis of the neurotransmitter from its precursors.

creasing the amount of neurotransmitters in the synapse, and for this reason they are called *selective serotonin reuptake inhibitors*, or SSRIs. One hypothesis of the biological basis for depression and possibly PTSD in the brain is that there is a deficiency of the neurotransmitter serotonin. The SSRI-induced increase in serotonin in the synapse is felt to be the reason why these antidepressant medications are effective in treating trauma-spectrum disorders such as PTSD and depression.

Chronic stress results in changes in the release or binding of the brain chemicals called neurotransmitters, and these changes are felt to underlie the symptoms of trauma-spectrum psychiatric disorders such as PTSD and depression. The brain chemical norepinephrine, commonly known as adrenaline, floods the brain during a situation of danger. Most of the cell bodies that contain norepinephrine are located in an area called the *locus coeruleus*, which is in the brainstem. These cell bodies have long axons that extend throughout the brain and release norepinephrine at the drop of a hat. When norepinephrine floods the brain during a situation of danger, it causes an increase in alertness and vigilance, and sharpens the mind to deal with the danger. Norepinephrine also causes an increase in heart rate and blood pressure, which can be beneficial in responding to life threat. The neurotransmitter serotonin has especially been implicated in depression. Reduced levels of serotonin are felt to be involved in the development of depression. Chronic stress in animals results in a reductions of serotonin levels in the frontal cortex with associated deficits in behavior, which reverse with administration of serotonin in the frontal cortex.

Hormones are a type of chemical that form an interface between the brain and the body. The brain triggers release of hormones, which travel throughout the blood supply, and have a number of physiological effects. Stress results in release of a hormone called *cortisol*, which is critical to survival. Cortisol has effects on the physical organism that are beneficial for acute survival. For instance, cortisol results in a shunting of energy away from the gut's digestive processes and reproduction and toward the brain and the muscles, which allow quick thinking and fast moving that can be beneficial to survival. Another neurotransmitter, epinephrine, is released from the adrenal, which causes an acceleration of heart rate and blood pressure. This has the effect of increasing delivery of blood flow with necessary energy requirements for the increased demand of dealing with the stressor. These neurochemical and hormonal systems play a critical role in the response to life-threatening stressors.

There are millions of neurons in the brain, and each neuron has thousands of connections with adjacent neurons. Changes in the connections between neurons are felt to underlie processes such as the laying down of new memory traces and the development of mental capacities with early development. Until recently, it was thought that we are born with a fixed number of neurons, and it is not possible to replace lost neurons through new growth or development. In fact, in the first years of life there is a reduction or "pruning" of neurons, the reasons for which are not completely understood. However, in recent years Elizabeth Gould (Gould, Tanapata, McEwen, Flugge, & Fuchsa, 1998) at Princeton and Rusty Gage at the Salk Institute in San Diego (Eriksson et al., 1998) have showed that it is possible to grow new neurons in adulthood. Interestingly, this process has been shown to occur only in the hippocampus and possibly the prefrontal cortex, two regions that are of particular interest to trauma-spectrum disorders.

Most of the cell bodies of neurons are located in the gray matter of the brain, which is the highly convoluted substance on the brain's outer rim (Figure 2.2). The axons of the neurons travel through the white matter, and they are covered with special sheaths called *myelin* that are white, giving the white matter its

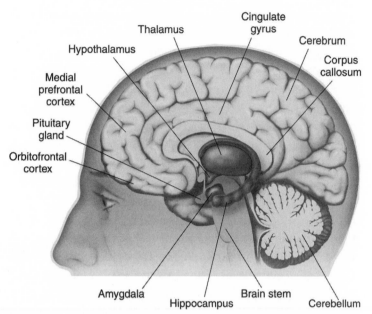

Figure 2.2 Diagram of the human brain. The cerebral cortex is the outer covering of the brain, where neurons are located. The hippocampus is a long, sausage-shaped organ present on both the left and the right sides of the brain. At the head of the hippocampus sits the amygdala. The thalamus acts as a gateway from the outside world into the brain, and the hypothalamus regulates bodily changes like heart rate and temperature. The cingulate gyrus sits just over the corpus callosum, which connect the left and the right sides of the brain. The frontal cortex, especially the medial prefrontal and orbitofrontal cortex, plays a critical role in the regulation of emotion.

distinctive color. This outer gray matter portion of the brain is called the *cerebral cortex*. Different parts of the cerebral cortex have different functions; for instance, the occipital cortex (in the back of the brain) is responsible for vision, while the motor cortex (on top of the brain) is responsible for movement. Deficits in these areas (e.g., with strokes), in which there is an interruption of blood flow to that part of the brain, result in a failure in these functions.

The development of the brain in different animal species tells us something about how the brain probably developed during human evolution. Some of the primitive brain structures in the center of the brain (called "*subcortical*" because they are under the cortex, which surrounds the outside of the brain, and also known as limbic brain structures) are more or less equally seen in more primitive animal species, like rats, just as they are in humans. These brain areas include the hippocampus, amygdala, hypothalamus, thalamus, orbitofrontal and medial prefrontal cortexes, and cingulate. In addition, there is a primitive part of the brain that is involved in smell (important for survival in lower animal species) and emotional behaviors that lies just over the eyes, and is therefore called the *orbitofrontal cortex*. In contrast, the outer rim of cerebral cortex is more developed the higher one travels up the animal chain, and it is most developed in humans. One of the last feats of evolution, which distinguishes us from monkeys, is the extraordinary development of the prefrontal cortex, that part of the cerebral cortex that sits in the front of the head. In fact, the human skull transformed itself, pushing the typical animal snout back into the head so that the frontal cortex could extend out over the top of the face. This brain area is responsible for higher cognitive processes, planning and executing of behaviors, and abstract thought.

A Network of Brain Regions that Plays a Role in Both Stress and Memory

Many of the primitive brain areas play an important role in stress. The involvement of primitive brain areas seen in all animal species in the stress response is logical, because avoiding threats to life is a crucial behavior in all animal species. These brain areas also tend to play an important role in memory. One of these areas, the *hippocampus*, is a long sausage-shaped organ in the central part of the brain is critical to learning and memory. Like most structures in the brain, there is a hippocampus on both the left and right sides, and the two have slightly different functions. The famous case of H. M. illustrates the important role that the hippocampus plays in learning (Scoville & Milner, 1957). H. M. had a stroke (an interruption of blood supply that causes brain damage) that specifically involved the hippocampus, on both the left and right sides. Following this accident, H. M. could not learn anything new; for instance he couldn't remember what to buy at the grocery store, and he couldn't remember what someone told him only a few minutes before. However, H. M. could converse normally and interact in a social way, and in those circumstances seemed like he was perfectly normal. He could also remember very clearly the events that occurred before the accident, such as his marriage, his career, and events from his childhood. Interestingly, H. M. was very happy reading the same copy of *Reader's Digest* over and over again. Traumatized patients report experiences similar to those of H. M., often remembering what happened to them years ago better than what they had for breakfast that morning.

The role of the hippocampus is more complex than a simple storage of new facts and lists. Memories are continuously strengthened and formulated—a process called *consolidation*—perhaps for weeks or months after the original event. We know this from animal studies showing that a lesion of the hippocampus that occurs for up to a month after the original event results in a loss of the memory. However, after that time hippocampal lesions do not disrupt the memory trace, probably because the memory has been stored in other parts of the brain. This window of memory consolidation represents an opportunity to modify traumatic memories before they become indelible or firmly engraved in the mind, a process that probably occurs when the memory becomes stored in the cerebral cortex.

The hippocampus has also been described as placing the individual in the context of space and time; it tells us where we are and what is happening in relationship to the future and the past, relating present information to other memories and experiences that we have collected (Nadel & Bohbot, 2001). As such, the hippocampus plays an integrative role in our experience (Zola-Morgan & Squire, 1990). It is perhaps for this reason that damage to the hippocampus, or conversely electrical stimulation of the hippocampus, is associated with increases in symptoms of dissociation, which are defined in the *Diagnostic and Statistical Manual of Mental Disorders* as a "breakdown in memory, consciousness, or identity." Seen in this context, it is the hippocampus that tells us who we are, and a breakdown in function of this brain area leads to a disintegration of the sense of self and a loss of the context of our memories, with associated gaps in memory. The most extreme form of dissociation is the controversial diagnosis of dissociative identity disorder, in which there is a breakdown of the sense of identity, so that patients will attribute different identities to different fragmented aspects of their selves and their memories and experiences. Consistent with the idea that stress-induced hippocampal damage contributes to these disabling symptoms is the finding that, in traumatized patients, the greatest decreases in volume of the hippocampus are associated with the most pronounced symptoms of dissociation. The hippocampus also plays an important role in memory for the emotions related to the context of an event. Studies in animals showed that lesions of the hippocampus resulted in a forgetting of the context of a fear-inducing situation (e.g., the sights, smells, and sounds related to a threatening event). The hippocampus pulls together these individual elements and stimulates the emotions related to the original event.

Another primitive brain area that plays a critical role in emotion is the *amygdala*, an almond-shaped structure that sits right at the front of the hippocampus. This structure is involved in fear and emotional responses (Chapman et al., 1954). Animal studies by Joseph LeDoux (1993), Michael Davis (1992), and others showed that the amygdala is involved in primitive fear conditioning. In basic animal experiments, if something aversive like an electric shock is paired with a neutral event like a bright light, reexposure to the bright light alone results in a fear response. This phenomenon is known as *fear conditioning*. With time, reexposure to the light alone will result in a diminishing of the fear response, a process known as *extinction of conditioned fear*. The amygdala has important connections (through a brain area called the *hypothalamus*) to the body that stimulate the fight-or-flight response. Amygdala activation results in increases in heart rate and blood pressure, and stimulated release of cortisol and epinephrine, the body's stress hormones (Gunne & Reis, 1963; Hilton & Zbrozyna, 1963). The amygdala also has connections to norepinephrine neurons, which stimulate release of that stress related neurotransmitter.

The orbitofrontal cortex and *medial prefrontal cortex* sit just over the eyes and regulate human emotion and social behavior (Carmichael & Price, 1994, 1995). The old surgery of frontal lobotomies involved lesions of the orbitofrontal cortex by entering around the eye socket. It is well known that patients with frontal lobotomies had flat and dull behavior, did not interact socially with others, and had a blunting of the normal range of human emotion. Other observations of individuals who had damage to this part of the brain—such as the famous case of Phineas Gage, who had a railroad spike enter this part of his brain—show that the orbitofrontal cortex and medial prefrontal cortex are involved in normal emotional and social behavior (Damasio, Grabowski, Frank, Galaburda, & Damasio, 1994). This part of the brain also seems to regulate the sense of what is right or wrong, or what is socially appropriate. For instance, studies by Damasio and colleagues found that patients who had damage to this area from early childhood were more likely to grow up and break the law or engage in other antisocial behaviors.

The *cingulate* gets its name from the ringlike appearance of this structure that extends from the front to the back of the brain

(Devinsky, Morrell, & Vogt, 1995; Vogt, Finch, & Olson, 1992). The cingulate sits just above the corpus callosum, the part of the brain that connects the left and the right side. There are two aspects of the cingulate. The front part, or anterior cingulate, is involved in concentration and inhibition of responses, and planning and executing of behavior. Recent imaging studies also show that the anterior cingulate is involved in normal emotion, and decreased function in this area has been seen in trauma spectrum disorders. The posterior cingulate (at the back of the brain) is involved in processing information in space and time, which may be important for rapid response to life-threatening situations.

The *hypothalamus* and *thalamus* are primitive structures that sit at the center of the brain. The thalamus is the central relay point where information from the senses comes in and is distributed to different parts of the brain. I once heard the thalamus referred to as a "good secretary," who screens what is and is not important from getting access to the boss. The hypothalamus is just below the thalamus, and is the door from the brain to the body. It is here that neurons interface with messengers called *neuropeptides* that travel to the pituitary gland, stimulating release of hormones throughout the body. These hormones are responsible for a diversity of functions, including growth, appetite, body temperature, and metabolism. The hypothalamus is also an important gateway for the brain to stimulate stress responses in the body, such as increased heart rate, elevated blood pressure, and shunting of energy to the muscles and the brain.

The laying down of memory traces and other activities of these brain regions are modulated by brain chemicals and hormones such cortisol and norepinephrine, which are released during stress. For example, cortisol acts at the level of the hippocampus to impair the laying down of memories, while the catecholamines norepinephrine and epinephrine have been shown to strengthen the formation of memories (Cahill, Prins, Weber, & McGaugh, 1994; De Weid & Croiset, 1991; Gold & van Buskirk, 1975; Keenan, Jacobson, Soleyman, & Newcomer, 1995; Kirschbaum, Wolf, May, Wippich, & Hellhammer, 1996; Liang, Juler, & McGaugh, 1986; Liang, McGaugh, & Yao, 1990; McGaugh, 1989; McGaugh, Castellano, & Brioni, 1990). The catecholamines have also been shown in animal studies to act at the level of the amygdala to strengthen the emotional valence associated with specific memories. These findings may explain why some aspects of traumatic memories are very strong and others appear to be missing. Also, in chronic stress there is dysregulation of cortisol and norepinephrine function, which leads to alterations in the laying down and retrieval of memories.

Two areas that made an explosion of knowledge possible in the field of neuroscience and mental disorders are brain imaging and genetics. It is no accident that most major medical schools in the United States have prioritized imaging sciences and genetics as the two most important areas on which to focus their resources for the 21st century. Through imaging we can visualize physiological processes in a detail that would have been unimaginable 20 years ago. We can image the activation of neurons (the cells of the brain) when they respond to a variety of inputs, ranging from the memory of an old friend, to the sensation of sadness related to a relative's death, or the perception of a painting in an art museum. In the area of genetics we have recently cracked the genetic code, so that we know the sequence of the thousands of building blocks of the genetic code that determine who we are and what we will become.

The Application of Brain Imaging to the Study of Stress-Related Mental Disorders

In the fields of psychiatry and neuroscience, the developments of imaging technology have been especially fruitful. Imaging of the brain can provide a bridge between what is happening with the

smallest molecules and the expression of the most complex behaviors. The past two decades have seen an explosion of this
technology, so that we now have a window into the brain and
other bodily organs, and can see what is happening during "real
time" while the individual is experiencing any type of thought,
sensation, or mental process. New technology also makes it possible to even provide an image of the expression of genes or processes at the molecular level.

Neuroimaging studies include all studies that take advantage
of radiological techniques to provide information about the structure and function of the brain (Figure 2.3). Modern medicine
uses imaging techniques that are based on passing radiation
through the body (x-ray or computed tomography, or CT), inject-

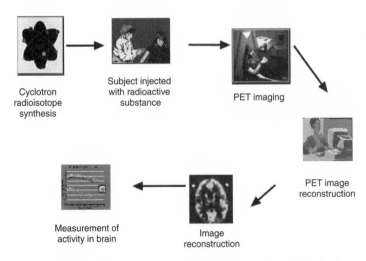

Figure 2.3 Diagram of brain imaging with positron emission tomography (PET). Radioactive substances are injected into the brain, where they travel to areas where
neurons are active. They release radioactivity, which is detected by the PET camera.
Powerful computers create images of the brain showing where these neuronal processes are taking place, and provide information about where, for example, neurons
turn on during a specific memory.

ing radiation and measuring how it passes out of the body after injection (single photon emission computed tomography—SPECT— and positron emission tomography—PET), or delivering powerful electromagnetic pulses and measuring how they affect the properties of the electrons in the tissues in the body (MRI). In the case of x-ray and CT, the properties of the tissue determine how radiation is attenuated, or slowed down, as it passes through the body, and information on attenuation is used to create a map, or an image, of the body. In SPECT and PET, radiation travels to where a particular physiological process is taking place, depending on what the radiation is tagged or attached to, and information about the location of the radiation in the body provides information about the body's physiology. In the case of MRI, the properties of the tissue determine what effect the electromagnetic pulse will have on the spins of the electrons in different parts of the tissue, which allows the imaging device to create a map, or image, of the body.

Modern imaging sciences were made possible by the discovery of radioactivity in the 19th century. At the end of the 19th century, the Curies discovered that some elements exhibit properties of radioactive decay. Studying radon, they determined that it decayed at a constant rate, meaning that if one started out with the same amount of activity, after a given time period the amount of radioactivity that was left over was always the same. An arbitrary amount of radon was determined to represent a unit of radioactivity, designated as a unit of measurement known as the "Curie." Since that time all elements that have properties of radioisotopic decay are measured in terms of the Curie unit. It has since been determined that a radioactive substance that exhibits 37,000,000,000 radioactive disintegrations per second represents one Curie of radioactivity. Different radioactive substances have different rates of decay. The *half-life* is used as a measure of the time it takes for half of the material to decay. Therefore, the half-life is an important measure of the radioactive properties of a particular substance.

Since the Curies' time, it has been determined that radioactive decay involves a fundamental change in the properties of a compound. The basic building block of all matter is the atom. All atoms are made up of electrons, protons, and neutrons. Electrons have a negative electrical charge, protons have a positive charge, and neutrons are neutral. The center of the atom—the *nucleus*—is made up of tightly packed neutrons and protons. Revolving around the nucleus like planets orbiting the sun, are the electrons. It makes sense that there should roughly be an equal number of positively charged protons and negatively charged electrons so that the electrical charge is balanced. Some unstable atoms may have too many protons in the nucleus relative to the number of electrons, or too few protons. If they have too many protons they may emit a particle or a light photon to achieve a more stable level, and the detectors in an imaging device will detect the emission of this light ray. The radioactive decay of millions of atoms will be used to create an image of all of the radioactive decay events in the body.

The discovery of radiation has been an important element in the advance of the imaging sciences. The past century's advances in the field of imaging sciences have their basis in the discovery and development of x-rays for the imaging of the human body. At the turn of the 20th century, a physician named Roentgen discovered that passing x-rays through the human hand with a photographic plate on the other side created a ghostly image on the photographic plate that represented the bones of the hand that are hidden from the naked eye. Soon, physicians discovered that x-rays could provide a wealth of information about the structure of the human body, both in sickness and in health. The principle of x-rays is based on the creation of an x-ray beam. The x-ray beam is created when electrons travel from an anode to a cathode, which travel through space like light or sound and have their own specific energy.

X-rays travel through different parts of the body at different speeds, depending on the type of tissue that is present. Tissue that is denser or has physical properties will slow down, or "attenuate," the x-ray beam to a greater extent than will tissue that is less dense. For example, bone is denser than water (which is basically what the cerebrospinal fluid—the water that bathes the brain—is made of, and in fact most of the brain has a density that is fairly close to water). X-rays will have a harder time traveling through bone than through water. Fewer of the x-ray photons that travel through bone will be able to make it to the other side of the skull and hit the photographic film in the area corresponding to where bone is present, making the part of the film corresponding to the location of bone look different than the area where there is brain and cerebrospinal fluid. This basic principle, of what are essentially variant forms of light waves (or "photons") passing through the body, and the degree to which the photons are slowed down or deflected in their path providing information about the physical properties of the body that can be used to provide a picture or image of our insides that we cannot see with our naked eye, underlies most of the radiological sciences.

An advance over the use of simple x-rays came with the development of the computer after World War II. An engineer named Hounsfield working in London in 1967 found that images of the interior of the body could be produced by passing x-rays through the body at multiple angles and measuring the degree to which the tissues of the body attenuated, or slowed down, the x-rays. With computers, x-rays could be passed through the body at multiple angles, and the information could be reconstructed in an image that provided a map of the interior of the body in exquisite detail. This new technique was used to turn the x-ray images into displays of fine slices, or tomographs, throughout the human body; hence the term *computed tomography* (CT). This technology provided images of not only normal human anatomy but also of disease, often giving clues of very small tumors in the body that were less than one-half inch in size. Another advance that boosted the resolution of CT over earlier x-ray imaging techniques was the use of photomultiplier tubes over regular radiographic film. With photomultiplier tubes, the radiation reaching the other side of the body interacts with other electrons, resulting in a shower of electrons for each radiation that penetrates the body, effectively amplifying the signal as much as a 100 times over the old technique. The improvement is in a parameter known as *sensitivity*, or the ability to detect small amounts of radiation. Another factor, which is important in imaging, is called *resolution*, or the ability to image very small objects or to determine that two objects that are very close together actually represent two distinct objects. Sensitivity and resolution have been steadily improving in all of the imaging modalities over the past 40 years, which has led to increasingly precise maps of the body's structure and the function of the body.

CT has continued to improve since its first development, while the introduction of magnetic resonance imaging (MRI) about 20 years ago added another technological improvement in the imaging sciences. The atoms that make up the basic building blocks of life consist of cores (or "nuclei") of neutrons and protons surrounded by electrons that orbit the nuclei like planets around the sun. MRI uses a powerful magnetic to throw the electrons that make up brain tissue out of their normal patterns, and measures the time it takes for them to return to their normal "resting" state. This "relaxation time" provides information about the content of the tissue, which can be used to create an image of the brain. MRI images are obtained of successive slices that move through the entire volume of the brain a few millimeters at a time. With specialized image-processing software on a computer, the outline of individual brain regions in successive slices can be traced using a mouse-driven cursor, and the volume within the outlines quantitated and converted to real brain volume. These techniques have been shown to be highly reliable in the hands of well-trained operators, and have provided a wealth of information about brain structure in psychiatric disorders in general, and more recently in the field of PTSD.

More recently, MRI has been used to measure brain function, hence the name *functional MRI*, or fMRI. This technique takes advantage of the fact that blood cells have small amounts of a metal, called *heme*, which has magnetic properties that can be measured by MRI. Heme is actually the metal that is part of hemoglobin, the molecule inside of red blood cells that carry oxygen from the lungs to the tissues of the body. With activations of neurons in a specific part of the brain there is an increase in blood flow to that part of the brain. The increase in blood flow occurs automatically, and does so in response to the increased energy demands of the neurons, to deliver an increase in oxygen and glucose to that part of the brain. With the increase in blood flow the concentrations of red blood cells change, something that can be detected with fMRI. With this ability to detect changes in blood flow, fMRI can be used to measure brain function during a variety of conditions, such as experiencing a particular emotion, remembering something, or performing particular mental operations.

Another application of MRI that has proven to be useful is the field of MRI spectroscopy. Using MRI, it is possible to measure the physical properties, or spectra, of individual chemicals in the brain. Measuring the spectra of the chemicals in a particular region of the brain provides an estimate of the concentration of specific chemicals in that area. One example of this is the measurement of a chemical called *N-acetyl-aspartate* (NAA). NAA is an amino acid, the presence of which is felt to correlate with the integrity or health of neurons, which are the basic cells of the brain. Decreases in NAA are felt to represent a loss of neurons or changes in the integrity of neurons that indicate abnormalities. Other brain chemicals can be measured with MRI spectroscopy, including GABA, which is an inhibitory neurotransmitter in the brain.

An additional important development in technology is *positron emission tomography* (PET). PET can be used to provide a measure of brain function, measured with brain blood flow and metabolism. Glucose (sugar) is the primary energy source of the brain, and when there is an increase in firing of the neurons in a specific brain region, there is an increase in glucose uptake in that region to meet the demand. Similarly, with increased glucose demand there is an increase of brain blood flow to that region. With a regional increase in neuronal activity (e.g., in the visual cortex following exposure to a bright light), there is a shunting of glucose and blood flow toward that region that can be measured with PET as a real-time measure of brain function.

PET imaging is based on the principles of radioactivity. Radioactive substances are those that are unstable because they have too many positive or negative charges. As mentioned earlier, an atom wants to have an equal balance of negative and positive charges. If it doesn't, it will change by letting go a negative or positive charge. This letting go of the charges is what is known as *radioactivity*. Imaging devices like PET cameras can measure these charges when they are let go. If this process is multiplied millions of times, the camera can get a picture of where in the body all of these radioactive atoms are located, and reconstruct a picture of the physiological process of interest. The radioactive substances used in PET can be prepared in an on-site cyclotron and injected immediately into the patient for imaging. Brain blood flow is measured with radioactive water $H_2[^{15}O]$, and brain metabolism with radioactive glucose ($[^{18}F]$2-fluoro-2-deoxyglucose, or FDG).

These substances are produced in a cyclotron located on the site of the imaging facility. Cyclotrons are like the particle accelerators that are used to perform research in physics on the properties of atoms. Cyclotrons create a streamlined flow, or "beam," of protons that is the smallest atom (hydrogen) stripped of its only electron. The cyclotron uses magnets to spin the protons round and round in a circle, going faster and faster, until they spin off and barrel into another area of material called the "target." When the positively charged proton hits the target material it collides with the nucleus and joins it, adding one extra positive charge to the nucleus, thus changing the entire makeup of the atom. For example, when protons are hurled against the target material of nitrogen-15 (N-15), they add an extra positive charge to the nucleus, thus changing it from nitrogen to a form of oxygen (O-15). This form of O-15 is radioactive, meaning that it has an extra positive charge that it wants to get rid of. Sooner or later it will emit a proton from the nucleus in the form of a positron. Positrons emitted in the body collide with electrons, and there is complete annihilation of the positron and the electron. I often explain this as being like the *Star Trek* adventure where the world of matter met the world of antimatter and there was total annihilation of both.

In the case of positrons, the mass of the positron and of the electron are converted to energy in the form of two photons, or beams of light, with the energy of 511 KeV that travel in opposite directions. This obeys Einstein's law that the energy of a substance is equal to the mass of the object times the speed of light squared, or $e = mc^2$. These two beams of light travel away from each other in opposite directions and are "detected" by the camera. Computers recognize that two beams of light traveled in opposite directions at 180° from each other, and they determine this as representing an "annihilation" from an original emission of a positron from an atom that was originally injected in the body. The computers then use this information to reconstruct an image of the brain's metabolism or blood flow patterns.

The development of imaging technology has revolutionized the practice of medicine. Whereas 40 years ago physicians spent many hours tapping over the area of the liver or laying sensitive fingers over the stomach to glean indirect clues about possible disease, we now have the ability to look directly at disease wherever it may be, without having to surgically open the body to look inside. This revolution has led to a gradual abandonment of the archaic arts of "physical diagnosis." The modern physician typically listens to all of a patient's symptoms and presenting story, and then determines the best radiologic studies that will determine the patient's disease. The physician then integrates the findings of all of the radiological tests, and from that determines the treatment. Traditional physical diagnosis, such as listening to the heart with a stethoscope, or palpation, is basically extinct; however, physicians perpetuate the teaching of physical diagnosis out of tradition, much like an ancient priesthood that won't give up muttering spells and prayers in a lost language.

Imaging science has also had a major impact on the development of psychiatry and neuroscience. The ability to see within the brain has eliminated the need to rely on philosophy or second-guessing in evaluating psychiatric disorders. The first radiologic studies of the brain concerned pneumoencephalography, which involves injecting air into the cerebrospinal space and imaging with the use of simple x-rays. This technique was used to good effect to address the central question of this book, whether stress damages the brain. Pneumoencephalography was applied to World War II concentration camp survivors, in whom evidence of "[cerebral] atrophy of varying degrees" and "diffuse encephalopathy" was found in up to 81% of cases (Thygesen, Hermann, & Willanger, 1970). Following this there were several cases reported of individuals, such as political prisoners, who had been tortured and had diffuse atrophy of the brain.

In the 1970s and 1980s, the development of CT added to our understanding of psychiatric disorders. Scientists used CT to study patients who were given steroids for the treatment of medical conditions, and to study patients with the diagnosis of depression. Some medical conditions were treated with steroids that are similar to cortisol, the body's natural stress response hormone. Patients treated with steroids developed atrophy of the brain and enlargement of the large fluid-filled cavities of the brain, called *ventricles*, that also indicated atrophy of the brain. In a similar way, patients with depression have an increase in cortisol levels in many cases, and stress has been linked to the development of depression. CT studies in patients with depression showed atrophy and enlargement of the ventricles similar to that seen in patients treated with steroids. In some cases, patients with the highest levels of cortisol had the greatest amount of brain atrophy.

Many of these earlier CT studies lacked the resolution to look more carefully at individual parts of the brain that may be affected by stress. Magnetic resonance imaging (MRI) increased our ability to look at fine details of the brain. MRI made it possible to quantitate the size of individual brain structures that may be particularly relevant to trauma related mental disorders. As discussed elsewhere in this book, the hippocampus is a brain structure that is particularly sensitive to stress. The hippocampus plays a critical role in new learning and memory, and we hypothesize that abnormalities of the hippocampus underlie both the memory and cognitive problems seen in trauma-spectrum disorders, as well as many of the symptoms of mood imbalances and pathological fear and anxiety reactions in these disorders. In the past decade, researchers have been able to use MRI to quantitate the volume of the hippocampus. Patients with trauma-spectrum disorders—including PTSD, depression, and borderline personality disorder—have been scanned with MRI. The MRI scanner creates images of the brain in the form of "slices," moving through the brain every few millimeters. The MRI images are stored in a digital format on a computer, and researchers then draw around the borders of the hippocampus on each slice in which it is seen. The computer can then calculate the volume inside of each of these drawn regions and, by adding up the volumes on all the slices in which the hippocampus was seen; it determines the size of the hippocampus. Volume of the hippocampus is then compared in a group of patients with trauma-spectrum disorders to that of a group of normal individuals.

Determining the volume of the hippocampus is particularly relevant to trauma-spectrum disorders, because of the studies in animals showing the damaging effects of stress on the hippocampus. The hippocampus also plays a role in recording the emotions attached to a stressful event (Phillips & LeDoux, 1992). In the past decade, researchers have measured the volume of the hippocampus with MRI in a number of trauma spectrum disorders, including PTSD, depression, and borderline personality disorder. Our research group first measured the hippocampus in Vietnam combat veterans with PTSD, and published the results in 1995. In that original study, we reported an 8% reduction in hippocampal volume on the right side in the PTSD patients (Bremner, Randall, et al., 1995). Since that time we have also reported a 12% reduction in left hippocampal volume in patients with PTSD related to early childhood physical and sexual abuse (Bremner, Randall, et al., 1997). Other studies have replicated this finding, including a study by Stein, Koverola, Hanna, Torchia, and McClarty (1997) who found a 5% reduction in left hippocampal volume in women abused in childhood, most of whom had PTSD; and a study by Gurvits and colleagues (1996) who found a 29% reduction in both left and right hippocampal volume in combat veterans with PTSD. Two published studies used MRI spectroscopy to show a reduction in NAA, suggesting a decrease in neuronal integrity, in the hippocampus in combat-related PTSD. Two studies of depression, one from our group (Bremner, Narayan, et al., 2000) and another from Sheline, Wang, Gadon, Csernasky, and Vannier (1996), reported a reduction in hippocampal volume noted with MRI.

Other techniques such as positron emission tomography (PET) and functional MRI (fMRI) have been used to study function of the brain in trauma-spectrum disorders. PET can be used to measure blood flow in the brain while a patient is lying in the scanner. In typical studies, the patient lies in the camera and performs a task, such as trying to remember a list of words. While the patient is performing the task, the investigator injects radioactive water into an intravenous catheter, or tube. The PET scanner is immediately turned on and takes a picture of the brain for one minute while the patient continues to remember the list of words. The PET scan takes an image of where in the radioactive water travels in the brain. Because the radioactive water diffuses into the bloodstream, increases in blood flow in a particular part of the brain are associated with increases in delivery of the radioactive water to that area. Because the brain automatically increases blood flow to parts of the brain that have an increase in activity, the PET camera can measure these changes in blood flow. If a particular part of the brain increases plays an important role in the task—for example, the hippocampus in the attempt to remember a list of words—the neurons, or basic cells of the brain, increases the rate of their firing. This increase in firing uses up energy, and the brain automatically shunts an increased amount of blood to that area to deliver more oxygen and glucose, which is the energy source of the brain. The PET image therefore captures the areas of the brain that are most active, or "light up," during a task, and provides important information about function.

Functional imaging technologies such as PET and fMRI have supplied important information about trauma-spectrum disorders. One application is to see if patients have normal function in areas of interest, such as the hippocampus. In one study we had patients with sexual abuse-related PTSD try to memorize a paragraph while they were in the PET scanner, and we compared them to normal individuals performing the same task. Although the normal individuals lighted up the hippocampus during this memory task, the PTSD patients did not. From this we concluded that the PTSD patients' hippocampi were not working properly during the memory task. Another application is to try and measure the brain circuits that underlie symptoms of trauma-spectrum disorders. For example, we can use the PET scanner to see which areas of the brain light up when patients are experiencing traumatic memories. The way this is done is to show pictures and sounds of combat to combat veterans, or read an account of a person's traumatic event, while the patient is being scanned with the PET camera. Using this, we have found a circuit involving the frontal cortex, cingulate, and hippocampus to be abnormal in PTSD patients. We have had similar findings when we scan patients with depression after they become depressed.

The Use of Genetics in Understanding Psychiatric Disorders and Stress

Another critical advance in the neurosciences has been progress in the field of genetics and the mapping of the human genome. Together with neuroimaging, genetics represents the most important area that will help us understand the basis of mental disorders. Genetics represents the information passed on to us from our parents that provides a blueprint for how we will grow and develop. By understanding genetics, we understand what makes us vulnerable to the development of disease. Much of what determines what will happen in our lives is present in our genetic material. This material is present from the time our mother's egg, or ovum, is fertilized by our father's sperm. This microscopic single cell, the fertilized ovum, astonishingly contains within itself all of the information needed to map out our development over the entire lifespan. This fertilized egg goes on to multiply and divide thousands of times over the lifespan, leading to a fully developed human being. However, the information for all of this amazing architecture is contained in a tiny blueprint in the fertilized ovum, one that contains everything needed for the development of a complex organism, called the chromosomes.

We all have 23 pairs of chromosomes, one of the pair from our mothers and the other from our fathers (Figure 2.4). Each chromosome contains millions of tiny keys for the production of proteins, which are the basic building blocks of life. These chromosomes are incredibly long, very tightly wrapped, and contained within the microscopic center, or nucleus, of the fertilized ovum. The combination of genetic material from our mothers and fathers in the pairs of chromosomes contributes to the development of a unique individual—each of us—has a little bit of both of our parents. Our understanding of the genetic code as the blueprint for the development of who we are has important implications for medicine. As specifically applied to the field of PTSD, information contained in the genetic code may help us to understand questions such as why some individuals develop psychiatric disorders following exposure to stress and others do not. Indeed, research has shown that there is a genetic vulnerability to the development of PTSD that, at least in part, determines who will and will not develop PTSD following exposure to a stressor.

One of the most important scientific accomplishments of this century was the breaking of the genetic code. This was accomplished as part of the Human Genome Project, a joint project of

DOES STRESS DAMAGE THE BRAIN?

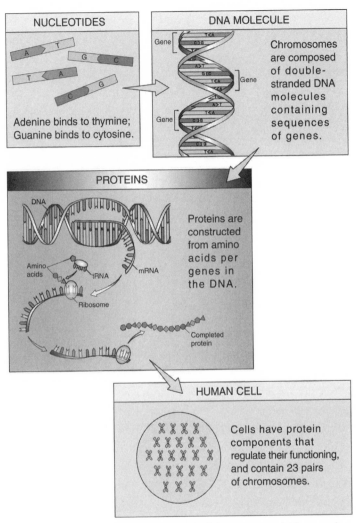

NUCLEOTIDES

Adenine binds to thymine;
Guanine binds to cytosine.

DNA MOLECULE

Gene

Gene

Gene

Chromosomes
are composed
of double-
stranded DNA
molecules
containing
sequences
of genes.

PROTEINS

DNA

Amino
acids

tRNA

mRNA

Ribosome

Completed
protein

Proteins are
constructed
from amino
acids per
genes in
the DNA.

HUMAN CELL

Cells have protein
components that
regulate their functioning,
and contain 23 pairs
of chromosomes.

Figure 2.4 Each human cell contains 23 pairs of chromosomes, which are made up of DNA containing the individual's genes. The DNA is composed of sugar-phosphate "ropes" and rungs of sequences of nucleotide bases: A (adenine), which binds with T (thymine); G (guanine), which binds with C (cytosine). The genes direct the construction of proteins from amino acids; the proteins both make up parts of the cell and control cell activity.

the National Institute of Health and private industry. In the end, the Human Genome Project deciphered over 3 billion basic units of the genetic code, at the cost of hundreds of millions of dollars and many years of effort by an international consortium of scientists. Some of the basic units of the genetic code have been determined to be the components of specific genes with specific functions; however, it is still not known what much of this information means. The breaking of the genetic code by the Human Genome Project has exciting implications for psychiatry in general and stress-related disorders in particular.

The foundation for the breaking of the genetic code lies in the pioneering work in the 20th century of James Watson and Francis Crick. In 1953, Watson and Crick made the amazing discovery that all of the information that determines who and what we will become is contained in a small space of 23 pairs of chromosomes, which are contained in a single cell. Watson and Crick described the double helix—two parallel strands of sugars called DNA or deoxyribonucleic acid—with the letters of the genetic alphabetic forming rungs of a ladder in between the two strands. The rungs of the ladder are composed of only four molecules, called *thymine, guanine, adenine*, and *cytosine*. Each rung is composed a pairing of either thymine and adenine or guanine and cytosine. Each thymine-adenine or guanine-cytosine pair is called a "base pair." These base pairs can form an infinite number of patterns, and a reading of their patterns forms the basis of the genetic code. These base pairs are "read" by another type of molecule called *messenger ribonucleic acid* (mRNA), which leads to the construction (or "transcription") of the code into proteins, which perform all of the essential functions of the body. For instance, blue eyes may be coded by a combination of thymine-guanine-adenine-adenine-adenine, whereas brown eyes are coded by adenine-adenine-thymine-guanine-adenine-cytosine. In fact, most genetic traits are coded by much longer strings of combinations of base pairs, but this simple example helps to illustrate how genetic material leads to the development of physical traits.

What is perhaps more fascinating is how the genetic material may be responsible for the development of personality traits, attitudes, and perhaps even philosophical points of view, namely those attributes that we currently think of as being encompassed by the concept of "mind." I remember being a young medical student in 1983 and hearing of a study that claimed to have found the gene for manic depression. At that time, this was an exciting finding that suggested the possibility of finding a biological basis for all of the psychiatric disorders. However, studies after that were not able to replicate this finding. Since then, other groups of scientists have triumphantly claimed to have discovered the gene for various psychiatric disorders, from schizophrenia to manic depression, only to have their findings not replicated by other groups. This has illustrated what may be an important principle, that there is no single gene for complex phenomena such as behavior or psychiatric disorders; multiple genes play a role in the development of these disorders.

An illustrative area of research related to this concerns the brain chemical serotonin. Low levels of serotonin have been found in a variety of disorders, such as depression, as well as in behavioral traits like violence and impulsiveness. The medication prozac, and other medications like it, are called *serotonin reuptake inhibitors* (SSRIs), because they act by blocking the action of what is called a *transporter*, which pumps serotonin back into the neuron after it has been released. This results in increased levels of serotonin in the space between the neurons (called the *synaptic space*), which is where all the action is, and where the neurons talk to one another. This increased serotonin in the synaptic space is thought to represent the mechanism by which patients with depression get better when they take medications like prozac. However, the serotonin transporter—like all things—is genetically determined, and genetic differences in the transporter have been found to be related to a variety of behavioral factors, including being "neurotic," impulsive, and even smoking, or how often one likes to have sex. In addition, this gene was found to be only one of probably several that determine psychiatric disorders like anxiety and depression.

CHAPTER THREE **Evolving Concepts for the Biology of Stress**

Indietro, via di qui, gente sommersa,
Andate. Non ho soppiantato nessuno,
Non ho usurpato il pane di nessuno,
Nessuno e morto in vece mia. Nessuno.
Ritornate all vostra nebbia.
Non e mia colpe se vivo e respire
E mangio e bevo e dormo e vesto panni

[Go away you partially submerged phantasms,
go away. I did not supplant anyone,
I did not take bread from anyone,
No one is dead because of me, no one.
Return to your mists and fogs.
It's not my fault if I live and breathe
And eat and drink and sleep and eat bread]
(translation by the author)

—"Ad Ora Incerta" ("At This Uncertain Hour"),
   by Primo Levi (1988)

The Two-Thousand-Year Perspective on Trauma

The past century saw a remarkable transformation in our view of the processes involved in the generation of emotion. In earlier times, there were a variety of ways in which people thought about how emotions are regulated and produced. In the Middle Ages, the conceptualization of most things was determined by views carried over from the Ancient Greeks and the dictates of religion and the church. Thus, there were various ideas of the basis of the emotions, such as a dysregulation of the "bodily humors" (an imbalance of the natural elements of matter) or, using a more theological framework, that emotions were created by possession by spirits or the influence of evil supernatural forces. In the last century, there has been an increased emphasis on examining the anatomy of the brain, the use of animal models, and most recently using neuroimaging to measure brain function, which has led to a radical change in our understanding of how the brain mediates emotion.

Prior to the last century, there were only vague concepts of how emotion is mediated. During most of this time there were no additions to the knowledge base, because of both the lack of a tradition of scientific research and strong societal and religious pressures against scientific approaches to these types of questions. For example, throughout most of the Middle Ages there were religious laws against opening up the human body after death to perform human autopsies. It was therefore impossible to learn more about the function and structure of the brain. With the 19th-century relaxation of rules prohibiting human autopsy, it was possible not only to learn more about normal human anatomy, but also to look at the brains of individuals with known neurological or behavioral problems and determine if there were any lesions such as those caused by strokes (interruption of blood supply), tumors, or other changes that could explain the deficits. (For instance, if someone has a stroke in the occipital, or visual, cortex, he/she may develop problems with vision, and lesions seen in the brain on autopsy would link that brain area with the function of vision.) Studies of patients with a variety of strokes, tumors, or other pathologies—called "lesion studies"—provided a wealth of knowledge about the function of the normal brain. For example, patients with lesions in the orbitofrontal cortex, that part of the brain that lies just above the eye sockets, were found to have increased fear reactions as well as attacks of anger and dysregulation of emotions.

Even before the advent of modern neuroanatomy and neuro-physiology, there were physicians who recorded the apparently physiological effects of exposure to extreme stress. As mentioned in Chapter 1, the American physician Da Costa (1871), treating casualties of the American Civil War, described symptoms of irritability, arousal, and elevated heart rate in soldiers exposed to combat, which became described as "Da Costa's Syndrome" or "Soldier's Irritable Heart." This represented the first connection between stress-related symptoms and a possible formulation for a stress-related physiological disturbance that involved neurohormonal and neurobiological systems involved in the stress response.

However, it was not until physicians first began consistently performing autopsies of the brain in the 19th century that our modern understanding of emotion and psychiatric disorders first took off. One of the first physicians to look at the brains of patients with mental disorders was the Swiss neuropsychiatrist Kraepelin. Kraepelin examined the brains of patients who had been diagnosed with what at the time was called *dementia praecox*, or what we would call today *schizophrenia*. Kraepelin performed these examinations because he believed that the symptoms of *dementia praecox* had their basis in the brain, and that it could be seen on postmortem examination. Kraepelin also described a condition following extreme stress called *schreckneurose* or "fright neurosis" (Saigh & Bremner, 1999b), a psychiatric condition "composed of multiple nervous and psychic phenomena arising as a result of severe emotional upheaval or sudden fright which would build up great anxiety; it can therefore be observed after serious accidents and injuries, particularly fires, railway derailments or collisions" (Kraepelin, 1896/1985, p. 737). Freud conceptualized the phenomena of hysteria as representing a mental condition that had its basis in a physiological disturbance in the brain. My reading of the cases of hysteria from Freud have led me to the strong suspicion that these patients had a history of sexual abuse. The symptoms these patients exhibited may have been related to trauma-induced changes in neurobiology. However, it would take another hundred years before advances in technology would permit these hypotheses to be examined directly.

World War I brought the important effects of traumatic stress on the individual to the attention of physicians everywhere. Freud was asked to consult about an increasing number of battle casualties. He provided the diagnosis of "war neurosis," which he felt was related to a conflicted urge to run from the battlefield. An English soldier who was trapped behind enemy lines for several days stated:

> I am subject to dreams in which I hear these shells bursting and whistling through the air. I continually see my sergeant, both alive and dead, and also my attempts to return are vividly pictured. I sometimes have in my dreams that feeling of intense hunger and thirst which I had in the village. When I awaken, I feel as though all the strength had left me and I am in a cold sweat . . . during the day if I do nothing in particular and find myself dozing, my mind seems to immediately begin to fly back to France. (Mott, 1919, pp. 126–127)

Other authors described a number of symptoms related to the extreme stress of combat, such as forgetting one's name on the battlefield, being in a daze, or forgetting important things such as all of the events that had occurred during a major battle. These types of symptoms were labeled as "shell shock," and today would be described as symptoms of dissociation. Specifically, forgetting one's name or important information, or other gaps in memory that are not due to ordinary forgetfulness, are described as "dissociative amnesia."

One physician working at the time of Freud who had an intuitive grasp of the effects of psychological trauma on the individual was Pierre Janet. Janet saw the same kind of patients with hysterical neuroses as did Freud and Charcot, but he came to different conclusions about the etiology of their symptoms. Whereas Freud saw mental life in a horizontal framework, with repressed urges being squelched by a top-heavy "superego," Janet viewed things in a more vertical fashion. He felt that extreme stressors or upsetting events could cause consciousness to split, so that mental life had two parallel processes operating side by side, which may or may not have been aware of one another. Janet observed patients who were exposed to extreme stressors and had symptoms of viewing things as if they were in a tunnel, seeing things in black and white, having time stand still, or feeling as if they were in a dream—all symptoms we would describe today as symptoms of dissociation. These patients also had classic PTSD symptoms, like hyperarousal, intrusive memories, increased startle, and fear reactions. Janet felt that some individuals were more vulnerable to stress than others. In these individuals there was a disintegration of the psyche in the face of traumatic stress that led to a "neurophysiologic breakdown of the mind." These were the individuals who later went on to develop symptoms of dissociation. In addition, Janet felt that those individuals who had a dissociative reaction to stress would be more likely to have dissociative reactions in the future. Consistent with this idea, research from both our group and Charles Marmar and colleagues found that individuals who had dissociative reactions at the time of stress were more likely to have dissociative reactions with subsequent stressors, as well as to have long-term dissociative and PTSD symptomatology, indicating that dissociative reactions to stressors were a bad reaction to stress.

Mapping of the Neural Circuitry of Stress and Emotion

While physicians were describing the effects of traumatic stress during the first half of the 20th century, scientists were describing the neuroanatomical and neurophysiologic foundations of stress and emotion (Figure 3.1). Walter Cannon (1927) first described the physiological reactions to stressors, or the "fight or

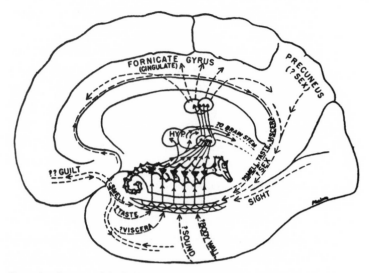

Figure 3.1 Diagram of the limbic brain, incorporating the ideas of neuroanatomists Cannon and Papez. The hippocampus (shown as a sea horse, the literal translation of the term) was felt to play a central role in the emotional brain, as well as cingulate, hypothalamus, and thalamus.

flight" response. He proposed that blood flow was shunted away from areas that were not needed for short-term survival (e.g., the stomach) in order to deliver an increase in energy stores to those areas, and shifted to areas that were critical for survival, like the brain and the muscles. The fight or flight response was important in sending energy to important parts of the body to aid in survival, and thus was "selected for" during the course of evolution. Cannon first described the role of the sympathetic nervous system in the stress response, which is responsible for activating the heart and peripheral responses to stress like sweatiness and muscle tension.

Cannon also performed studies in animals to attempt to learn about the neurological basis of emotion. The cerebral cortex is the layer of gray matter that completely surrounds the outer surface of the brain. Underneath the cerebral cortex is a layer of white matter, below which are the subcortical structures—the primitive brain areas that have been most persistent and well-preserved in the animal kingdom for the longest period of evolution, including the amygdala, thalamus, cingulate, hippocampus, and hypothalamus. Removal of the cerebral cortex in cats led to an increase in fear responses to potentially threatening or novel situations, and were accompanied by adrenaline activation, with increased blood pressure, sweating, hair standing on end, and increased release of the stress hormone epinephrine from the adrenal gland (Cannon, 1927). This behavioral response became termed as "sham rage," and led to the original hypothesis that subcortical brain structures above the level of the midbrain—such as the hypothalamus, hippocampus, cingulate, and thalamus—are involved in the generation of emotion. Cannon's own studies involved the elimination of several brain areas until he demonstrated that elimination of the hypothalamus led to an elimination of emotion. Based on this, he concluded that the hypothalamus is the seat of emotion in the brain. Cannon also discovered that the hypothalamus was the main gateway from the brain to peripheral autonomic responses. Thus, it made sense that the hypothalamus would represent the pathway by which sophisticated parts of the brain, like the frontal cortex, are related to systems such as the sympathetic nervous system that mediate peripheral autonomic responses to stressors.

The neuroanatomist Papez (1937) proposed a wider circuit of brain areas as being involved in emotion, including the subcortical regions—the hypothalamus, thalamus, medial temporal cortex (including the hippocampus and adjacent structures), and cingulate (Figure 2.2). This circuit of brain areas was described as the "limbic brain" or literally "rim brain," based on the fact that it appeared like a rim, extending from the hippocampus and other parts of the medial temporal lobe, thalamus, and hypothalamus, and around through the ring of the cingulate from the back part of the brain to the front. Cannon specifically included the cingulate and hippocampus as playing a role in emotion based on the effects of lesions or disease in these areas on emotion. This part of the brain is the oldest in evolution, making up a large portion of the brain and being well represented in lower-animal species such as rabbits, whereas the cortex makes up an increasingly larger part of the brain in higher-animal species extending up to the level of the human. The "limbic brain" was later described as "rhinencephalon" due to its relationship to the sensation of smell, and neuroanatomists pointed out the important role that smell plays in defense and other primitive behaviors in lower-animal species. The neuroanatomists noted that this "primitive brain" is preserved in all animal species and plays a critical role in "deep-seated emotions." Papez hypothesized a "circuit" of brain structures involved in emotion, which later became known as the "Papez circuit," in which information flew from the hypothalamus through the cingulate and hippocampus and other medial temporal structures and back to the hypothalamus. Information came from the bodily senses through the "gateway" of the brain—the thalamus—and was transmitted to the hypothalamus. From there the hypothalamus controlled bodily responses to emotion, as well as transmitted information to the cortex that enabled subjective experiences of emotion.

Another observation that contributed to our understanding of the neural correlates of emotion was made by Kluver and Bucy (1937, 1939), who noted that removal of the temporal lobe in monkeys resulted in an inability to recognize the psychological significance of objects, what they called "psychic blindness." Monkeys who had undergone this procedure had normal visual discrimination and motor abilities, but they would pick up objects randomly and put them in their mouths until by chance they found the object that they could eat as food. The monkeys also appeared to be without fear or emotions. Patients who had lesions in the temporal lobe are known as having "Kluver-Bucy

Syndrome." These findings suggested that the temporal lobe is involved in generating emotions and attaching psychological significance to situations.

MacLean (1949) put together the findings of Papez and Kluver and Bucy, and developed an integrative model for how the brain mediates emotion. He took the subcortical regions of the brain known as "rhinencephalon" and renamed them the "visceral brain" to emphasize the important role they played in generating peripheral visceral responses, like activation of heart rate and blood pressure and increased respiration. MacLean emphasized that the visceral brain played an important role in executing the peripheral response to emotional responses. The visceral brain was critical for a number of core processes, including response to threat, as well as feeding, reproduction, and regulation of bodily functions. The visceral brain integrated information from the senses with internal emotional states and executed a coordinated response. The brain areas involved in the visceral brain and the responses they elicited also played a critical role in the survival response. MacLean felt that abnormalities in this "primitive brain" could play a role in the development of psychiatric disorders or psychosomatic conditions, like asthma and gastric ulcers, that are not subject to the conscious control of the cerebral cortex. MacLean placed a particular emphasis on the hippocampus, which he felt articulated primitive responses like fears and phobias outside of the controlling influences of the cerebral cortex, thus leading to psychiatric disorders that could not be controlled by the conscious will. He later added other brain areas to the visceral brain—including the amygdala, septum, and prefrontal cortex—and changed the description to "limbic brain."

One fact that becomes apparent from the work done by these early neuroanatomists is that the brain areas involved in emotion are also involved in memory formation. This makes sense at a face value, because emotion is so important for survival, and one of those most important functions for survival is the fear response. Another critical function for survival is memory. If we are to survive the attack of a hungry lion, we have to be able to check the information presented to us (the charge of a large, yellow creature with sharp teeth and a furry mane) with our prior store of information (last year we were approached by a similar large, yellow creature with sharp teeth and a furry mane, and it very nearly ate us). Pulling up this memory as quickly as possible could be critical for survival. For example, if I can pull up the memory in a tenth of a second, and it takes you half a second, that may make me a survivor and you lunch. If I survive to go on and spread my genes around through lots of children and you don't, that means that the quality of having a quick recall will be selected through evolution. Thus, the hippocampus with the "fastest draw" will prevail and be perpetuated through the generations.

Some of the research by Cannon and others on fight-or-flight responses probably influenced the approach of military psychiatrists to understanding the effects of combat stress on individuals during World War II. After World War I, physicians lost interest in the effects of stress on the individual, because they no longer had to deal with the casualties of combat. Thus set in an attitude that unfortunately became all too common: that outside of major world wars there was no need to study the effects of stress on the individual, implying that stress was uncommon in civilian life, and that the effects of combat stress were transient and insubstantial. With the advent of World War II there was a renewed interest in traumatic stress. Grinker and Spiegel (1945), in their landmark volume *Men Under Stress*, addressed the psychological effects of combat, which they termed "Combat neuroses." They described symptoms of increased fear responses, shakiness, sleep disturbance, and nightmares. Grinker and Spiegel noted that many of the symptoms appeared to be related to an excessive production of the stress hormone adrenaline, and proposed surgical removal of the adrenal gland as a treatment for this condition.

Another theme that emerged from observations of combat casualties was the effect of stress on memory. Several authors noted that combat soldiers had important gaps in memory related to combat situations. For instance, in one major combat engagement in North Africa, 5% of individuals had no recall of the combat immediately after the engagement (Torrie, 1944). It was also found that the stress of combat, or of being interned in a concentration camp, had lasting effects that persisted for many years after the war. For instance, a substantial percentage of combatants had difficulties with memory for many years after combat had ceased. Also, studies of survivors of concentration camps showed that lasting effects on memory, concentration, and fatigue persisted for many years after release from the camps (Thygesen et al., 1970).

Neurohormonal Concepts of the Stress Response

In the aftermath of World War II, there was an increased focus on physiological responses to stress. A number of researchers, including Hans Selye, began to map out hormones and brain chemicals that mediate the stress response. Selye and others pointed out the critical role played by hormones such as cortisol. Cortisol is released during times of threat and is critical to survival. It redistributes the energy of our bodies when we are under attack in order to help us survive. This includes suppressing functions that we don't need for immediate survival, such as reproduction, the body's immune response, digestion, and the feeling of pain. Cortisol also promotes what we do need, increasing heart rate and blood pressure, and shifting energy to the brain and muscles, so that we can think fast and make a quick getaway. Selye emphasized the ability of stress responsive systems like cortisol to rapidly respond to a stressor and then return the organism back to a stable baseline, or "homeostasis," when the threat was past.

Another critical hormone in the stress response that was studied at this time is adrenaline (the scientific word for which is *catecholamines*, or *norepinephrine* and *epinephrine*, referred to as *adrenaline* from here on out for simplicity's sake). Stress results in a massive outpouring of adrenaline. Adrenaline is released in both the brain and the body and has several functions that are critical for survival. Adrenaline sharpens the senses, focuses attention, raises the level of fear, quickens the heart rate and blood pressure, and in general prepares us for the worst. The adrenaline system is like a fire alarm that tells all of the cells of the brain (called *neurons*) that something really bad is about to happen if everyone on the team doesn't get their act together real fast. In other words, this system sacrifices the ability to convey specific information to specific parts of the brain in order to obtain more speed. It is very good at rapidly communicating information that things are not all right, but it can't tell you exactly what, or why. However, this type of system is very useful, and can serve to focus the senses (by activating the neurons that collect information obtained by the senses) in order to rapidly and efficiently obtain information about threatening situations in the environment. The adrenaline system is also very efficient. At the same time it stimulates the cells of the brain to more efficiently collect information about what is happening in the environment, it also stimulates the heart to beat more rapidly and blood pressure to increase. This promotes an emergency transfer of oxygen and nutrients needed for survival to all the cells of the body. The beauty of the system is that the same chemical messenger that "turns on" the brain also stimulates the heart (as well as other bodily organs) in order to facilitate survival. This close coordination may underlie what poets and philosophers have intuitively known for centuries, that the heart and mind are closely linked.

At the time that Hans Selye and others were performing studies of the effects of stress on cortisol, John Mason conducted a number of studies, using monkeys as models for combat pilots, to examine the effects of combat stress on the individual. Mason showed that stress was associated with increases in a number of physiological parameters—including adrenaline (epinephrine), noradrenaline (norepinephrine), cortisol, and thyroid hormone—and with decreases in the sex hormone testosterone. One of the true pioneers in psychiatry at this time was the psychiatrist Lawrence Kolb, a keen observer who picked up on telltale signs in his veteran patients in the period after World War II. He was treating veterans who had problems adjusting to civilian life after returning from the war, patients who were suffering from what we would call today posttraumatic stress disorder (although this was not officially recognized as a diagnosis by the American Psychiatric Association until 1980). While his patients were in his waiting room, Kolb could look out of his office and see them sitting there with their backs to him. He noticed that every time his secretary's typewriter came to the end of a carriage return and made a loud dinging sound, his patients would jump out of their chairs. He speculated that this response, known as the *startle response* and now recognized as a symptom of PTSD, was secondary to excessive levels of norepinephrine release in his traumatized patients.

Scientists like Mason and Selye emphasized the adaptive role of stress hormone release and were interested in understanding the physiological bases for resilience to stress. This research did not, however, focus on the long-term effects of stress on physiology.

Development of a Psychiatric Diagnosis for the Stress Response

The experience of World War II was still fresh in the minds of psychiatrists when the first edition of the *Diagnostic and Statistical Manual* (*DSM*) was formulated in 1952, and the philosophy of a short and reversible effect of stress on the individual guided their approach to thinking about psychological trauma. Psychiatrists quote chapter and verse in formulating their psychiatric diagnoses and assessments. However, the *DSM*-guided approach to psychiatry is not without its controversy or detractors. The *DSM* has taken a "splitters" approach to diagnosis, as opposed to a "lumpers" approach, and this has resulted in every new edition of the *DSM* becoming progressively larger than the previous version. In fact, one of the central tenets of this book is that several diagnoses in the *DSM* that are related to stress are best thought of as linked together in a cluster of what I have termed "trauma-spectrum psychiatric disorders" which, in turn, are best thought of as neurologically based disorders that result from the effects of stress on the brain.

Since its introduction in 1952, the vagaries of the *DSM* over time have reflected the changing attitude of psychiatrists and the field of mental health in general toward the effects of psychological trauma on the individual. For instance, at the time of World War II (as mentioned earlier), people thought that the effects of stress on the individual were normally time limited and reversible. This philosophy was incorporated into the diagnosis of gross stress reaction, which was first incorporated into the *DSM* in 1952. Gross Stress Reaction described a series of stress-related symptoms in response to an extreme stressor that would be traumatic for almost anyone. This disorder did not take into account the fact that individuals with preexisting psychiatric disorders may develop a new disorder that is specifically related to the stressor, or that acute responses to stress can translate into long-term pathology. It is as if gross stress reaction was a response to the reality that extreme stressors such as war can lead to psychiatric outcomes that are not secondary to "bad personalities." (Military psychiatrists in WWII had tried in vain to find premilitary personality traits that would help them predict who was most vulnerable to the stress of combat.) Embodied in gross stress reaction was the ambivalence that has pervaded psychiatry until the current time about whether stress has merely transient effects, or whether it can lead to permanent psychopathology.

It was not until the Vietnam War that the potentially permanent effects of traumatic stress on the individual were recognized. At that time, there was controversy regarding the effects of stress on the individual. One theory, the *stress evaporation theory*, stated that the actual effects of combat stress "evaporated" within a few months of traumatic exposure, and that what was left was only the psychopathology or defects in character that were present in the individual prior to their combat experiences. This theory was largely the foundation of earlier diagnoses in the *Diagnostic and Statistical Manual* from the 1940s and 1950s, such as gross stress reaction, which viewed psychological symptoms in the aftermath of trauma as a normal response to trauma that would rapidly resolve. The other theory of traumatic stress, called the *residual stress theory*, held that the symptoms seen in veterans of the Vietnam War were related to the effects of combat itself, not to premorbid personality or other unrelated factors. The truth is probably somewhere in the middle, in that prior stress does play a role in the response to the current stressor, but it is not the only determining factor.

Two other theories that have dominated stress research are the theories of *stress inoculation* and *stress sensitization* (Figley, 1978). The theory of *stress inoculation* holds that a history of prior stress strengthens the individual's ability to deal with future stressors. This theory is embodied in popular belief by the common movie story line of, for example, the individual who crashes a small plane in the Arctic wilderness and somehow through his/ her wits survives and becomes a better person for it. The alternative theory, *stress sensitization*, first outlined by the famous stress researcher Hans Selye in the 1940s, holds that repeated stress increases the risk for development of abnormalities in both neurobiology and behavior following reexposure to stress. A number of studies in animals have shown that reexposure to stress results in increased physiological responding relative to animals that have never been exposed to stress. Studies in human subjects exposed to extreme stress are also consistent with the idea that a prior history of exposure to stress is a risk factor for the development of stress-related psychopathology. These findings are consistent with the *stress sensitization* viewpoint; however, we still do not understand the physiological basis of resilience that we see repeatedly on a practical basis in trauma survivors.

The development of PTSD as an established diagnosis—and with it the concept that stress can have permanent detrimental effects on the brain—permitted studies of the neurobiology of traumatized patients who met criteria for this disorder (Bremner, Southwick, & Charney, 1999). This led to a time when it was accepted as a given fact by many researchers that PTSD was a real diagnosis, and these researchers set about studying both the neurobiological correlates of this disorder and new treatment approaches. Much of this work began at the West Haven Veterans Hospital and Yale University in the 1980s. I was a resident in psychiatry at this institution in the late 1980s, at the time when Congress mandated a National Center for Posttraumatic Stress Disorder at this site, so that more could be learned about the long-term effects of the Vietnam War on combat veterans. In the aftermath of the Vietnam War, pioneers at West Haven VA included the psychiatrist Art Blank, who advocated for a systematic assessment and treatment of combat veterans with mental complaints, and later promoted the development of a national Vietnam Veterans Outreach Center program to seek out veterans in need of treatment who did not have access to VA hospital facilities. Also at this time the first controlled trial of antidepressant medication for the treatment of PTSD was conducted, and John Mason and colleagues ran the first studies of the stress hormones cortisol, norepinephrine, and epinephrine.

An Expanding Body of Knowledge
on the Neurobiology of Stress

The background of studies of PTSD neurobiology was an increasing body concerning knowledge of the effects of stress on physiology gleaned from animal studies. There is a long history of creating animal models for the first study of depression, and more recently that of anxiety. Most methodologies for animal models for depression and anxiety involve exposing the animal to extreme stress. In one of the more popular animal models, animals are exposed to repeated stress from which they cannot escape. This eventually leads to certain behaviors that are termed "learned helplessness," which correlate with specific biological changes such as depletion of brain norepinephrine. Behavioral changes related to stress include weight loss and decreased food intake, decreased active behavior in novel environments such as "open fields," decreased competitiveness and normal aggressiveness, decreased grooming and play activity, decreased responding for rewards, decreased self-stimulation of brain reward centers, deficits in memory and attention, sleep disturbances, and increased defecation (indicative of "anxiety" in the rat, Weiss, Simson, Ambrose, Webster, & Hoffman, 1985). Behaviors seen in rodents exposed to stress in many ways parallel behaviors seen in humans with a history of traumatic stress. For instance, decreased exploration in open fields can be seen as avoidance, decreased grooming and play activity as being cut off from others, and decreased responding for rewards and self-stimulation as emotional numbing.

One of the most extensively studied stress response systems has been the norepinephrine (noradrenaline) system (reviewed in Bremner, Krystal, Southwick, & Charney, 1996a, 1996b). The majority of norepinephrine cell bodies in the brain are located in a brainstem site called the *locus coeruleus* (*dorsal pons*), with long neurons that project to multiple brain sites for direct release of norepinephrine neurotransmitter. Scientists such as Gary Aston-Jones (Aston-Jones, Chiang, & Alexinsky, 1991) have extensively studied the anatomy of the norepinephrine system. This system responds to a variety of stressors as well as signs of internal distress (e.g., a drop in blood pressure due to a loss of blood), representing a "central relay station" that responds to information from a variety of sources, and rapidly and globally activates the peripheral response to stress as well as the brain. During states of rest, feeding, and grooming, this system is in a quiet state, but with stressors there is a rapid activation that is associated with an increase in heart rate and blood pressure, and norepinephrine in the blood. There is also an increase in behaviors that are characteristically seen during situations of stress and fear. Infusion of norepinephrine or electrical stimulation of this system results, similar to administration of drugs like yohimbine that stimulate the systems, in an increase in fear-related behaviors. All of these findings point to the important role that norepinephrine plays in the stress response.

The adrenaline system, however, does not work like an all-or-none phenomenon. Gary Aston-Jones performed an experiment in which he stimulated electrically the source of the norepinephrine cells in the brain. This resulted in an increase in the levels of norepinephrine in the brains of monkeys who were playing a video game in which they had to focus on a point on a screen in order to get their favorite bananas. Aston-Jones found that increasing stimulation caused the monkeys to be more awake and alert and to perform better on the video game, but only to a certain point. Beyond that point, the monkeys merely became more anxious and distracted, and their performance on the video game started to decline (Aston Jones et al., 1991). The findings are consistent with an inverted U-curve for norepinephrine, where lower levels of norepinephrine stimulation increase the efficiency of the brain, whereas very high levels make it more inefficient (Figure 3.2). Similar results have been obtained in

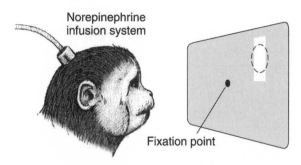

Figure 3.2 A monkey performs the task of pushing a bar when he sees a certain shape on a screen, which requires concentration. Increasing levels of norepinephrine are infused into his brain and his performance is measured. With mild increases in norepinephrine, his performance on the task improves. However, with very high levels of norepinephrine, his performance begins to worsen. This illustrates the Yerkes-Dodd inverted U effect, as well as one of the mechanisms by which stress can impair cognitive function.

traumatized patients, as reviewed in more detail later in this chapter.

Studies in animals showed that repeated exposure to stressors over a lifetime resulted in exaggerated norepinephrine responses. Elizabeth Abercrombie and others have demonstrated that animals that have a history of prior exposure to stress have increased release of norepinephrine with repeated exposure to a stressor, as compared to animals without such a prior history (Abercrombie, Keller, & Zigmond, 1988). There was specifically increased release of norepinephrine in the hippocampus (Madison & Nicoll, 1982), which has also been shown to be very sensitive to stress. In animals for whom the production of norepinephrine is not fast enough to keep up with the demands of increased stress, there is a depletion of brain norepinephrine content with associated behavioral changes that have been termed *learned helplessness* (Weiss et al., 1985).

Norepinephrine also plays a critical role in the human stress response. Individuals given injections of norepinephrine have increases in blood pressure, breathing rate, and subjective sensations of anxiety. Individuals jumping out of airplanes, driving race cars, or flying combat jets experience an increase in both norepinephrine and epinephrine. During public speaking, plasma epinephrine levels increase twofold, whereas during physical exercise, plasma norepinephrine levels increase threefold (reviewed in Bremner, Krystal, Southwick, & Charney, 1996a, 1996b).

Noradrenergic function is increased in patients with PTSD (reviewed in Bremner, Krystal, Southwick, & Charney, 1996, and Murburg, 1994). Initial studies collected urine over a 24-hour period in Vietnam combat veterans with PTSD and compared it to that of normal individuals. It was found that PTSD patients had higher levels of norepinephrine and epinephrine (adrenaline) in their urine than did the normal individuals (Mason, Giller, Kosten, & Harkness, 1988; Pitman & Orr, 1990). Other studies showed that exposure to reminders of Vietnam in the form of combat-related slides and sounds resulted in increased release of norepinephrine in the blood (Blanchard, Kolb, Prins, Gates, & McCoy, 1991; McFall, Murburg, Ko, & Veith, 1990). Studies by Roger Pitman and others consistently found increased heart rate and blood pressure reactions to traumatic reminders (McFall, Veith, & Murburg, 1992; Pitman, Orr, Forgue, De Jong, & Claiborn, 1987). PTSD patients who were given the medication yohimbine, which stimulates release of norepinephrine in the brain, showed much higher levels of norepinephrine release (as measured by metabolites of norepinephrine in the blood) than did normal individuals without PTSD. In addition, stimulating the norepinephrine system recreated the symptoms of PTSD, including flashbacks, excessive arousal and hypervigilance, and increased startle responses (Southwick et al., 1993, 1997).

These studies suggest that excessive norepinephrine release underlies many of the symptoms of PTSD, including trouble with concentrating, being excessively vigilant and fearful when there is nothing to worry about, being easily startled, and having trouble sleeping. Some of the PTSD patients I have treated have increased usage of substances such as heroin, alcohol, and benzodiazepine-type medications like Valium. Many of the patients who came in to the specialized inpatient unit for the treatment for PTSD at a veteran's hospital in Connecticut where I worked came off of heroin for the first time in many years. I noticed that withdrawal from heroin made their symptoms of PTSD much worse. This made sense, because heroin, alcohol, and benzodiazepines act by decreasing activity of the norepinephrine neurons in the brain. In order to test this, we asked patients whether these substances made their symptoms better or worse. The majority of patients said that these substances, especially heroin, made their symptoms of hyperarousal, hypervigilance, startle, and intrusive memories much better. In addition, patients started using these substances after their PTSD started, and as their PTSD symptoms became worse their use of these substances increased (Bremner, Southwick, Darnell, & Charney, 1996).

In order to see if the brain response to stimulation of the norepinephrine system was different in PTSD patients, we administered a medication that stimulates the norepinephrine system and measured brain responses using *positron emission tomography* (PET), a type of brain imaging. This technique allowed us to see what was happening to brain neurons when patients were experiencing symptoms, for example when symptoms were provoked by stimulation of the norepinephrine system with medications. What happened was that normal individuals had an increase in brain function, as if they were at the low end of the norepinephrine dose response curve, whereas brain function in PTSD patients shut down, which told us that they had very high levels of norepinephrine release. In particular, the areas most affected were the frontal lobe, which plays an important role in planning and thinking as well as maintaining attention, and the hippocampus, a brain area involved in learning and memory (Bremner, Innis, et al., 1997). These studies told us that this shutdown of the brain in the PTSD patients may have been associated with an impairment in thinking that is particularly pronounced when they are under stress—the precise time when they most need their wits about them. That stimulation of the system causes it to overreact.

Another hormonal system that plays an important role in the stress response is cortisol (Figure 3.3). Like norepinephrine, cortisol is released during times of threat and is critical to survival. Cortisol redistributes the energy of our bodies when we are under attack in order to help us survive. Release of cortisol is driven by a protein in the brain called *corticotropin releasing factor* (CRF). Normally CRF is released from the hypothalamus—a window

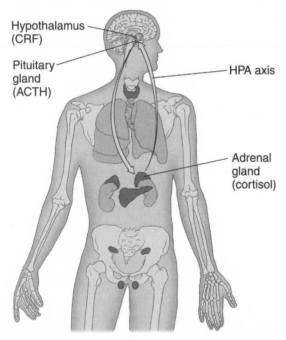

Figure 3.3 Each of the glands produces and releases hormones into the bloodstream. The arrow shows the hypothalamic-pituitary-adrenal (HPA) axis, which controls the release of the stress hormone cortisol.

DOES STRESS DAMAGE THE BRAIN?

from the brain to the body. The hypothalamus allows the brain to regulate the body's stress response system. CRF stimulates the pituitary gland, (a small almond-shaped gland that releases hormones in the body), to release another hormone called *adrenocorticotropin hormone* (ACTH), which in turn stimulates release of cortisol from the adrenal gland, which is near the stomach. Animals that are chronically stressed have increases in CRF and cortisol that persist throughout life (Coplan et al.,1996; Ladd, Owens, & Nemeroff, 1996; Levine, 1962; Levine, Weiner, & Coe, 1993; Plotsky & Meaney, 1993). High levels of CRF also seem to increase behaviors of fear and anxiety. Studies in animals also showed that CRF did not normally stimulate ACTH, which indicated that the pituitary gland was overstimulated by excessive levels of CRF.

Studies in human subjects have validated the important role of cortisol in the stress response. Underwater demolition team training (Rubin, Rahe, Arthur, & Clark, 1969), landing aircraft on aircraft carriers (Miller, Rubin, Clark, Crawford, & Arthur, 1970), and other highly stressful experiences (Rose, Poe, & Mason, 1968; reviewed in Miller, 1968) resulted in elevations in serum cortisol relative to background levels. The exact relationship between stress and cortisol in human subjects, however, is complex, and is highly dependent on psychological factors. For instance, in one study measuring levels of urinary cortisol in helicopter ambulance medics, there was no difference between ground time and time flying on combat missions with the threat of death. Overall, the medics had lower cortisol levels than expected from normal samples. The authors noted that psychological factors—such as feelings of being in control, invulnerability, and downplaying the threat of death—probably played an important role in their findings (Bourne, Rose, & Mason, 1967). Consistent with this, combat veterans under threat of an impending attack in Vietnam showed differing levels of cortisol depending on their role. The officers and the radiomen, who were actively planning the response, had elevated levels, whereas the enlisted men, who had no part in the preparation, had lowered levels (Bourne, Rose, & Mason, 1968). Miller (1968) summarized this literature, and concluded that psychological factors, including feelings of controls and competency, play an important role in the cortisol response to stress.

When PTSD patients were first studied, it was found that cortisol levels appeared to be lower than normal, the opposite of the increased cortisol levels found in stressed animals (Mason, Giller, Kosten, Ostroff, & Podd, 1986). A number of studies by Rachel Yehuda have shown that cortisol is lower or unchanged compared to normal individuals (Yehuda, Southwick, et al., 1991). Yehuda and colleagues also found an increased feedback sensitivity to cortisol, such that the system appeared to turn itself off more actively than normal (Yehuda et al., 1993). However, there are other aspects of the cortisol system in PTSD that suggest increased activity. For instance, we found that levels of CRF were increased in the cerebrospinal fluid that bathes the brain (Bremner, Licinio, et al., 1997). Also, ACTH response to CRF stimulation was blunted, suggesting increased CRF release, similar to that seen in stressed animals (Smith et al., 1989). During exposure to stressors such as challenging mental tasks, or with reminders of the trauma, we have found an increased cortisol release. These studies suggest a chronic dysregulation of the cortisol system, with possibly increased cortisol responses to stress.

There are other brain chemical systems besides cortisol and norepinephrine that are involved in the stress response. For instance, our brains contain receptors that bind Valium, the anti-anxiety sedative benzodiazepine medication. In animals, chronic stress leads to reductions in this receptor in the frontal cortex of the brain. Similarly, we used brain imaging to measure the Valium-type receptors in the frontal cortex of human patients with PTSD, and found a similar reduction (Bremner, Innis, et al., 2000). The brain also has natural receptors that bind opiates (like heroin), and the brain can make endogenous opiates similar to heroin. These endogenous opiates are released during stress and may serve a useful purpose in reducing pain, which may have survival value. Studies in patients with PTSD have suggested a decrease in pain sensitivity during traumatic reminders, possibly linking the opiate system to the symptoms of PTSD (van der Kolk, Greenberg, Orr, & Pitman, 1989).

The serotonin system is also involved in the stress response. Serotonin is important because it is the system on which medications such as prozac and paxil act, and these medications have been shown to be useful in the treatment of PTSD. Stressors resulted in increased release of serotonin in the frontal cortex, and serotonin medications or administration of serotonin in the frontal cortex brought about a reversal of stress-induced behaviors (Petty, Kramer, & Wilson, 1992; Sherman & Petty, 1982). Some studies of PTSD have shown a reduction in the receptors for serotonin, or that drugs that stimulate the serotonin system result in an increase in PTSD symptoms (Fichtner, O'Conner, Yeoh, Arora, & Crayton, 1995). We have recently found that the medication paxil, which blocks the reuptake of serotonin from the synapse (the space between neurons) improves PTSD symptoms as well as memory and concentration, and increases the size of a brain area sensitive to stress that is involved in learning and memory (the hippocampus).

Involvement of the Amygdala in the Stress Response

In parallel with these neurobiological studies in PTSD patients, neuroanatomical investigations in animals have continued that have furthered the work of Cannon, Papez, and MacLean, and have further informed thinking about the neurobiology of PTSD. These studies have validated the work of the early neuroanatomists in showing that brain regions involved in memory also play an important role both in fear-related behaviors seen naturally in the wild, and in manifestations of increased peripheral responses to stressors. One brain area that MacLean added to the fear circuit that has subsequently been shown to play a critical role in fear responses is the amygdala. Early studies in cats showed that electrical stimulation of the amygdala resulted in signs of increased stress responses and fear-related behaviors seen in the wild when the animal was being attacked or was attacking, including alerting, chewing, salivation, piloerection, turning, facial twitching, arching of the back, hissing, and snarling. In addition, the animals had an increased output of the stress-responsive hormone, adrenaline (Hilton & Zbrozna, 1963). Electrical stimulation of the amygdala in humans also resulted in signs and symptoms of fear and anxiety, including an increase in heart rate and blood pressure, increased muscle tension, subjective sensations of fear or anxiety (Chapman et al., 1954), and increases in peripheral adrenaline release (Gunne & Reis, 1963).

Over the past decade or two, Joseph LeDoux, Michael Davis, and others have elucidated the pathways by which the amygdala plays a critical role in the stress response (Figure 3.4). These studies have shown that the amygdala is involved in conditioned

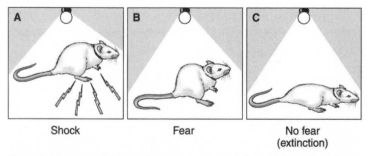

Shock   Fear   No fear
(extinction)

Figure 3.4 Diagram of fear conditioning. A rat exposed to a light and an electric shock simultaneously will later develop a fear reaction to the light alone. With repeated exposure to the light, however, the fear reaction subsides, a phenomenon known as extinction to fear. The amygdala has been shown to play a critical role in the acquisition of fear responses, and the medial prefrontal cortex, through inhibition of amygdala function, is hypothesized to play a role in extinction of fear.

DOES STRESS DAMAGE THE BRAIN?

fear reactions. A basic laboratory model of conditioned fear responses involves pairing a neutral stimulus (like a bright light) with a fear-inducing stimulus (like electric shock). These pairing leads to fear responses to the light alone. This phenomenon, known as *fear conditioning*, is mediated by the amygdala, an ancient and primitive brain area located in the center of the brain. The amygdala—a small walnut-shaped brain region—hangs off of the most forward part of the hippocampus. Repeated exposure to the conditioned stimulus (the bright light) alone normally results in the gradual loss of fear responding. The phenomenon, known as *extinction to conditioned fear responses*, has been hypothesized to be secondary to the formation of new memories that mask the original conditioned fear memory. The extinguished memory is rapidly reversible following reexposure to the conditioned–unconditioned stimulus pairing (bright light and electric shock), even up to one year after the original period of fear conditioning, suggesting that the fear response did not disappear but was merely inhibited (Bouton & Swartzentruber, 1991; McAllister & McAllister, 1988). In fact, recent evidence suggests that extinction is mediated by medial prefrontal cortical inhibition of amygdala responsiveness.

The neuroanatomy and neurophysiology of conditioned fear responses in animals have been well characterized (Davis, 1992). Lesions of the central nucleus of the amygdala have been shown to completely block fear-potentiated startle (Hitchcock & Davis, 1986; Hitchcock, Sananes, & Davis, 1989), whereas electrical stimulation of the central nucleus increases acoustic startle (Rosen & Davis, 1988). The central nucleus of the amygdala projects to a variety of brain structures, including the brainstem, to stimulate peripheral stress responses. These findings demonstrate that the amygdala is involved in emotional memory (even conditioned fear responses), as well as effecting the stress response.

Studies in human subjects support a role for the amygdala in emotion and the stress response. Such studies have demonstrated that the threat of electric shock results in an increase in startle response (Grillon, Ameli, Woods, Merikangas, & Davis, 1991). Patients with lesions of the amygdala showed impaired acquisition of fear conditioning relative to normal.

Studies have also detected abnormalities of the startle response in patients with PTSD (Morgan, Grillon, Southwick, Davis, & Charney, 1995). Increased startle magnitude has been found in Vietnam combat veterans with PTSD, in comparison to Vietnam combat veterans without PTSD or normal individuals. The heightened responsiveness to reminders of the original trauma (or conditioned emotional stimuli) and abnormalities of the startle response are probably mediated by the amygdala, in addition to other brain regions mediating the stress response.

PTSD patients show evidence of symptoms that may be related to altered function of the amygdala. One of my patients who had been sexually molested in childhood told me:

> I want to be physically close to other people but I feel so shocked and betrayed when they want to make it into something sexual. If anyone (including myself) has a sexual urge I feel betrayed. I have the mind of a child. I just want to cuddle but it always turns into something sexual, and then I become very afraid. When I was a child I freaked out when people wanted me to dance with boys.
>
> I put myself in bad situations, thinking if I expose myself to men that I can desensitize myself, but it's really bad, and I just get violated again. If someone touches me I say to myself "ug" and I become very afraid. Then I think about what they are doing and if they are slow I can think about it and desensitize myself to their touching me. But they never go slow and they just want to keep going and get into the genital thing and that just freaks me out. I'd be happy to have a relationship that doesn't involve sex at all, like an animal that just touches and rubs your belly or whatever but never does anything sexual.

DOES STRESS DAMAGE THE BRAIN?

This patient had problems with conditioned fear responses to reminders of traumatic sexual experiences. She was unable to extinguish fear responses to these traumatic reminders. We hypothesized that this was related to dysfunction of medial prefrontal cortical areas that normally should suppress the amygdala, which plays a critical role in fear responding. This is outlined in more detail in later chapters.

Nature and Nurture in PTSD

Work on the neurobiology of PTSD in some ways has set many ideas of American psychiatry on its head. For the first half of the 20th century, American psychiatry was dominated by Freud's theories. These views held sway until the advance of biological approaches to psychiatry, which have become increasingly prominent over the past 30 years. Biological psychiatrists aimed to replace Freud's theories of psychopathology (based on the notions of imbalances of psychological forces) with what they felt was a more scientific approach. In their view, psychopathology was secondary to disruptions of physiology that had their foundation in genetic vulnerability. This framework placed great emphasis on genetic abnormalities leading to physiological changes, with their phenomenological expression in psychiatric disorders. In the early phase of biological psychiatry, there was great emphasis on finding the genetic basis for psychiatric disorders, and little emphasis on the role of environment in the genesis of psychopathology. As is often true in the history of the development of ideas, the biological psychiatrists effectively leaped backward over 50 years of psychoanalysis to psychiatrists such as Kraepelin (1919). Kraepelin also believed that psychiatric disorders had their basis in constitutional abnormalities that expressed themselves in the brain, and performed neuroanatomical studies of the brains of schizophrenics in order to find a lesion to explain their illness.

The biological psychiatrists who used this model, however, were really not much different from the psychoanalysts who preceded them. Both groups gave little or no credence to the role that *environment* could play in the development of psychiatric illness. Biological psychiatry emphasized the deterministic effects of genetics, whereas psychoanalysts focused on unconscious mechanisms upon which the environment had little impact (e.g., it was at one time considered radical that children should be observed in order to understand their internal psychology). Thirty years after the start of the biological revolution in psychiatry, although we still haven't found the genes for schizophrenia or mania, it is clear that genetic factors do play an important role in psychiatric disorders. Most likely, a *combination* of genetic and environmental factors—of nature and nurture—is involved in the development of psychopathology. In terms of possible environmental causes of psychopathology, stress is a good candidate.

When some of the initial studies of changes in the brain and neurobiology in PTSD were published several years ago, the editor of the *American Journal of Psychiatry*, Nancy Andreasen (1995), wrote an editorial on the "Manichean Duality of PTSD." She referred to the conception up until that time of PTSD representing a psychological disorder, while disorders such as schizophrenia were thought to have a biological basis in their etiology. According to this thinking, stress was a psychological condition that led to psychological disorders such as PTSD, whereas schizophrenia had its basis in genetics and haywire neurodevelopment due to bad neuronal wiring. The idea that what you saw, felt, or otherwise experienced purely through your sensations could have lasting effects on your neurophysiology had a potentially revolutionary implication for understanding psychiatry. In spite of the fact that thousands of studies, all the way up to the level of the primate, had shown that stress can have lasting effects on neurophysiology, it was difficult to accept the fact that the same could be true for humans. This upset the normal conception of the dichotomy between nature and nurture, mind and brain, biology and psychology.

However, a careful consideration of this debate reveals the artificial nature of the dichotomy. The more we learn about the nature of genetics, the more we realize that our genetic material is not as fixed as we may have believed. In fact, the expression of our genetic material can be modified by environmental events, including stressors. Likewise, our response to environmental events like stressors, and perhaps even our vulnerability to exposure to stress, is influenced by genetics. These false dichotomies between nature and nurture, mind and brain, and biology and psychology beg the question of whether we should be thinking in polar terms of the effects of psychological stress as being related to mind or brain. In fact, these questions raise the issue of whether PTSD should be considered a purely psychiatric disorder. What we are learning points to the fact that psychological trauma has a broad-based effect on all aspects of physiology, suggesting that we should think as much about the effects of stress on heart disease as on mental function. This leads again to some of the central tenets of this book: (a) the effects of psychological trauma are best understood as a physiological effect on the brain resulting in neurological dysfunction that in turn results in psychiatric symptoms of PTSD and related conditions; (b) that other disorders like depression and substance abuse are similarly related to the effects of stress on the brain, and should be considered together with PTSD as being part of a trauma-spectrum of disorders; and (c) stress has a broad range of effects on the organism, and we should stop limiting our thinking to psychiatric disorders, and instead broaden our conceptualizing to include the effects of stress on the heart, mind, brain, immune system, and metabolism, as well as on the soul.

CHAPTER FOUR

**Effects of Stress
on Memory and
the Brain**

*Terrible were the methods of torture they devised in their quest for food. They
stuffed bitter vetch up the genital passages of their victims, and drove sharp
stakes into their seats. Torments horrible even to hear about they inflicted on
people to make them admit possession of one loaf or reveal the hiding-place of
a single handful of barley.*

—From *Josephus: The Jewish War*, translated by G. A. Williamson

Lasting Effects of Stress on the Brain

Research in only the past decade or so has shown that extreme
stress has effects on the brain that last throughout the lifespan
(Bremner, Southwick, & Charney, 1999; Charney, Deutch, Krystal, Southwick, & Davis, 1993; Friedman, Charney, & Deutch,
1995). The brain areas most sensitive to stress are the same systems that we call upon for survival in a situation of extreme
threat, such as the norepinephrine and cortisol systems described
in previous chapters. Brain areas involved in memory also play
a critical role in the stress response; these brain areas are very
sensitive to the effects of stress. Such observations have led to
one of the main points of this book, that traumatic stressors have
neurological consequences that in turn mediate symptoms of
stress-related psychiatric disorders like PTSD and depression. Below we will look in more detail at the bad effects of stress on the
brain and the body, and think about the possibility that stress can
damage the brain, especially brain areas involved in memory.

At both the levels of science and society we are increasingly interested in the relationship between stress and memory. An interesting area of research is related to so-called flashbulb memories (Brown & Kulik, 1977). This refers to the phenomenon of remembering things that happened around the time of a significant event; for instance, we remember where we were when we heard that planes had crashed into the World Trade Center. Several studies were done on memories surrounding the time of the Space Shuttle *Challenger* disaster (which exploded on the launch pad while thousands of children watched live from their schoolrooms). These studies found that the stress and novelty of an event like the *Challenger* disaster will strengthen memories for other events surrounding that time, like what you had for lunch that day or where you were, so that these memories are more strongly engraved than other memories occurring on a more mundane day. However, the researchers found that part of the enhancement of memory was related to a "rehearsal effect," in which people tended to talk in later days about what they were doing that day, which led to a strengthening of memory. These rehearsal effects can actually lead to distortions in memory, in that you remember what you (inaccurately) recalled about the day, and the memory of rehearsing the event becomes stronger than the reality (Winograd & Neisser, 1992).

There is also evidence that stress can inhibit the laying down of memory. An important area in the legal arena is the accuracy of eyewitness testimony related to violent crime. Often convictions are based on the ability of eyewitnesses to identify someone at the scene of a crime. However, detailed information based on the recollection of the eyewitness is often patchy and distorted. Experiments by the psychologists Christiansen and Loftus found that memory for a picture with a threatening scene (e.g., a man holding a gun) was biased toward the part of the picture that held the greatest threat, namely the gun (Christiansen, Loftus, Hoffman, & Loftus, 1991). Because of this, memory for other parts of the picture were more vague, which led to the unwanted effect that memory for the face of the individual holding the gun was more vague. This showed that memories for stressful events involve a biased preference for the aspects of the memory that showed the most immediate threat, namely the gun. These findings have negative implications for the use of eyewitness testimony in criminal court trials.

Delayed Recall of Abuse and Other Traumas

Another area of interest to the legal system is the memory of episodes of childhood abuse that happened many years ago. Over the past decade or so there has been an explosion of court cases in which individuals sue parents or others whom they claim abused them as children. Often these plaintiffs claim that the memory of abuse came many years later, rushing into their consciousness with a flood of graphic memories and emotions. One has only to pick up a newspaper to read about controversies related to the validity of memories of long-ago childhood abuse. There has been considerable controversy surrounding such validity, with some experts criticizing self-reported abuse as representing false memories suggested by over-zealous psychotherapists or the media and popular culture. Memories can, in fact, be susceptible to insertions, deletions, and distortions, often resulting in a situation in which the individual remains convinced of the validity of the memory as experienced in its altered form.

Scientists have developed paradigms to attempt to experimentally manipulate memories (Loftus & Loftus, 1980). For example, Elizabeth Loftus and her coworkers showed a story in slides in which a person came to a stop sign, turned right, and hit a pedestrian. Later, suggestions were offered that the person came to a yield sign before hitting the pedestrian. This later confounding information caused a significant number of people to falsely recall that the original story involved a yield sign (Loftus, Miller, & Burns, 1978). Studies by Ira Hyman and others involved interviewing individuals repeatedly over time about the details related to an event such as a relative's wedding that occurred when the individual was a child (Hyman, Husband, & Billings, 1995). During these interviews, the researchers would offer misleading information, like "Remember when you spilled the punch bowl on the bride?" At first, the subjects would not remember, but with repeated interviews many individuals would falsely reconstruct elaborate memories related to the "spilling the punch bowl incident," filling in many peripheral details such as what happened immediately before and after the supposed incident. Another experimental method for assessing so-called "false memory effects" involves learning lists of words that are all highly associated with a primary word that is not, however, part of the list of studied words. For example, during recall of a list of words like *thread, pin, eye, sewing, sharp, point, prick, thimble, haystack, thorn, hurt, injection, syringe, cloth, knitting,* the "critical lure" *needle* (which is highly associated with the other words) is falsely recalled about half the time (Roediger & McDermott, 1995). These findings have been used to build up the claim that memories for events such as childhood abuse are subject to distortions and modifications.

Both myself, working with Katy Shobe and John Kihlstrom (2000), and a group from Harvard including Clancy, Schacter, McNally, and Pitman (2000), found that women with self-reported childhood sexual abuse and the diagnosis of PTSD showed high levels of false recognition using this paradigm. We have also found that patients with PTSD have other types of memory problems, including problems remembering facts and lists or a paragraph that was read to them a few moments before. Based on this research, we concluded that abuse and PTSD is associated with a broad range of memory disturbances, and that PTSD patients may in fact be more susceptible to problems with memory recall than are normal individuals. However, we also have hypothesized that the stress of abuse leads to changes in the brain involved in memory that in turn result in greater problems with memory recall. The sticky issue is whether these individuals who have presumably been abused are accurately recalling the details of their abuse. I am reminded of a woman involved in our research studies who reported memories of her family being involved in satanic ritual abuse and seeing babies hung from meat hooks in her basement. I don't really believe that there were babies tortured in her basement, but I do believe that she was abused in some way in childhood and that she currently suffered from PTSD. This belief is based on my clinical judgment and many years of evaluating people for the diagnosis of PTSD. Some would say that I have no basis for making this "judgment" and that my impression is probably incorrect, and with the difficulty in validating self-reported abuse there probably is no way to determine the truth for sure. My feeling is that there are a number of individuals who truly have been abused who don't have a clear memory of their abuse, and may have inserted false and distorted memories related to their childhood, who nevertheless have PTSD symptoms related to actual traumatic events in childhood.

Neurohormonal Modulation of Memory

Hormones released during stress can modulate the laying down of a memory trace. For instance, as reviewed in Chapter 2, norepinephrine and epinephrine can strengthen the laying down of memories, acting at the level of the hippocampus and other brain regions involved in memory, whereas cortisol can inhibit the laying down of memories. It makes sense that the body should have a way of modulating the laying down of memories in order to facilitate the memory of something really scary, like seeing a bear, so that the next time you see it you can remember it quickly in order to get away and survive. With chronic stress there is dysregulation of these stress hormones so that the laying down of memories is different than normal. This, combined with the changes in brain areas that mediate memory, leads to distortions and other changes in memory in traumatized individuals.

These very hormones that are dysregulated by chronic stress are also critical for survival. When I was a medical student, I spent my summers working in Alaska in the fisheries industry, and would hike for several weeks in the tundra by myself. One of the dangers there was that if you surprised a grizzly bear in the brush, you might be attacked. The shops of Alaska are full of "true story" magazines about people who were mauled by bears and survived to tell the tale. A grizzly never did attack me, although I did have a caribou run up to my tent early one morning and scare me practically to death. If I were confronted by a bear while walking in the brush, it would have been necessary to be able either to get away very quickly or stay and fight (and defeat!) the bear. Either choice, by the way, is very unlikely, since a bear can both outrun you and take you out fairly easily, which means that your best hope is that you do not surprise a bear when she is with one of her children (bear cubs). This can only be prevented by carrying a bell or by singing at all times while walking through the Alaskan brush. When the caribou ran up to my tent I had a massive outpouring of stress-responsive brain chemicals and hormones. These brain chemicals and hormones form the chemical basis of the flight-or-fight response. When confronted with a life-threatening situation (fur-covered or otherwise), there is a massive outpouring of adrenaline (*catecholamines*, or norepinephrine and epinephrine), which is critical for survival.

As we discussed in the prior chapter, animal studies have shown that increasing norepinephrine release up to a certain level improves cognition and attention, but beyond that point there is a reduction in performance. Using positron emission tomography, which allows us to measure brain activity while we stimulate norepinephrine release in the brain with medications, we found that lower levels of norepinephrine stimulate brain activity, but at very high levels (as seen in PTSD) the brain shuts off. The findings are consistent with an inverted U-curve for norepinephrine, where lower levels of norepinephrine stimulation increase the efficiency of the brain, whereas very high levels make it more inefficient. Everyone knows that a little bit of stress can be a good thing. For instance, it's always hard to study if you don't have any real reason to learn the material, especially if you don't find it all that interesting. However, we learn better and faster if we have an important exam to study for that we don't want to mess up. But sometimes people get so stressed out that they "choke" and actually do worse. This happens when they release too much norepinephrine in their brains. This concept lies behind the common practice of taking propanolol (which blocks the effects of norepinephrine in the brain) to improve performance during public speaking.

What determines who will choke under pressure and who will come through on that big exam? Or why some people will make the game-winning free throw whereas others will not? A lot of it has to do with releasing the right amount of norepinephrine at the right time, just enough to help us think quickly when we're attacked by a bear in the brush, without our brain cells becoming so rattled that we can't think straight. How this tight balance is tipped will determine whether we get out alive so we can keep our cherished genes in the gene pool.

This all-important act of surviving the immediate danger just long enough to shovel our genes off to the next generation may not be affected at all by whether we can think straight or act normally in our later years when we are doddering around the front porch, which may explain the paradox of why exposure to an extreme fright may permanently affect the ability of the body's norepinephrine system to appropriately respond to minor stressors in later life. One can imagine a scared and jumpy caveman who had one too many close calls with a wooly mammoth in his younger days, who has already fathered a child and then lived beyond his initial brushes with death to father some more. Now he spends his free days and nights lurking around the fire, eyes darting at every sound in the bushes. Although he is unable to be close to other members of the clan because of this excessive jumpiness, he is ignored and tolerated as long as he doesn't hurt anyone, because he continues to be a fine hunter.

Neurobiological Responses to Stress and Long-term Dysregulation

Even today there are many among us who have traveled to the other side of an extreme fright. On the surface they continue to go through the motions of daily life, although to themselves and the few who really know them they act very differently. Many survivors of psychological trauma, whether it is combat stress or childhood abuse or a train wreck, continue to bear hidden scars that are invisible to the naked eye yet are very real. One important outcome is long-term dysregulation of the brain chemical systems that we need to survive the immediate threat to our lives. Norepinephrine and other stress responsive brain chemicals act like temperature regulators in the body. When the "heat" gets too high (i.e., there is too much norepinephrine release in the body) it is detected by the body's self-regulation system, which shuts the system down, thus returning things back to normal. It is this system that keeps us from jumping out of our skins when we should be dozing around the fire. However, with extreme frights in some people (we don't entirely understand why some more than others, in the same way we don't understand why some people choke on the big exam and others come through with flying colors), the system never really works again. The body keeps things hot all the time, and is not able to crank up the heat quickly when it is really needed. Much like a broken thermometer that is unable to respond to temperature changes anymore, the stress response system doesn't serve these people well anymore either.

The cortisol system, as mentioned earlier, also plays an important role in the stress response. Like norepinephrine, cortisol is released during times of threat and is critical to survival. Cortisol redistributes the energy of our bodies when we are under attack in order to help us survive, such as suppressing functions that we don't need for immediate survival, including reproduction, the body's immune response, digestion, and the feeling of pain. Cortisol also promotes what we need, increasing heart rate and blood pressure, and shunts energy to the brain and muscles, so we can think fast and make a quick getaway. Although cortisol has actions that are beneficial for short-term survival, it may perform these functions at the expense of long-term viability of the body. For instance, chronically high cortisol levels cause gastric ulcers, thinning of the bones, and possibly even brain damage. Again, evolution may have preferred the caveman who could survive attacks by wooly mammoths long enough to pass his genes to the next generation, even if it meant that he couldn't remember where he left his favorite spear when his was old. In other words, evolution prefers short-term survival at the expense of long-term function.

Effects of Stress on the Hippocampus

Work from the laboratories of Robert Sapolsky at Stanford University and Bruce McEwen at Rockefeller University provided evidence for the startling observation that cortisol (*glucocorticoids* is the generic term, which applies across all animal species) released during stress may cause damage to the brain. (McEwen et al., 1992; Sapolsky, 1996; Uno, Robert, Finch, & Sapolsky, 1990). When male and female vervet monkeys are caged together, the female monkeys attack the males, leading to such extreme stress in the males that it is often fatal. Robert Sapolsky and his colleagues found that monkeys who were improperly caged and died spontaneously following exposure to severe stress had gastric ulcers and enlarged adrenal glands, which told the scientists that the monkeys had been releasing large amounts of glucocorticoids (Sapolsky et al., 1990). Sapolsky et al. also found that the monkeys had specific damage to the hippocampus (a part of the brain involved in memory). In order to test whether glucocorticoids were the culprit, the researchers applied pellets of glucocorticoids to one hippocampus but not the other (the hippocampus occurs on both the left and the right sides of the brain). They found that only the hippocampus with the glucocorticoids applied showed the damage. Further studies confirmed that glucocorticoids were associated with damage to this part of the brain. The scientists found both a decrease in the normal branching of neurons, as well as actual death of the neurons (Magarinos, Verdugo, & McEwen, 1997; Uno, Tararan, Else, Suleman, & Sapolsky, 1989; Virgin et al., 1991; Woolley, Gould, & McEwen, 1990). The mechanism appeared to be a potentiation of the harmful effects of naturally occurring brain chemicals that paradoxically play a role in memory, called *glutamate* (Sapolsky, Packan, & Vale, 1988; Sapolsky & Pulsinelli, 1985).

Stress has important effects on impairing memory—an important function of the hippocampus (Luine, Villages, Martinex, & McEwen, 1994)—as well as long-term potentiation, felt to represent the molecular basis of memory in the hippocampus (Diamond, Branch, Fleshner, & Rose, 1995; Diamond, Fleshner, Ingersoll, & Rose, 1996). Stress is also associated with problems in new learning and memory (Arbel, Kadar, Silberman, & Levy, 1994). Other neurochemical systems interact with glucocorticoids to mediate the effects of stress on memory and the hippocampus. Stress resulted in a decrease in serotonin $5HT_{1A}$ receptor binding within the hippocampus with associated atrophy in the CA3 region of the hippocampus and memory impairment (McEwen et al., 1997). Glucocorticoids modulate serotonin

5HT$_{1A}$ receptor binding (Chalmers, Kwak, Mansour, & Watson, 1993) and may mediate the effects of stress on serotonin receptor binding in the hippocampus. *Neurotrophins* such as brain-derived neurotrophic factor (BDNF), a recently isolated neuropeptide that has important trophic effects on the hippocampus and other brain regions, may also play a role in stress-related changes in the hippocampus (Smith, Makino, Kvetnansky, & Post, 1995). Stress resulted in a reduction in BDNF in the hippocampus, an effect that may be partially related to glucocorticoid release (Smith et al., 1995) or serotonin 5HT$_{2A}$ receptor stimulation (Vaidya, Marek, Aghajanian, & Duman, 1997). Given the trophic effects of BDNF, these findings suggest that decreased levels of BDNF, in stress may result in hippocampal atrophy or cell death (Smith, 1995).

Early interventions during the time of early development can have a positive as well as a negative effect on development. Postnatal handling is an animal model that has been applied to studying beneficial early interventions. It has important effects on the development of behavioral and endocrine responses to stress. For example, daily handling within the first few weeks of life (e.g., picking up rat pups and then returning them to their mother) resulted in increased Type II glucocorticoid receptor binding, which persisted throughout life. This was associated with increased feedback sensitivity to glucocorticoids, and reduced glucocorticoid-mediated hippocampal damage in later life (Meaney, Aitken, Bhatnager, van Berkel, & Sapolsky, 1988; Meaney, Aitken, Sharman, & Sarrieu, 1989). These effects appear to be due to a type of "stress inoculation" from the mothers repeated licking of the handled pups (Liu et al., 1997). Considered together, these findings suggest that early in the postnatal period there is a naturally occurring brain plasticity in key neural systems that may "program" an organism's biological response to stressful stimuli.

In 1990, my colleagues and I saw these fascinating findings presented at a scientific meeting and wondered if they were applicable to humans exposed to psychological trauma. If so, this would have profound implications. Was it possible that being abused as a child or being a war veteran could cause brain damage, just from the things that one saw, heard, smelled (Bremner, 1999b)? My interest in memory function in traumatized patients had been sparked the year before, when I was a Yale resident in psychiatry on call at the Veterans Hospital in West Haven, Connecticut. I was awakened in the middle of the night by a veteran who called and asked to speak to the doctor on call. All he could say to me was "Got to get them out, got to get them out," over and over again. I tried to talk to him but was unable to communicate with him. After about 20 minutes I was able to get through to him and found out that he had just rescued some children from a burning house. He had run into the house and pulled them out, putting himself into danger. But in doing so he had put himself at great risk. When he was in the Vietnam War he worked as a fireman, putting out fires on helicopters and other aircraft after enemy attacks. Many times during the war he had to go into burning aircraft and pull out the pilots and crew. Sometimes all that came out were charred bodies. He continued to relive those events as if they had happened yesterday. He saw the smoke, the fire, he heard the screaming of the victims. When he had to run into the house and save the children, he had done it at the expense of his sanity. He had triggered a flashback, and was replaying the memory of the event as if it were playing like a movie in front of his eyes.

This experience convinced me that PTSD was a brain-based disorder. These flashbacks were automatic and uncontrollable, almost like seizures. As a budding physician scientist I made the deduction that if the disease's symptoms involved abnormal memories that played in the mind without any control, then it must involve abnormalities of the parts of the brain that play a role in memory.

Later that year, at the VA hospital in West Haven, Connecticut, we started one of the first specialized hospital-based treatment programs for veterans of the Vietnam War. This program had been mandated by Congress to address the needs of these veterans. I was working as the Medical Director on that unit, and I noticed that my patients had trouble remembering to come to their psychotherapy appointments with me. My supervisors were rooted in the psychoanalytic tradition of psychiatry, and they told me that this behavior was due to my patients' resistance to treatment. However, I was not convinced. I linked these observations with my experience with the fireman and the reports of the damaging effects of glucocorticoids released during stress on the hippocampus. Could it be that my veteran patients were suffering brain damage caused by the stress of the Vietnam War?

Another thing I noticed about these patients is that they remembered things that happened in Vietnam very vividly. One of my patients would bring me scrapbooks with pictures of him and his friends in Vietnam. He would talk about his friends as if he had seen them the day before. However, he couldn't remember what he had for breakfast that morning, and could only vaguely describe what was going on in his current daily life. Similarly, in a special ceremony we held for these veteran patients at the Vietnam War Memorial in New Haven, the veterans would write down the names of their friends they had lost in Vietnam, and then burn them and throw them into Long Island Sound, as a sort of grieving ceremony. Most of the veterans could remember long lists of names. In one poignant moment, a veteran remembered someone who had been in Vietnam such a short time that he hadn't had time to learn the soldier's name. However, he remembered the soldier's face very clearly and wanted to try to let him go, so he threw into the water a paper with the words "the guy with the red hair."

These PTSD patients appeared to be suffering from an inability to learn new things. However, their memories of long-ago events were intact. These patients were very similar to patients suffering from what we call *neurological amnesia*, which is caused by strokes or tumors that specifically affect the hippocampus. A well-known example of this is the patient H.M., who had strokes affecting the hippocampus on both sides of his brain. He could carry on normal conversations, and remember everything that happened in his life very clearly before the stroke occurred. However, since the time of the stroke he couldn't learn anything new (Scoville & Milner, 1957). He spent his days reading one copy of the *Reader's Digest*. When he got to the end, since none of the articles stayed in his memory, he would just start all over again, like Sisyphus of Greek legend who was condemned for eternity to push a boulder up a hill, only to have it roll down again once he had almost made it to the top, at which point he would have to start rolling the boulder up all over again. My patients with PTSD have similar experiences.

Based on these observations and the studies of the effects of stress on the hippocampus, my colleagues and I became interested in studying memory disturbances in our PTSD patients. We administered tests of memory, such as remembering a story or a list of words, that had been shown to be related to neuron (the basic cells of the brain) loss in the hippocampus. We used neuropsychological testing to measure declarative memory function in PTSD. To be specific to hippocampal function, we selected measures that were validated in studies of patients with epilepsy. Sass and colleagues in the Yale Neurosurgery Program administered the Wechsler Memory Scale (WMS)–Logical Subscale (paragraph recall) and verbal Selective Reminding Test (vSRT) to patients with epilepsy who subsequently underwent surgical resection of the hippocampus. The investigators found that decreases in percent retention of the WMS paragraph after delayed recall, and deficits on the Long-Term Retrieval (LTR) subscale of the vSRT (a test that involves learning a list of words), were correlated with decreases in neuronal number of the CA3 region of the left hippocampus (Sass et al., 1990, 1992). The findings were specific to verbal, not visual, memory. In an initial study we found deficits in verbal declarative memory function in combat-related PTSD, including deficits in paragraph recall as measured by the WMS–Logical Component, for immediate and delayed recall and percent retention, as well as with the vSRT LTR, but no deficits in IQ or visual memory (Bremner, Scott, et al., 1993) (Figure 4.1).

These studies led us to conclude that stress may have resulted in damage to the hippocampus in PTSD patients, and that this could explain the memory problems we had observed. PTSD pa-

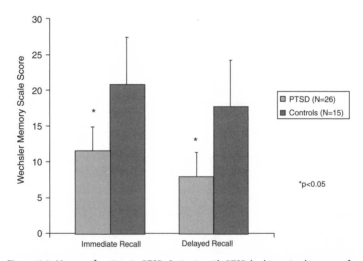

Figure 4.1 Memory function in PTSD. Patients with PTSD had impaired memory for a paragraph that was read to them (measured with the Wechsler Memory Scale) both immediately after the paragraph was read and following a delay, relative to normal individuals.

DOES STRESS DAMAGE THE BRAIN?

tients have trouble remembering things like what to buy at the grocery store, or appointments they have made. I often tell my patients to write things down to remind themselves. Many patients have difficulty studying for exams if they are in school, or memorizing material. This can be a problem for PTSD patients who are referred to rehabilitation programs, which commonly advise patients to go back to school in order to learn a new trade or profession for their "disability." This is the wrong advice for such patients, who have problems with new learning and memory that will impair their ability to perform in a school setting.

We next looked at survivors of childhood physical and/or sexual abuse with the diagnosis of PTSD, and compared them to healthy subjects matched for age, gender, race, years of education, and years of alcohol abuse. We found deficits in short-term memory as measured by the Wechsler Memory Scale–Logical Component (verbal memory), for immediate and delayed recall, and percent retention, as well as the vSRT LTR, in the patients with abuse-related PTSD in comparison to controls. Deficits in short-term memory in the childhood abuse patients were significantly correlated with level of abuse as measured with the composite severity score on the Early Trauma Inventory (Bremner, Vermetten, & Mazure, 2000). There was no difference in IQ or visual memory (Bremner, Randall, Capelli, et al., 1995).

Based on the animal studies mentioned earlier, we were interested in looking at hippocampal morphology in patients with a history of traumatic stress exposure and PTSD. We used a special imaging device called magnetic resonance imaging (MRI) that provides a clear picture of the structure of the brain. I drove all of the veterans in our specialized inpatient unit for PTSD at the VA Hospital to the imaging camera at Yale Hospital, and performed scans of their brains with MRI. We compared them to construction crew workers and others who were similar in many ways to the veterans, and carefully controlled for a number of factors including alcohol usage and educational status. The MRI scans were put into a computer where we could determine the exact size of the hippocampus. What we found is that the hippocampus was smaller in the PTSD patients than the comparison group, 8% smaller for the right hippocampus (Figure 4.2). We also found that the more problems the veterans had with memory, the smaller the hippocampus (Bremner, Randall, Scott, et al., 1995) (Figure 4.3). This was exciting news from the scientific standpoint—the first suggestion that stress may cause damage to the brain. However, needless to say it took some time before my psychiatrist colleagues could accept that this might be a possibility.

We wanted to see if these findings applied to other groups besides veterans, so we studied patients who had been severely physically or sexually abused as children. We found the same pattern of memory deficits (Bremner, Randall, Capelli, et al., 1995), as well as a reduction in size of the hippocampus. This time the effects were greater on the left side, a 12% reduction (Bremner, Randall, Vermetten, et al., 1997). Using MRI we measured hippocampal volume in 17 male and female adults with a history of severe childhood physical and/or sexual abuse and long-term

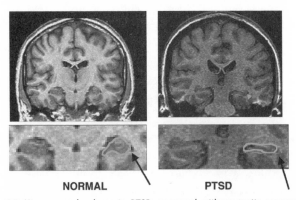

NORMAL   **PTSD**

Figure 4.2 Hippocampal volume in PTSD measured with magnetic resonance imaging (MRI). There is a visible reduction in volume of the hippocampus in a representative patient with PTSD relative to a normal individual (arrow).

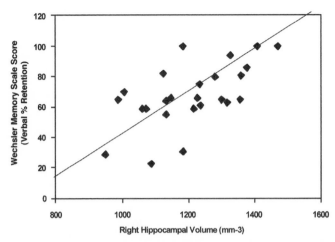

Figure 4.3 Relationship between memory dysfunction and hippocampal atrophy. Progressive reductions in hippocampal volume were associated with increasingly poor performance on a memory task in PTSD patients ($R = 0.64$; $p < .05$). Each point represents an individual PTSD patient, graphed according to hippocampal size and score on a memory task (Wechsler Memory Scale).

psychiatric consequences in the form of PTSD, who were compared to 17 healthy controls matched on a case-by-case basis for age, gender, handedness, race, years of education, and years of alcohol abuse. As stated above, there was a 12% reduction in left hippocampal volume in the patients with abuse-related PTSD in relation to comparison subjects, which was statistically significant. A 3.8% reduction in volume of the right hippocampus was not significant. There were no significant differences between patients and controls for temporal lobe, caudate, or amygdala volumes in this study (Bremner, Randall, et al., 1997).

Other studies found reductions in hippocampal volume in clinical populations of traumatized subjects. Stein et al. (1997) found a statistically significant 5% reduction in left hippocampal volume in 21 sexually abused women relative to 21 nonabused female controls. Hippocampal atrophy in this study was correlated with level of dissociative symptomatology (DES Score) in the abused women. Most (although not all) of the abused women had a current diagnosis of PTSD. Gurvits et al. (1996) compared hippocampal volume in seven patients with Vietnam combat-related PTSD to seven Vietnam combat veterans without PTSD, and eight healthy nonveteran controls. The authors found a 26% bilateral decrease in hippocampal volume, which was statistically significant for both left and right hippocampal volume considered separately. Although subjects were not case matched for alcohol abuse, there continued to be a significant difference in hippocampal volume after adjusting for years of alcohol abuse using analysis of covariance. There was no difference in ventricular, amygdala, or whole-brain volume among the groups. This study also found a significant correlation between level of combat exposure (measured with the Combat Exposure Scale) and reduction in hippocampal volume, as well as visual delayed recall errors. In summary, there are several replicated studies in more than one population of traumatized patients showing atrophy of the hippocampus that appear to be specific to PTSD diagnosis, with some evidence that hippocampal damage is related to dissociative symptoms. One study in children with PTSD did not find a reduction in hippocampal volume (DeBellis et al., 1999), suggesting that chronic exposure to stress over many years may be required for hippocampal atrophy. We also found that depression, which is commonly associated with stress, is associated with a 19% reduction in left hippocampal volume (Bremner, Narayan, et al., 2000), a finding that was consistent with Sheline and colleagues (1996) at Washington University in St. Louis.

The hippocampus demonstrates an unusual capacity for neuronal regeneration, or growing new neurons (brain cells) in adult life (Gould, Cameron, Daniels, Woolley, & McEwen, 1992; Kuhn, Dickinson-Anson, & Gage, 1996). Until recently, it was thought that whatever you had in the way of brain cells after early childhood was all you got, and you blew them all in one wild party, that was it. However, recently it has been shown that the hippocampus may be unique in being able to grow new neurons in adulthood. Elevated glucocorticoids such as cortisol (as are seen during stress) suppress the capacity for neuronal regeneration in the dentate gyrus of the hippocampus (Gould et al., 1992), and these effects may be mediated through the excitatory acid (*glutamate*) NMDA receptor (Cameron, McEwen, & Gould, 1995). Stress also results in an inhibition of neurogenesis in the dentate gyrus of the hippocampus, an effect mediated by the NMDA receptor (Gould, McEwen, Tanapat, Galea, & Fuchs, 1997). Recently, it has been demonstrated that changes in the environment (e.g., social enrichment) can modulate neurogenesis in the dentate gyrus of the hippocampus, and slow the normal age-related decline in neurogenesis (Kempermann, Kuhn & Gage, 1997, 1998). These results may have implications for PTSD patients, especially given recent findings that the human hippocampus also demonstrates the capacity for neurogenesis (Eriksson et al., 1998; Gage, 1998). Rusty Gage and colleagues (Eriksson et al., 1998) at the Salk Institute showed that these animal findings applied to humans, and thus demonstrated that the human hippocampus can regrow neurons, even in adulthood. This was very exciting news indeed. This suggests that hippocampal damage in PTSD may be reversible. PTSD patients with ongoing stressors, however, will be expected to have impaired ability to regrow damaged hippocampal neurons.

Fascinating work by Ron Duman and his group showed that selective serotonin reuptake inhibitor (SSRI) medications such as Prozac or Paxil that are used in the treatment of psychiatric disorders can counteract the negative effects of stress on the hippocampus (Duman, Heninger, & Nestler, 1997; Nibuya, Morinobu, & Duman, 1995; Nibuya, Nestler, & Duman, 1995). These scientists worked out the molecular mechanisms by which antidepressants exert this effect. Other medications, such as dilantin (commonly used in the treatment of epilepsy), were shown to block the damaging effects of stress on hippocampal neurons

(Watanabe, Gould, Cameron, Daniels, & McEwen, 1992). Based on this work, our group tested these medications to see if they could reverse the memory deficits and hippocampal atrophy associated with PTSD and depression. Eric Vermetten, working with myself and others at Yale and later at Emory, showed that a year of treatment with the serotonin reuptake inhibitor (SSRI) medication Paxil in PTSD patients resulted in a 5% increase in hippocampal volume and a 20% increase in hippocampal-based declarative memory function. These studies corroborated the beneficial effects of medications like Paxil on hippocampal structure and function following traumatic stress, applying findings from animal studies to humans.

Role of the Hippocampus in Fragmentation of Memory and Dissociation

Empirical studies on memory and the hippocampus may shed some light on the unusual changes in memory that follow traumatic stressors. The hippocampus plays an important role in integrating or binding together different aspects of a memory at the time of recollection, and is felt to be responsible for locating the memory of an event in time, place, and context. Atrophy and dysfunction of the hippocampus in PTSD may lead to distortion and fragmentation of memories. For instance, in an abused patient who was locked in a closet, there is a memory of the smell of old clothes, but no visual memory of being in the closet, and no affective memory of the feeling of fear. Perhaps with psychotherapy there is a facilitation of associations to related events that may bring all of the aspects of the memory together. Or, if the patient has an event such as being trapped in a dark elevator, the feeling of fear associated with darkness and an enclosed space may be enough to trigger a recollection of the entire memory.

The symptom area of dissociation may hold an important key to understanding the function of the hippocampus. In the fourth edition of the *Diagnostic and Statistical Manual*, dissociation is defined as a breakdown of normal memory, identity, or consciousness. These functions are felt to be mediated or at least supported by the hippocampus. For example, it is known that the hippocampus plays a critical role in memory. The hippocampus has also been hypothesized by Nadel (Nadel & Bohbot, 2001) to act as a "spatial map," localizing the person in time, space, and place. Identity can be thought of as a collection of memories related to events in one's life—with accompanying thoughts and feelings about those experiences—that play a critical role in shaping our sense of ourselves.

Evidence supporting a role for the hippocampus in dissociation comes from several lines of evidence. Patients with epilepsy who underwent electrical stimulation of the hippocampus during surgery developed a number of sensations similar to dissociation, including feeling strange, seeming to be out of body, feeling a sense of déjà vu, and experiencing distortions in perception. The hippocampus has a high concentration of NMDA receptors, which are hypothesized to play an important role in learning and memory. We have used the NMDA receptor antagonist, *ketamine*, as a probe of NMDA receptor function in human subjects. We administered ketamine at increasing doses to normal college students and measured dissociative states with the Clinician Administered Dissociative States Scale (CADSS). Increasing doses of ketamine were associated with marked increases in dissociative states as measured with the CADSS (Krystal et al., 1994). These symptoms included seeming to be out of body, experiencing time distortion, feeling like one is in a dream, and colors becoming very bright. The symptoms experienced by these normal college students were identical to those reported by trauma patients with pathological dissociation. These findings provided strong evidence for the idea of the NMDA receptor, probably acting through the hippocampus, mediating symptoms of dissociation, at least in part.

Hippocampal dysfunction may play a part in dissociative symptoms related to trauma (Bremner, Krystal, Charney, & Southwick,

1996). The hippocampus has an important role in integrating or binding together different aspects of a memory at the time of recollection. It is believed to be responsible for locating the memory of an event in time, place, and context. As described in greater detail in Chapter 6, symptoms of dissociation include feeling like you are in a tunnel, seeing things in black and white, seeming disconnected from your body, or feeling like you are in a dream or that time is standing still. At the time of trauma, dissociation is increased individuals who have an increase in pathology following exposure to trauma. Hippocampal damage may be responsible for the breakdown in normal memory, consciousness, or identity, which by definition constitutes dissociation. In addition, as noted previously, dissociation at the time of trauma is associated with long-term psychopathology. This dissociation may represent not a risk factor for later pathology, but instead the initial onset of a PTSD-dissociative spectrum disorder. Dissociation at the time of trauma may represent the subjective sensation of hippocampal damage at the time of stress, given the critical role that the hippocampus plays in the integration of both memory encoding and retrieval. According to this model, fragmentation of memory and dissociation would not be expected to occur in all individuals who were exposed to traumatic stress, only in those who developed psychopathology (PTSD) with associated hippocampal atrophy and dysfunction.

Hormones and neurotransmitters released during stress have important effects on memory function. These stress-responsive systems, which show long-term effects following exposure to stress, influence both the laying down as well as the retrieval of memories. Both cortisol and adrenaline have important effects on memory. For instance, cortisol released during stress can result in longlasting (for hours) impairments of memory, which may account for the "spaced out" feeling that comes with being under chronic stress. Adrenaline released with stress has a more acute effect, which accounts for the fact that stressful events are often better remembered than are more mundane events. In victims of psychological trauma, there are long-term changes in cortisol and adrenaline systems that also affect these individuals' memory function.

Studies in animals showed that the hippocampus inhibits the cortisol system, which, as stated before, plays an important role in the stress response. Damage to the hippocampus in animals was associated with an increase in the brain messenger system, called *corticotropin releasing factor* (CRF), which during stressful events is released from the brain and turns on the cortisol system in the body during stressful events (Herman et al., 1984; Jacobson & Sapolsky, 1991). Animals that are chronically stressed have increases in this brain chemical system. Similarly, in humans undergoing stress, there is an increase in cortisol levels (Guerra & Dibrell, 1995). We collected cerebrospinal fluid (the fluid that bathes the brain and can be sampled in order to tell us what is happening in the brain) in patients with PTSD, and found that they had increased levels of CRF (Bremner, Licinio, et al., 1997). This may be related to the hippocampal damage, as well as to the primary effect of stress on CRF in traumatized patients.

Studies in animals show that early stressors, such as being deprived access to one's mother, result in long-term changes in the cortisol system that persist throughout life. Recently we studied women with PTSD who were sexually abused in early childhood, and found further evidence of a hyperactive CRF system. Normally, CRF is released from a part of the brain called the *hypothalamus* that is a window from the brain to the body. CRF stimulates release of *adrenocorticotropin hormone* (ACTH) from the pituitary. We found that in the women with PTSD, CRF did not normally stimulate ACTH, which told us that the pituitary was overstimulated by excessive levels of CRF. Also, the cortisol response to both CRF and ACTH was low, suggesting that the adrenal gland was exhausted. This finding of low cortisol levels in PTSD was first reported by John Mason in 1986 (Mason et al.,

1986), was later found in other studies (Yehuda, Southwick, et al., 1991), and seems paradoxical given the findings related to the hippocampus. However, studies in children performed soon after being abused show that cortisol is high. With chronic stress and many years of PTSD symptoms, it may be that a pattern of dysregulation sets in, which suggests that the adrenal gland becomes exhausted. Consistent with this, we found that the lower the cortisol levels, the worse the memory impairment (which is a marker for hippocampal dysfunction). Studies have also shown an increased suppression of cortisol with negative feedback at the level of the brain or pituitary with synthetic cortisol (dexamethasone), which is also consistent with low levels of cortisol (Yehuda et al., 1993).

Criticisms have been raised about the proposed mechanism of hippocampal damage in PTSD. Animal studies suggested that high levels of glucocorticoids released during stress lead to damage of the hippocampus. The mechanism was felt to be related to an inhibition of glucose metabolism in the brain, which led to an increase in vulnerability to toxicity from excitatory amino acids. However, studies by Rachel Yehuda and others have shown low levels of cortisol in 24-hour urinary samples in patients with chronic combat-related PTSD (Mason et al., 1986; Yehuda, Southwick, et al., 1991; Yehuda et al., 1995). Other studies by Resnick, Pitman, Foy, and Yehuda (1995), have shown that cortisol levels in the aftermath of rape trauma were not elevated in patients who subsequently developed PTSD. In fact, women who had a prior history of trauma (which was associated with increased risk for PTSD) actually had lower cortisol levels than did women without a prior history of trauma, although low cortisol was not directly associated with subsequent PTSD in that original study. Based on these results, Yehuda argued (1997) that it is not possible for cortisol elevations at the time of trauma to cause hippocampal damage.

These studies do not preclude, however, the possibility that elevated levels of cortisol are associated with hippocampal damage in patients with PTSD. For one thing, lower baseline levels of cortisol in chronic PTSD have not been replicated in all studies. Pitman and Orr (1990) showed elevated levels of cortisol in 24-hour urine samples in patients with combat-related PTSD, and more recent studies showed no change in urinary cortisol levels in combat-related PTSD (J. Mason, personal communication, November 1, 2000). Other studies of women with childhood sexual abuse-related PTSD have also shown elevated levels of cortisol in 24-hour urine (Lemieux & Coe, 1995), as have studies of children with abuse-related PTSD (DeBellis, Baum, et al., 1999). In fact, our own studies of diurnal levels of plasma cortisol (which represents a more comprehensive measurement of cortisol) in women with abuse-related PTSD found lower afternoon cortisol levels. Initially, PTSD may be associated with elevations in cortisol, which with chronicity leads to long-term dysregulation and lower levels of cortisol in the periphery years after the original trauma. Decreased baseline cortisol many years after the original trauma does not preclude the possibility of higher levels of cortisol release at the time of the original trauma.

Previous studies have not looked at what happens to cortisol during, for example, the stress of traumatic reminders in patients with PTSD, because all studies were conducted in a baseline unperturbed state. The original study done in rape victims involved samples obtained up to several days after initial presentation to the emergency room. This data, although interesting, does not give us a true picture of what happens at the time of the original trauma. A more recent study by that group obtained cortisol levels 12 to 48 hours after the original trauma (Yehuda, Resnick, Schmeidler, Yang, & Pitman, 1998). The study also did not find elevated levels of cortisol in patients who developed PTSD. Although the measurements were obtained closer to the time of the original trauma, they still were not representative of cortisol at the time of trauma. Therefore, until such time as we are able to measure cortisol at the exact time of trauma in patients who develop subsequent PTSD, we won't be able to definitively answer this question. We have obtained data in women abused in childhood with PTSD showing that exposure to reminders of the traumatic event result in an increase in cortisol levels relative to women without PTSD. This is in spite of the fact that baseline cortisol, in these same women, is low. These studies suggest that PTSD may be associated with potentiated release of cortisol during stress, in spite of the fact that baseline cortisol is low.

Another finding from the previously mentioned study of Yehuda et al (1998) is that history of prior trauma was associated with low cortisol in the aftermath of the current rape. Several studies have shown that history of prior trauma increases the risk for PTSD with subsequent victimization (Bremner, Southwick, et al., 1993). The study, therefore, raises the question of whether patients with low cortisol and prior trauma had undetected prior PTSD.

Some authors have also criticized theories of the mechanism of stress-induced hippocampal damage. As mentioned earlier, original studies found that high levels of glucocorticoids released at the time of stress lead to hippocampal damage. However, some authors have found that physiological levels of glucocorticoids do not lead to neuronal loss in the hippocampus (Leverenz et al., 1999). Note, though, that the Leverenz et al. study did not examine changes in hippocampal cytoarchitecture. It may be that a change in morphology occurs with exposure to elevated levels of glucocorticoids, without loss of neurons.

Glucocorticoids may not act alone to mediate the effects of stress on the hippocampus, but instead may interact with other factors that are affected by stress and have trophic effects on hippocampal neurons. Stress resulted in a decrease in serotonin $5HT_{1A}$ receptor binding within the hippocampus with associated atrophy in the CA3 region of the hippocampus and memory impairment (McEwen et al., 1997). Glucocorticoids modulate $5HT_{1A}$ binding (Chalmers et al., 1993) and may mediate the effects of stress on serotonin receptor binding in the hippocampus. Tianeptine, which decreases serotonin levels within the hippocampus, blocked the effect of stress on memory and the hippocampus, suggesting that serotonin released during stress may also play a role in the etiology of hippocampal damage (McEwen et al., 1997; Watanabe et al., 1992, 1993). Brain-derived neurotrophic factor (BDNF) is a recently isolated neuropeptide that has important trophic effects on the hippocampus and other brain regions (Smith et al., 1995). Stress resulted in a reduction in brain-derived neurotrophic factor (BDNF) mRNA in the hippocampus, an effect that may be partially related to glucocorticoid release (Smith et al., 1995) or serotonin $5HT_{2A}$ receptor stimulation. In contrast, stress increased BDNF in hypothalamus and pituitary (Smith et al., 1995). Given the trophic effects of BDNF, these findings suggest that decreased levels of BDNF in stress may result in hippocampal atrophy or cell death.

The hippocampus demonstrates an unusual capacity for neuronal regeneration that may be relevant to chronic PTSD (Kuhn et al., 1996). Elevated glucocorticoids (as are seen during stress) suppress the capacity for neuronal regeneration in the dentate gyrus of the hippocampus, and these effects may be mediated through the excitatory acid NMDA receptor. Stress also inhibits neurogenesis in the hippocampus (Gould et al., 1997), and a positive environment can have the opposite effect (Kempermann et al., 1997, 1998). The chronic stress of PTSD (related to the stress of continuously reexperiencing symptoms and traumatic reminders) may inhibit the capacity for neurogenesis, which prevents the ability of the hippocampus to regenerate neurons in patients with a history of prior exposure to stress. This may explain the finding of no reduction in hippocampal volume in children with PTSD, in whom the disease chronicity was relatively short (DeBellis, Keshavan, et al., 1999). This field is rapidly evolving, and future studies will be needed to elucidate mechanisms mediating the effects of stress on the hippocampus.

It is well known that not all individuals exposed to traumatic stress will develop PTSD. Evidence from a range of populations shows that 85% of traumatized individuals do not develop PTSD (Schlenger, Fairbank, Jordan, & Caddell, 1999). A central question in the field is what determines why one individual will develop PTSD following a traumatic stressor, whereas another individual exposed to the same stressor will be unaffected. This has led to a search for risk factors for the development of PTSD. Roger Pitman has argued that smaller hippocampal volume at birth may represent a risk factor for the subsequent development of PTSD. According to this argument, stress does not cause hippocampal damage; rather individuals who were born with smaller hippocampal volume were at increased risk for the development of PTSD. To support this theory, Pitman cites a study by McNally and Shin (1995) showing that intelligence was lower in combat veterans who subsequently developed PTSD. In this study, investigators were able to obtain from military records measurements of intelligence conducted before the individual's actual military service. The authors interpreted these findings as consistent with the idea that lower intelligence is a risk factor for the development of PTSD. By extension, small hippocampal volume (which plays a role in cognition and contributes to IQ) would be seen as increasing the risk for development of PTSD.

However, one problem in the interpretation of this study is the finding, mentioned earlier, that prior history of traumatic stress increases the risk for development of PTSD with reexposure to traumatic stressors. In fact, this phenomenon, known as *stress sensitization*, can be modeled in the laboratory. For example, animals with a history of prior exposure to electric shock have a potentiated release of norepinephrine in the hippocampus with reexposure to shock as compared to naïve animals. Also, clinical

DOES STRESS DAMAGE THE BRAIN?

observations suggest that cognitive function deteriorates in the aftermath of traumatic stress in patients who subsequently develop PTSD, which argues against a preexisting lower level of cognitive function being a risk factor for PTSD. Therefore, from a clinical perspective, it would be surprising if all of the cognitive deficits in PTSD represent a risk factor for the development of PTSD rather than a consequence of exposure to stress. In order to investigate the relative role of genetics and environment (i.e., stress) in the findings of smaller hippocampal volume in PTSD, our group and Pitman and colleagues at the Manchester VA hospital are studying twins with and without Vietnam combat-related PTSD. These studies should provide more information about the relative role of genes and environment in the reduction in hippocampal volume in PTSD.

Role of the Frontal Lobe in PTSD and the Stress Response

Another brain area that is very sensitive to stress is the *frontal lobe*, the part of the brain that lies just behind the forehead. The frontal lobe is a very special part of the brain, perhaps the one thing that makes us different from other animals. Our ancestors who spent their afternoons dragging their knuckles around the African savanna, like *Homo Australopithecus* or *Homo erectus*, were very similar to us in many ways, including the ability to use tools and work together in groups. The things that make the modern version of humans, or *Homo sapiens*, so special are the ability to plan and execute actions, and most importantly to interact with others, including using language and employing social and emotional interactions.

At some point between the time we were dragging our knuckles in the Savannah and started doing the foxtrot on the Champs Elysée, our brains underwent a very radical change. Originally, our brains had a reasonable structure, with the snout in the front and the brain matter wagging around somewhere behind it. This is an arrangement that the vast majority of the animal kingdom would consider quite reasonable and in fact elegant, from Mr. Mouse to Ms. Monkey and even *Homo erectus*. However, at some point our cranial physiognomy underwent a most unfortunate change, with the face being pushed in as if someone had flat-handed us in the face, in a way that most cats and monkeys would consider to be very unaesthetically appealing (Figure 4.4). A considerable portion of the brain grew out and over our newly submerged eye sockets, in a newly created space that most closely resembled the fore compartment of a U-Haul trailer. This new compartment was exclusively reserved for a very important brain area, the frontal cortex.

The frontal cortex is the part of the brain that makes us different from monkeys and other animals. It also was a major factor in our recent evolution from earlier forms of humans or "Homo" species—what distinguishes us from our more ignorant ancestors. Thus, one can see why the frontal lobe plays an important role in planning, thinking, and executing responses, all functions that we have developed as a specialty of modern humans. The frontal lobe also is involved in changes in mood, another specialty of our kind. It is therefore understandable that abnormal-

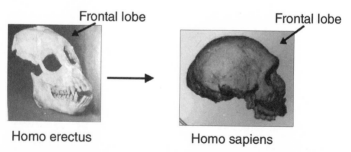

Figure 4.4 Evolution of the frontal cortex in history. Early species like Homo erectus had a much smaller space for the frontal lobe (the part of the brain above the eyes) in comparison to modern humans. With evolution, the nose and jaws receded, creating room for the expanding frontal cortex over the face (instead of behind the face).

DOES STRESS DAMAGE THE BRAIN?

ities of this area are a factor in most psychiatric disorders, including PTSD and depression. The barbaric use of "psychosurgery" in the form of "frontal lobotomy" to dampen the emotional responses of psychiatric patients, although such procedures haven't been conducted for many years, nevertheless continues to be legendary. These surgeries involved putting the patient to sleep, going in around the eye socket, and damaging a part of the brain just over it. This area is the middle and lower portion of the frontal lobe, and is particularly important in regulating mood and emotion.

The part of the frontal cortex that lies just above the eyes, or *medial prefrontal cortex*, plays a significant role in regulating emotion (Hamner, Lorberbaum, & George, 1999). The medial prefrontal cortex inhibits lower, more primitive areas that are equally well developed in rats and men. These primitive areas lie at the center of the brain and generate primitive fear reactions that are common to all of the animal species. What makes us unique is that we, as humans, have the ability to consciously quell our own fear reactions. For example, we humans find "entertainment" in watching scenes of blood and gore, seeing young mothers raped and killed, and other depictions of tragedy and deprivation in made-for-TV movies and other forums. We can watch these scenes and feel a sense of thrill, but we can also inhibit our urge to get up and run out of the room, because we tell ourselves that "this is only a movie." The brain area responsible for saying that is the frontal cortex, and more specifically the medial prefrontal cortex. This "higher brain area" is responsible for inhibiting the "lower brain areas" involved in fear conditioning, like amygdala, so that we don't jump up out of our seats when we watch a horror movie. However, if while we are watching a horror movie someone breaks into our house and pulls a gun on us, we need to be able to quickly identify that this person poses a true threat, unlike the villain in the movie. That ability to distinguish true threat from artificial threat could make the difference in surviving or perishing. It is our medial prefrontal cortex that tells us, "Calm down, it's only a movie, that bad guy can't get you," or "Wake up, there's a real killer in the house!" One of the sad things about PTSD patients is that they can't normally distinguish between these artificial and real threats, so they are always "on guard" and see life-threatening circumstances in the most banal of events.

For instance, when we showed pictures and sounds of the Vietnam War to combat veterans with PTSD, they became extremely frightened and wanted to get out of the room, even though their "higher brains" *should* have been telling their "lower brains" that there was no true life threat (Figure 4.5). However, when we showed the pictures and sounds to combat veterans who did not have PTSD, they were able to distinguish that the pictures and sounds were not real threats from Vietnam but instead only pictures and sounds, and appropriately they did not become afraid. This difference between these two groups was that the medial prefrontal cortex did not turn on normally in the PTSD compared to the non-PTSD veterans (Bremner, Staib, et al., 1999).

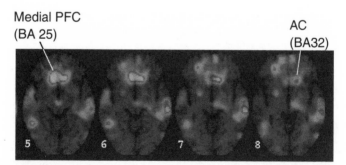

Figure 4.5 Brain activation with exposure to traumatic reminders. Combat veterans with PTSD had a decrease in brain function in the medial prefrontal cortex (PFC), including anterior cingulate (AC), during exposure to combat-related slides and sounds.

DOES STRESS DAMAGE THE BRAIN?

The trick behind all of this is that the higher brain areas of the frontal cortex (which is responsible for our ugly flat face) normally inhibit the more primitive lower brain areas located in the center of our skulls (the areas we share in common with rats and monkeys; Morgan & LeDoux, 1995; Morgan, Romanski, & LeDoux, 1993; Romanski & LeDoux, 1993) (Figure 4.6). Such inhibition turns off the activation of fear responses that are "conditioned" or outside of "conscious" (i.e., frontal cortex) awareness. This brain area may turn off fear responses through inhibition of primitive areas like the amygdala that play a critical role in conditioned fear reactions.

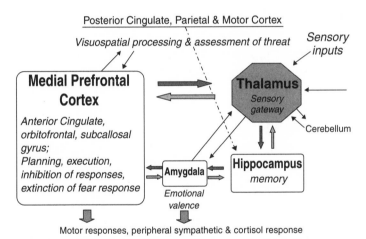

Figure 4.6 Neural circuitry of PTSD. A dysfunctional network of brain regions including medial prefrontal cortex, amygdala, and hippocampus, are hypothesized to underlie the symptoms of abuse-related PTSD. The hippocampus is sensitive to stress, and stress-induced hippocampal damage is hypothesized to lead to deficits in hippocampal-based learning and memory. The hippocampus has important connections with the amygdala, which plays a critical role in the acquisition of fear responses. The thalamus acts as the gateway to the brain, filtering sensory input from the outside world, and coordinating different brain regions during the stress response. The medial prefrontal cortex has connections to the amygdala and hippocampus, and inhibitory inputs to the amygdala are hypothesized to play a role in extinction of fear responses. Dysfunction in these brain areas is hypothesized to underlie symptoms of PTSD.

In addition to the above example of the PTSD patients shown combat slides and sounds, we have found other evidence for dysfunction of medial prefrontal cortex in PTSD. When we used medications to turn on the adrenaline system in PTSD patients, we found that the medial prefrontal cortex did not activate normally. This was associated with an increase in PTSD symptoms (Bremner, Innis, et al., 1997). In another study, we read a script of a person's own childhood sexual abuse and looked at cerebral blood flow. We found that women with abuse-related PTSD, similar to the combat veterans, had decreased blood flow in medial prefrontal cortex, compared to women who had been abused but didn't develop PTSD. PTSD women also had decreased blood flow in the right hippocampus (Bremner, Narayan, et al., 2000). Other imaging studies have found alterations in function of the frontal lobe (Rauch et al., 1996; Shin et al., 1997). These imaging findings are consistent with dysfunction of medial prefrontal cortex in PTSD, which may underlie pathological emotions in survivors of psychological trauma.

These studies have led to an exciting understanding of the effects of traumatic stress on brain function that may have important implications for survivors of psychological trauma. This work, most of which has occurred over the last decade, has helped to establish that psychological trauma can have real effects on the individual, and can lead to real psychiatric disorders. This knowledge has been particularly helpful for trauma survivors, for both their personal satisfaction and their getting compensation and support for disability. Two brain areas that appear to be particularly affected are the hippocampus, which plays a role in learning and memory, and the prefrontal cortex, which is involved in complex thinking as well as social judgments and emotion. The idea that stress could directly lead to hippocampal damage has raised the question of whether stress causes brain damage, a concept that has received considerable interest. Brain systems responsive to stress, including cortisol and adrenaline, have important modulating functions on these brain areas. In addition, chronic stress can lead to long-term dysregulation of these systems, which can affect memory function as well as other symptoms in survivors of psychological trauma. The effects of stress on brain areas involved in memory is relevant to clinical issues surrounding the effects of traumatic stress on the individual (Lewis, 1998).

part
two

THE WIDENING INFLUENCE OF TRAUMA IN THE WORLD TODAY

CHAPTER FIVE

The Scope and Breadth of Traumatic Stress in Society Today

What passing bells for these who die as cattle?
Only the monstrous anger of the guns,
Only the stuttering rifles' rapid rattle
Can patter out their hasty orisons . . .
 —From "Anthem for Doomed Youth,"
  by Wilfred Owen

Living with Traumatic Stress

In the first part of this book, we reviewed the physical consequences of stress, including some of the long-term changes that occur in the brain. However, ultimately our interest in the effects of traumatic stress on brain and body is driven by our desire to understand what effects stress has on the individual, hopefully with the goal of preventing or reversing them. The second half of this book examines the effects of traumatic stress on the individual, including psychiatric outcomes and the ability of individuals to relate to others and to work. The view of stress-related disorders, such as PTSD, representing a neurological disorder will be looked at in more detail. Thinking about stress-related psychiatric disorders as brain-based diseases makes sense, because it ties together many of the aspects of these supposedly distinct disorders that actually have a great deal of overlap. It is also known that not all traumatized individuals will develop psychiatric problems. This raises questions about why some people develop psychiatric problems following traumatic stress, and others do not, as well as related questions of resiliency and whether some types of stress can be beneficial as opposed to only destructive.

The images of traumatic stress are everywhere in our society today: Columbine, Kosovo, Ruby Ridge, Waco, South Central Los Angeles. The images of uncontrollable horror, fear, and devastation that these scenes evoke are becoming increasingly common. Traumatic stress is all around us in our modern age—in the newspapers, on television, in movies, in magazines, even waiting for the bus. Kosovo in Crisis. Tragedy in the Rockies. As a society we are both fascinated and repulsed by traumatic stress. Like bystanders at a highway accident, we want to look and turn away at the same time. Increasingly, we are beginning to realize that traumas are happening not only in our inner cities, but also in our suburbs, the heartland, the mythical sources of safety in America.

As I write this book, these events seem to pale in comparison to the terrible tragedy our country and the world is experiencing. On September 11, 2001, four airplanes and their passengers were hijacked by terrorists and flown into the World Trade Center in New York and into the Pentagon, leading to the collapse of the World Trade Center and the deaths of more than 3,000 people. This event was witnessed by millions on live television, and led to waves of trauma that radiated out from the epicenter of "Ground Zero" in New York to the country as a whole and the world. Our country is now trying to cope with the event that has monopolized our hearts and minds and led us all to rethink the way we see our lives and society. One survey I saw on television reported that 30% of Americans had trouble sleeping shortly after the event, which decreased to 16% a few weeks later—a classic stress response in which a large number are affected initially, and although many recover for some people the stress response becomes chronic. This trauma has led our country into a recession, because of the fear of flying and doing business that has resulted in a slowdown in the fast pace of our country.

Millions of people living in Manhattan are faced every day with the traumatic reminders of the total destruction at the site of the World Trade Center, smelling the smoke and burned rubber, coping with the loss of loved ones and acquaintances, and trying to continue working and living with the incredible feeling of vulnerability of living on a small but densely populated island. The images of the tragedy are played over and over on the television, and the event is discussed continuously on the radio and in newspapers. We are drawn to the news partly out of sense of survival, to see where the next hit is coming from, and yet the viewing increases the feelings of traumatization and disruption in our daily lives. No one in this country who heard of the events on September 11 was able to concentrate and work efficiently and effectively. I myself was drawn to the cafeteria of my hospital, where I watched the news on a television set up for the purpose of helping the employees cope with the event as it unfolded. And yet, for many people, the images, the problems with concentrating, sleeping, and coping will continue for many years to come. And, as this book goes to press, reports of anthrax infections via mail are beginning to spread. This latest form of terrorism raises the question in many people's minds of whether they will be able to continue their normal lives when once-mundane tasks like opening the mail become life threatening.

Psychological trauma changes the way we view the world, ourselves, and our place in the world. The events surrounding a traumatic stress become strongly engraved in memory, and sometimes certain details seem to become shrouded in fog. We all have some traumatic event that stands out from the backdrop of our lives, even if it does not qualify as a traumatic stress.

I remember very clearly my own personal encounter with a major disaster when I was a young premedical student at a small liberal arts college in western Washington. For years, in Washington State, there were predictions that one of the many mountains in the Cascade Range, which are actually dormant volcanoes, would explode. We all thought that it would be Mount Baker, a mountain at the furthest northern reaches of the Cascades, almost to the Canadian border. I myself had climbed to the summit of Mount Baker and looked down into its smoking and sulpherous crater, which seemed to me like peering into the depths of hell. The heat from the crater was slowly melting the massive glaciers that had lain on the flanks of Baker for centuries. There was a special exhibit at the Seattle Science Center showing the progression of the volcano, diagramming the forces at work beneath the ground and the mechanisms that were leading to the inevitable explosion. Seeing that exhibit and the confidence of the scientists, we were convinced that any explosion would come from Baker, a mountain far away from our homes, and in any case we were confident that the scientists would take care of things.

That was why it was such a shock when another mountain unexpectedly blew. After a day of class at my college, I sat down to watch the television news with some other students. The image was a live camera shot of someone stumbling through thick, hot dust and talking as he went. The dust increasingly covered and blotted out everything, including the sun. As we watched, it became clear that this man was dying; indeed, in front of our eyes the cameraman died and the filming came to an end. This was the first view that many of us had of Mount St. Helens exploding. The first blast covered the entire eastern part of the state with ash. Half of the mountain blew off and instantly torched thousands of acres of pristine wilderness, along with all of its living inhabitants (including the people). Spirit Lake, a large mountain lake where I spent my summers in camp, was gone. Hot mud swamped the Tuttle River for several hundred miles, overflowing its banks, and raising the temperature to 80 degrees so that all living things inside of it were killed. After that, the mountain exploded several more times. Later that summer, I was working in a 10-story hospital when one of the explosions occurred. I looked out the window and saw a large plume of dark gray ash slowly moving across the sky. Hours later, we were covered with several inches of that ash. It blotted out the sky at noon. People had to carry boxes of air filters in their cars and change them every few miles, because they would become clogged by the ash.

In the time of the explosion of Mt. St. Helens, we didn't know what was happening to us. Our familiar sense of things was turned upside down. The order and reasonableness that we assumed was always there no longer seemed to exist. The scientists whom we implicitly counted on to solve every problem and predict every possible unexpected outcome let us down. It was as though the veil of illusion that the world was a meaningful, safe, and predictable place had suddenly been torn away, leaving only the terrible reality that anything can happen to you at any time and any place, and there's nothing you can do about it.

Yet, somehow, we all eventually went back to the illusion of safety that we so cherish, because we need that illusion in order to survive. Can you imagine what life would be like if we could foresee the future, if we knew everything that was going to happen to us? We wouldn't be able to survive. We would become like trembling and terrified infants, afraid to take a single step on our own. It is our ignorance of the true nature of the world that keeps us sane.

Traumatized patients with the diagnosis of posttraumatic stress disorder do not see the world as a safe place. A woman who has a child snatched from her arms by a kidnapper will forever after live with the knowledge that anyone at any time could suddenly take another one of her children from her. In a sense, it is as if PTSD patients are the ones who see things clearly, who know the truth. And yet knowing the truth makes it impossible for them to live in the world. Strange thing.

When I first started writing this book, I planned to call it *Hidden Scars*, because the effects of psychological trauma on the individual are typically hidden from view. However, they are all too apparent to the people who suffer from the effects of psychological trauma, to those who are trained to recognize the effects, and sometimes to friends and family who know these patients best. Psychological trauma (defined by the American Psychiatric Association as a threat to life to yourself or someone close to you, accompanied by intense fear, horror, or helplessness) is more common than we would like to believe, affecting about half of Americans at some time in their lives. The most common types of psychological traumas meeting these criteria are assault, rape, and motor vehicle accidents, with events such as combat or natural disasters less common. Traumas such as assault, physical abuse, and rape or molestation in childhood are among the most common causes of long-term stress-related psychiatric disorders in adulthood, including PTSD, depression, and alcohol and substance abuse. Scientists are just beginning to understand how extreme stress can have lasting effects on one's mind, brain, and physical health.

The Invisible Epidemic of Traumatic Stress

Our society has not appreciated the magnitude of traumatic stress today, and until recently this attitude also applied to mental health professionals. There are about one million veterans of the Vietnam War who experienced the stress of combat between 1963 and 1975, which included seeing others killed or wounded, and being exposed to artillery or gunfire. Several hundred thousand veterans of the Gulf War experienced the stress of being in the Gulf War theater in 1990 and 1991. These soldiers were exposed to the constant stress of SCUD missile attacks, air raid alarms, participating in the assault on Kuwait that involved bulldozing Iraqi soldiers into their trenches, or passing hundreds of charred bodies who had been torched by the airstrikes that preceded the land assault. Add to this the stress of exposure to burning oil wells and the possibility (or reality) of chemical attack, and this was not a happy time for many military personnel. Equal or greater numbers of veterans participated in combat in our previous wars, including Korea, WWI, and WWII. And who knows what the future holds in store for our troops in the Middle East?

A few years ago, most mental health professionals felt that trauma only affected war veterans. Over time, professionals have come to realize that psychological trauma is much more common outside of veteran populations. In fact, there are probably at least 10 times as many people in our country with PTSD with no military affiliation as there are with military affiliation. As mentioned above, roughly half of Americans (the estimates vary) will experience a psychological trauma at some time in their lives. Even stressors that we would not consider to be extreme traumas probably have effects on our minds, brains, and bodies in ways that we don't yet fully understand.

The invisible epidemic of civilian traumas represents a major public health problem in our society today. Childhood abuse, car accidents, combat, rape, assault, and a wide variety of other severe traumas can all be associated with lasting effects on the individual. The definition of a traumatic event (something threatening to oneself or someone close to you, accompanied by intense fear, horror, or helplessness) is based on the definition in the *Diagnostic and Statistical Manual*, which is required for the diagnosis of posttraumatic stress disorder (PTSD). We make a distinction between traumatic stressors such as these and what we call *minor stressors*, such as stress on the job or getting a divorce. We are not arguing that getting a divorce is not upsetting, but in order to study this area we must have a definition of a severe stress that is clearly beyond the range of typical human experience. Nevertheless, as mentioned earlier, about half of the general population will experience a traumatic stress at some time in their lives. Of these, about 15% will develop chronic symptoms of posttraumatic stress disorder (Kulka et al., 1990). As mentioned elsewhere in this book, PTSD affects 8% of the population at some time in their lives (Kessler et al., 1995). Traumatic stress is also associated with increased rates of depression, which affects 10% to 15% of Americans at some time in their lives. Other disorders that are increased following exposure to traumatic stress include anxiety disorders (panic disorder and generalized anxiety disorder), somatic disorders, dissociative disorders, and alcohol and substance abuse (Kulka et al., 1990).

Traumatic stress has a particularly dramatic toll on our littlest citizens, who are not able to protect themselves physically or verbally, and who lack the large and well-financed lobbying and advocacy groups that support people who own handguns or who want to sell cigarettes. There are about a million documented new cases of childhood abuse each year. Studies using large samples of the national population showed that 16% of women reported being sexually abused at some time before their 18th birthday (McCauley et al., 1997), with sexual abuse defined as rape, attempted rape, or sexual molestation. These figures add up to the startling fact that about 25 million U.S. women report being sexually assaulted in childhood, and probably about half as many men. Traumatic stress not only has effects on psychological function; there are also a range of physical disorders that are increased by traumatic events, including depression, alcohol and substance abuse, anxiety disorders, somatic disorders, and dissociative disorders, as well as physical problems including heart disease, cancer, increased infections, gastric ulcers, and cognitive disorders. PTSD is 10 times more common than cancer, but our society spends one-tenth as much for research on this disorder as for cancer research. This discrepancy is growing as our senators have recently urged a greater expenditure for cancer research, while no one is speaking out on behalf of victims of childhood abuse and other traumas.

The extent of psychological trauma continues to be underrecognized by our society. Issues of guilt and shame lead many victims of trauma to not admit that they have been traumatized. Trauma victims are often powerless in our society, and there are few advocacy networks to speak on their behalf (unlike other areas of public health, like cancer, or even psychiatric disorders like schizophrenia that are actually much less common than PTSD). The consequences of disclosure may lead to a permanent removal from one's family and lengthy litigation that can cause additional traumatization. Also, families of trauma victims often develop a pattern of denial and avoidance—based on fear and pathological family relationships—that helps to keep psychological trauma a secret and adds to the invisibility of this epidemic. Many trauma survivors do not wish to be removed from their families in spite of the severe toll that the abuse has taken on them. The powerful effect of children's bonds to their parents, in spite of the fact that they may be victimized, should not be underestimated. All of these factors conspire to perpetuate the invisible epidemic of childhood abuse and other traumas.

Risk Factors for the Development of PTSD

One of the most common questions about psychological trauma is why some people develop PTSD following exposure to extreme stressors and other people exposed to a similar trauma do not. Exposure to a traumatic stressor is not the only factor that determines who will develop psychiatric disorders such as PTSD and depression. It is commonly assumed that traumatic stressors override other factors that influence the development of psychopathology. However, there is little evidence to support this idea. In addition, we don't know what effect the contributions of daily hassles, or stressors that don't meet criteria as a major traumatic stress, have on the development of psychopathology. In fact, the diagnostic criteria for PTSD have vacillated in the definition of a traumatic stressor. Much of this has represented an effort to keep out the wide range of slings and arrows of outrageous fortune that are threatening to create patients out of vast swaths of the population. Prior editions of the *Diagnostic and Statistical Manual* defined a traumatic event as "something beyond the range of normal human experience." However, recent epidemiological studies have found that events such as natural disasters, motor vehicle accidents, rape, assault, or witnessing violence—which have traditionally been defined as beyond the range of human experience—probably affect about half of the population at some time in their lives (Kessler et al., 1995). More recently, we have defined traumatic stress more simply as "a threat to life or to the life of someone close to you accompanied by extreme fear, horror, or helplessness." However, it is fairly obvious that there are a number of stressful events that do not meet this strict criteria but nevertheless may have a negative impact on the individual. This has left researchers scratching their heads and wondering about individuals who meet all of the criteria for PTSD except for the traumatic event.

There is a long history, especially in the military, of attempting to understand what factors other than traumatic stress determine which individuals will develop psychopathology following exposure to trauma. Evidence supports a number of factors that we will review below—including the person's constitution, childhood experiences, and what happened after the trauma—that may influence the response to stress (Bremner, Southwick, & Charney, 1994). The famous father of psychoanalysis, Sigmund Freud, originally proposed that unresolved developmental conflicts predisposed some soldiers of World War I to develop "war neurosis" (or what we describe today as PTSD) (Nemiah, 1998). Freud argued that unresolved conflicts from childhood erupted on the battlefield and led to the development of neurotic symptoms. War neurosis was seen as a conflict between unconscious suppressed urges to run from the battlefield and the conscious mind's desire to follow orders of the field commander to stay and fight the enemy. This theory placed emphasis on developmental conflicts from early childhood. Freud's theories were dominant in the first half of the 20th century, especially in America, and this led the military to assess the impact of factors such as personality on the development of war-related psychopathology. During World War II, military psychiatrists attempted to determine which men would develop stress reactions to combat. They evaluated the impact of personality factors, largely based on psychoanalytic theory, that determined who would develop "war neurosis." Although these studies were unable to determine any factors related to personality that predicted who would develop PTSD, other studies did show that factors such as family environment in childhood predicted the development of war-related problems.

The aftermath of the Vietnam War saw the most focused effort to understand why some individuals developed psychopathology after combat and others did not. Those studies found that about 15% of individuals would develop PTSD (which actually was only defined as a diagnosis in 1980). Studies in the 1980s, based on samples of the national population, examined childhood-related variables for the development of PTSD. In general, some of these studies showed that childhood factors such as being antisocial in childhood, family environment, family alcoholism, and academic performance predicted the development of PTSD, although other studies did not replicate this finding. Studies in disaster victims found that having a preexisting psychiatric condition increased the risk for the development of PTSD. A number of studies were conducted on Vietnam War veterans to determine possible predetermining factors for PTSD. Factors such as being very young at the time of joining the military, or having less education, were found to predict the development of PTSD (Schlenger et al., 1999).

There were several theories about what determined who would develop psychopathology after the war. One theory, the *stress evaporation* theory, stated that the actual effects of combat stress "evaporated" within a few months of traumatic exposure, and what was left was only the psychopathology or defects in character that were present in the individual before he or she went to Vietnam. This theory was largely the foundation of earlier diagnoses in the *Diagnostic and Statistical Manual* in the 1940s and

1950s, such as gross stress reaction, which as stated earlier in this text, viewed psychological symptoms in the aftermath of trauma as a normal response that would rapidly resolve. In fact, gross stress reaction required the absence of premorbid psychiatric disorder or personality problems to make the diagnosis. In addition, there were no diagnoses before 1980 that captured chronic psychopathology related to traumatic stress. The other theory of traumatic stress, called the *residual stress theory*, held that the symptoms seen in veterans of the Vietnam War were related to the effects of combat itself, and not to premorbid personality or other unrelated factors (Figley, 1978). These authors pointed to the correlation of increasing risk for the development of PTSD with increasing exposure to combat. More recently, Goldberg, True, and Henderson (1990) showed that combat exposure increases the risk of PTSD by nine times in Vietnam combat veterans as compared to their identical twins without PTSD. Like anything, however, there is no absolute truth in this area; rather, the truth lies somewhere in the middle. We know that the severity of traumatic stress plays a critical role in the risk for developing PTSD. However, we also know that other factors, including genetic constitution and previous history of exposure to stress, are also important.

Two theories that have dominated stress research, which were discussed earlier in this text in relation to the physiology of stress, are *stress inoculation* and *stress sensitization*. The theory of *stress inoculation* holds that a history of prior stress strengthens the individual's ability to deal with future stressors. Animal models suggest that repeated stress has a detrimental effect. However, there are many human trauma survivors who make substantial contributions to society—who feel that their experiences have made them better people in many ways. The alternative theory, *stress sensitization*, holds that repeated stress increases the risk for development of abnormalities in both neurobiology and behavior following reexposure to stress. There is now ample evidence in support of the stress sensitization view. For example, animals exposed to chronic stress have a potentiated release of adrenaline in the brain when reexposed to stress compared to animals who have never been exposed to stress. Studies in human subjects exposed to extreme stress are also consistent with the idea that a prior history of exposure to stress is a risk factor for the development of stress-related psychopathology.

In fact, one of the best predictors of who will develop PTSD following a traumatic stress is history of exposure to previous stressors. I have heard Dr. Robert Ursano of the U.S. Armed Services say that we all have multiple miniature episodes of PTSD, whether from a fender bender or a bad breakup. The important question is whether these mini-episodes will develop into a chronic disorder. Probably the most important factor that determines whether this will happen is the frequency of exposure to stress. For instance, we compared Vietnam combat veterans with and without PTSD, and found that childhood abuse was a strong predictor of the development of PTSD. Thirty-one percent of patients with PTSD from combat had a history of severe childhood physical and/or sexual abuse, compared to only 7% of the veterans without PTSD. Other factors—including family alcoholism, loss of a parent, adoption, and parental separation—did not predict PTSD (Bremner, Southwick, et al., 1993). Similarly, childhood sexual abuse increased the risk of PTSD in women who were raped in adulthood. Israeli military veterans who developed stress reactions to one conflict were found to be more likely to develop stress reactions with reexposure to combat stress in subsequent wars (Solomon, Garb, Bleich, & Grupper, 1987). These finding make sense from the standpoint of theories of stress sensitization, which states that a prior exposure to stress increases the risk of developing PTSD following reexposure to stress.

Other factors are related to the risk of developing PTSD. As mentioned above, a family history of antisocial behavior increases the risk for the development of PTSD. Increased rates of alcoholism and anxiety disorders have also been seen in patients with PTSD. Lack of education, emotional immaturity, preexisting psychiatric disorders, and lack of social support have additionally been linked to the development of PTSD following a trauma. McNally and Shin (1995) hypothesized that lower IQ scores before the trauma are also associated with the development of PTSD.

In spite of how strange this may seem, genetic constitution has been shown to make a substantial contribution to the development of PTSD following exposure to traumatic stress. In an early study, children of patients with PTSD were found to be more at risk for the development of psychiatric disorders, most commonly attention deficit disorder (Davidson, Smith, & Kudler, 1989). Work by William True, Jack Goldberg, and colleagues (True et al., 1993) showed that as much as 17% of the risk for developing PTSD could be predicted based on genes alone. In addition, these scientists showed that certain individuals were more likely to be *exposed* to traumatic stress than others. In other words, there was a genetic risk behavior that would put you in harm's way, that could not be explained by education, race, or other factors. This has prompted me to coin the term "the family of walking disasters" to describe families of related individuals who seem to get into a lot of trouble. In my opinion, this may be related to differences that are passed on from generation to generation in behavioral attributes, such as risk-taking behavior, a lack of ability to detect true threats in the environment, and in the ability to detect social cues. These may represent families of dangerous characters, as shown by studies demonstrating that a history of antisocial behavior in the family background increases twofold the risk for developing PTSD (Breslau, Davis, & Andreski, 1991).

It also may be that individuals with a history of exposure to trauma and the diagnosis of PTSD are less able to cope with stress and avoid traumatic stressors. PTSD patients have their fear alarm systems essentially "turned on" at all times, so they don't have the ability to make the fine distinctions that will help them determine when a true threat enters their environment. This can put them at a singular disadvantage. Using an example I give elsewhere in this book, an incest survivor has extreme fear reactions whenever a man does so little as to brush up against her, let alone touch her in an intimate way. However, she knows that this is not a normal response, and because she would like to have intimate relationships with others she sometimes tries to turn off her own feelings about her body so she can get closer to a man. This results in her completely dissociating, however, so she feels like she has been put to sleep. The dissociation, in turn, increases her risk for being taking advantage of, which may underlie the fact that she was the victim of rape in adulthood. As she described it, the man had penetrated her before she even knew what was happening. This story is typical of childhood sexual abuse survivors and may at least partially explain why they are at increased risk for rape in adulthood.

Factors related to the time of the traumatization or the type of trauma have been related to severity of PTSD. As noted earlier, there is a wealth of evidence that amount and severity of trauma are associated with severity of PTSD. Some specific traumatic events are also associated with worse outcomes, including being wounded, seeing others killed, personal identification with the dead, and having friends killed. Participation in atrocities during combat is associated with a particularly bad outcome. There is no clear evidence that alcohol or substance abuse before or at the time of traumatization influences outcome, although there is a clear increase in alcohol and substance abuse after the trauma in patients who develop PTSD, which is related to the self-medication seen in these patients. Severity of trauma exposure in other populations—such as victims of rape, childhood abuse, natural disasters, and criminal assault—has also been associated with degree of PTSD symptomatology. Several studies have shown that people who dissociate during trauma are at increased risk to have long-term negative effects from it. These individuals act like they are in a daze or a dream, see things as if they are in a tunnel, and have changes in how they perceive the environment or their own bodies. When they are later reexposed to minor stressors, they continue to respond with dissociative responses (Bremner et al., 1992; Bremner & Brett, 1997; Bremner & Marmar, 1998; Marmar et al., 1994).

Things that happen in the aftermath of the trauma, such as the support that one gets from family and friends, have been shown to decrease the trauma's negative impact. This includes how much the individual talks about the event with others, and how much understanding the individual receives from family and friends. Also, the support of a spouse has a positive effect relative to individuals who are unmarried. The extended kinships of the Kosovar Albanians provide them with an important moderating influence for the traumatizing effects of the Kosovo War. In contrast, when our Vietnam veterans returned from the war, they were met at the airport by protesters who spit or threw blood on them, and were often viewed by friends as murderers or terrible people when they returned to their communities. Needless to say, this did not help veterans very much. It was especially tragic because many veterans had been drafted into the war and young men from the working classes who did not attend college were preferentially selected. The ritual these veterans were denied—of the returning war hero who is gratefully greeted in celebrations by society as having protected and sacrificed for the community (e.g., the Fifth Avenue ticker tape parade)—has a long history. In the ancient world, from the Sumerians to the Romans, it was common for citizens to turn out to welcome their returning victorious heroes. In fact, the pragmatic Romans even built a special road (the *Via Trionfo*, or "Road of Triumph") so that the returning triumphant Roman Legions would not clog the roads and interrupt normal commerce and traffic. In light of our shameful treatment of the Vietnam veterans, our society needs to decide whether or not we want to use war as a means of obtaining our ends. If we don't, we should stop engaging in military conflict. If we do, we should stop blaming the military for the negative consequences of war, and provide a more supportive environment for our veterans who engage in the conflicts. In spite of the fact that the military is currently seen in a very positive light, we must be cognizant of sheltering the armed forces from the political winds that can blow storm clouds across the horizon without advance notice.

Resiliency to Traumatic Stress

Traumatic stress does not always have negative psychological consequences on the individual. Even some particularly horrific traumas can leave some individuals mentally unscathed. This raises questions about resiliency to traumatic stress, and why some people are able to get through relatively clean, whereas others with even less severe levels of trauma develop chronic psychiatric disorders that they take with them to the grave. As a physician and a psychiatrist, I have traditionally been trained to recognize pathology and to think about ways to treat defects. Therefore, as a physician and a psychiatrist with expertise in the field of psychological trauma, I have gotten used to thinking about the deficits induced by psychological trauma and the ways that these deficits can be treated. Naturally, the only individuals that we see as psychiatrists are those who feel they have some problem related to their traumatic experiences, whether it be as war veterans, or victims of childhood abuse, survivors of a natural disaster, or people subjected to other negative traumatic events.

With this background, I found it very surprising to interact with veterans of the Vietnam War who had been prisoners of war but had gone on to lead very productive lives after being released from captivity. I was giving a presentation for a group of scientists, physicians, and repatriated prisoners of war on the possible effects of the stress of captivity on heart disease, when one POW challenged me and asked me why I assumed that the POW experience was necessarily negative. Why couldn't it be, he asked, that the POW experience didn't have a positive effect on the heart? Why did everyone assume that the stress of being a POW was necessarily negative? This veteran had the perspective that there were certain aspects of the POW experience that had been positive: The knowledge that one could encounter adversity and survive led to the conclusion that one could survive anything that life had to offer. Being confined to small spaces with other individuals increased the tolerance that one had for others in future life settings. During captivity, many veterans developed impressive mnemonic capacities (the ability to memorize) that they later used, for example, to complete medical school or other studies. One veteran said that he memorized all of the names of the POWs in the "Hanoi Hilton" camp in North Vietnam in blocks of 10. When someone new arrived in the camp, he would merely add it into the list. Thirty years after the end of the war, he could continue to recite the list as if he had been there only a few days before.

I was impressed by my encounters with the Vietnam Repatriated Prisoners of War (RPOW), and felt that I had finally met the *übermenschen*, or "overmen," of Friedrich Nietzsche. These are the individuals who possess extraordinary physical and emotional capacities that set them above the ordinary individuals of daily existence. In fact, when listening to the veterans' stories, I heard of situations of extreme violence and torture that I did not think that I personally would have had the strength to resist. This led to the idea that these men had abilities above the average person. In fact, many of the RPOWS are functioning at levels above that of the common person, the best case being that of Arizona Senator John McCain. An alternative view is that these men were merely ordinary Americans who had risen to the challenge they encountered, as many Americans would do in similar circumstances.

What Constitutes a Stressor?

There is a long history of debate in our society and among mental health professionals on what constitutes a traumatic stress. It is important to be able to differentiate a truly stressful event, such as being assaulted, from something that may be upsetting but typically is considered not to have lasting effects, such as being fired from your job or having your car stolen. It is important to make such distinctions for a variety of reasons, including compensation for disability and legal issues related to litigation for personal injury and other areas. It may be arbitrary to make distinctions about whether or not a particular event constitutes a trauma based on the event type, because the same event may affect people in different ways based on the meaning that event has for the individual, the extenuating circumstances, a prior history of traumatic exposure, and other factors. The idea that a person might be particularly vulnerable to a traumatic event has been captured in legal frameworks as the notion of the person with an "eggshell skull." According to this idea, an event may not appear to be particularly traumatic, but the person with an "eggshell skull" is particularly vulnerable and should be compensated for injury from the event in any case.

Historically, only easily identifiable traumas were considered to constitute traumatic stressors, such as exposure to combat or being in a train wreck or other major accident. As outlined earlier in this chapter, even exposure to these major traumas was considered to have a passing effect on the individual. However, it is obvious that there are other types of traumas that affect the individual in a serious way that do not come under the categories of combat or accidents. In order to operationalize the definition of psychological trauma, earlier versions of the *Diagnostic and Sta-*

tistical Manual defined psychological trauma as an "event beyond the normal range of human experience," and the diagnosis of posttraumatic stress disorder required exposure to such an event ("Criterion A") for the diagnosis. Obviously, it may be very difficult to determine which events are beyond the normal range of human experience. Also, there are some human experiences—such as being the victim of assault or robbery, or having a loved one die suddenly—that unfortunately may not be beyond the range of human experience, especially for some sociodemographic groups.

However, the implementation of a definition for traumatic stress was a first step, and it represented the first time that traumatic stressors were outlined, defined, and represented as events with potentially negative consequences. In response to the limitations of the original definition of psychological trauma, a second version appeared in later versions of the *Diagnostic and Statistical Manual* as an "event with threat to life or significant other, accompanied by intense fear, horror or helplessness." This second definition avoided the problems of determining whether events were beyond the range of normal human experience, and incorporated the idea that traumatic events are essentially life threatening. However, there are a large number of normal individuals who experience a threat to their life or to someone close to them, or witness such an event, such that qualification for "Criterion A" for PTSD becomes so nonspecific as to be almost useless. An important question arises then as to whether a particular traumatic event is the one responsible for the development of PTSD, and whether individuals who have symptoms of PTSD that are not necessarily linked to a particular event are worthy of consideration for treatment by mental health professionals. What happens in practice is that patients learn that they need a specifically identified traumatic event in order to receive attention from their health care professionals, so patient and treator happily collude in finding that "special event" to focus on in treatment, when in fact the reality is that a lifetime of experience has led the patient to be walking in the door of the treatment facility with the particular list of problems, symptoms, and disabilities on that particular day. Modern psychiatry and the mental health profession have not solved the problem of "Criterion A" or the definition of psychological trauma. However, there is a healthy appreciation for the limitations of this area of psychiatric diagnosis that did not exist 10 years ago.

Mental Health Outcomes Related to Traumatic Stress

The psychiatric outcome of traumatic stress is also not always uniform, but instead can be a range, including depression, PTSD, dissociation, somatic disorders, and alcohol and substance abuse. One important question is why some individuals develop one type of psychiatric disorder and others develop something different. For example, why is it that one person will develop depression following a traumatic stress, and another individual exposed to a similar stress will develop PTSD? We don't entirely understand why, although there are some patterns that seem to be emerging. Individuals traumatized very early in life where the pattern of traumatic exposure continued throughout childhood seem to have difficulty escaping from long-term changes in character and personality, which can lead to diagnoses of personality disorders. Individuals traumatized later in life who have a more stress-free childhood will develop classic symptoms of PTSD characterized by excessive arousal symptoms, with less of the personality disturbances seen in early trauma victims.

Two of the common outcomes of psychological trauma are depression and PTSD. It is not known why some individuals develop depression and others PTSD following exposure to a similar stressor. One idea is that depression is a milder response to trauma, whereas more extreme trauma leads to PTSD, and the most extreme response is dissociative disorders. We also know that early trauma victims commonly develop symptoms of depression that last their whole lives. When the effects of trauma are not as severe, they may develop depression that resolves with treatment. However, with more extreme trauma, they often develop coexisting PTSD and depression that becomes chronic. In this case, the depression seen in conjunction with PTSD is not the same as typical depression seen in patients who do not necessarily have a history of trauma, and in whom the depression is probably more linked to factors such as a genetic vulnerability to develop depression.

There is a variety of evidence that the depression seen in PTSD is different than the typical depression. PTSD and depression differ in terms of biological findings and treatment response. I discussed in Chapter 1 and elsewhere in this book how there is considerable overlap between the symptoms of depression and the symptoms of PTSD as listed in the *DSM–IV*. There is also considerable overlap between PTSD and the dissociative disorders. The dissociative disorders, especially those involving a disturbance in personality, seem to require a history of traumatization that dates back to early childhood. It also appears that individuals who dissociate at the time of trauma are more likely to develop dissociative disorders later in life, although we don't understand why some individuals are more likely to dissociate at the time of trauma. Patients with severe dissociative disorders, such as dissociative identity disorder, almost always have the comorbid disorders of PTSD and depression, which indicates that the dissociative disorders represent an extreme of pathology among the trauma-spectrum disorders.

Other disorders, such as substance abuse, may develop following exposure to trauma for other reasons. We know that alcohol and substance abuse have a genetic component that certainly contributes to the vulnerability to develop these disorders. However, we also know that alcohol, drugs, and even cigarettes decrease the anxiety and symptomatology associated with reminders of the trauma in PTSD patients. Additionally, we have conducted survey studies showing that use of alcohol, heroin, marijuana, and benzodiazepines increased after the Vietnam War in parallel to the increase in PTSD symptoms in combat veterans with PTSD. The veterans also reported that these substances improved symptoms of PTSD, especially in the hyperarousal and intrusion categories, whereas other substances like cocaine actually made these symptoms worse. We know from biological studies in animals reviewed in Chapter 3 that these substances decrease activity of the noradrenergic system, which is abnormally increased in PTSD patients. Therefore, there is a theoretical rationale for the idea that PTSD patients "self-medicate" themselves to treat their PTSD symptoms.

Anxiety disorders seem to be generally more common in trauma victims (Kulka et al., 1990). This could be related to the fact that PTSD is associated with increased anxiety and therefore represents an artifact of psychiatric diagnosis. There are other ways in which the anxiety disorders may be specifically linked to psychological trauma. Patients may have conditioned fear reactions to a traumatic situation, as described in Chapter 3, very similar to the animal model of conditioned fear where a bright light is paired with an electric shock and reexposure to the bright light alone results in a stress response. In a similar way, if someone is attacked in an elevator, then exposure to confined spaces will result in a fear response, even though the true stressor is no longer present. Years later, the individual may have forgotten the circumstances that led to the fear of confined spaces, so that he or she has attacks of panic anxiety that seem to come out of the blue, leading to the diagnosis of panic disorder. Therefore, one theory of panic disorder is that patients are having conditioned responses to triggers that are associated with an original traumatic event, even though they no longer remember the association. Similarly, in obsessive-compulsive disorder, there may be repetitive behaviors, such as checking the doors to make sure they are locked, that seem to have no logical basis. However, there may have been a prior history of assault, and the individual has repetitive memories below the level of conscious thinking of the possibility of another assault that leads to the behavior. These are simplistic examples but serve to illustrate the point.

Somatization disorder is another disorder linked to stress that may have specific connections to trauma. Somatization disorders involve a preoccupation with physical illnesses or symptoms when there is no organic explanation for the disorder. These disorders include pain with intercourse, pelvic pain, or other symptoms that can interfere with sexual function or intimacy. Somatic disorders may be linked to exposure to the original trauma. For example, if someone was raped in childhood and associates that attack with pelvic pain, later in adulthood she may experience pelvic pain that has no conscious link with the original event. Somatic disorders also represent the overlap between the effects of stress on mind, brain, and body. Scientists have moved away from thinking about somatic disorders as something "in your head" to disorders that represent the interface between mind and body.

Why Do People Perpetrate Trauma on Others?

Perhaps a more difficult question than why individuals develop different disorders following stress is why people perpetrate violence on one another in the first place. During the most recent conflict in the Balkans, the North Atlantic Treaty Organization (NATO) forces bombed the tiny ex-autonomous republic of Kosovo while Serbian paramilitary forces swept through Kosovo, knocking on doors of families' homes, and giving them one hour to leave or be killed. Two million Albanian people, who made up 90% of the population, were forced from their homes by brutal killers who made a religion out of dominating, suppressing, and abusing those of their neighbors who had the misfortune to be of a different ethnic and religious group. Every night, politicians, pundits, and other talking heads wrung their hands and bewailed the fact that we were "heading for another Vietnam" (whatever that means) or regaled us on the television that we had lost two soldiers in Macedonia. I do not intend to belittle the value of one human life, but we must remember the fact that manifold more individuals of Albanian ethnicity were killed or severely traumatized while our debates about American involvement were going on.

Recent events, although tragic on the individual level, are a drop in the bucket compared to the grand list of atrocities committed by human beings on each other in the course of the 20th century. The reader does not have to be reminded about the 8 million Jews, Gypsies, and other unfortunate peoples that were systematically exterminated by the Nazis during World War II. Add to that several million Cambodians exterminated by Pol Pot in the aftermath of the Vietnam War. Other mass exterminations that have not received as much attention are the slaughter of what is estimated to be several million ethnic Armenians by the Turks at the time of World War I, and the destruction and deportation of countless more in the former Soviet Republic. These are all examples of genocide, the systematic destruction of one people by another because of their race or religion. When violence becomes organized, it is a terrible thing.

At the time of this writing violence from another part of the world, the Middle East, has been brought literally to our doorstep. Over the last decade of the 20th century an increase in chaos in Afghanistan allowed the emergence of a particularly brutal and oppressive group called the Taliban that dominated much of that country. These people developed particularly creative brutalities such as chopping off the arms of individuals who used drugs, or forbidding women to go outside alone, even if it meant starvation in their own homes. The growth of the Taliban is a harsh reminder that when law and order are allowed to lapse, we quickly fall back in time to a brutal and chaotic way of life that existed centuries ago, and that is too terrible for most of us to imagine. Civilization is a fragile and priceless gift that we should not readily toss aside.

The Taliban also fostered the growth of the terrorist organization, Al Quaeda, with its ring leader, Osama bin Laden, whose outrageous conduct grew until it culminated in the hijacking of airliners that were crashed in the World Trade Center and the Pentagon. The cruelty of flying innocent passengers into those buildings was so novel that it shocked us, because it is an idea we had never considered. It also took the nation by storm, as it unfolded in front of our eyes of national television. In the ensuing weeks we wondered why someone would hate us so much to commit such a terrible crime, and in our wondering we sought to learn more about the Islamic terrorists who did so.

Violence and destruction have been going on for several millennia. Our species has been committing atrocities upon each other for the past 12,000 years. This is a relatively recent chapter, however, that represents only a fraction of our long history as a species. For 99% of our history we wandered the earth (mostly in Africa), hunting for our food with simple spears and stone throwers and gathering nuts and berries wherever we could find them. In this simple state we never accumulated anything worth stealing, certainly not worth the effort of killing for. It was only about 10,000 years before biblical times when we started to cultivate grains and raise domesticated cattle, that we could accumulate wealth and possessions. When some people had less than others, they would fight and sometimes kill to get what the other person had, especially if their own families were going hungry. What some modern people don't realize is that the history of the ancient world was of a collection of walled cities engaged in continual warfare. These cities would attack each other, and if successful at breaching the defenses, steal everything of value, slaughter all of the males, and sell the women and children (if they were lucky) into slavery. Hence, violence and destruction is nothing new; it is only in the past century that we have become sufficiently organized and technologically advanced to take the numbers of mass destruction to such dizzying heights.

In the past century, there has been much soul searching and self-questioning about the causes of mass atrocities such as that committed by the Nazis, and the capacity of human beings for evil. As I noted above, most of our history over the past 12,000 years is in fact a history of death, destruction, and atrocities perpetrated largely on defenseless men, women, and children. The cause of all this mayhem is, in fact, very easy to understand: it is simple human greed. If one group wants to take what the other group has, they will use whatever means they have at their disposal to get it, including murder. The events leading up to the Holocaust in Germany (and most of Europe, for that matter, for let us not think that other citizens of the continent did not also play a role in that drama) were based on feelings of envy—envy that the Jews in Europe had more material wealth than did the Christian population of the time. It helped that the Jews could be identified as different than the rest of the population based on their religion. If the Jews could be categorized, identified, and easily characterized and therefore dehumanized, it would be easy to turn them into objects that could be dispatched so that the rest of the people could get their houses, bank accounts, and gold fillings. And this is exactly what happened.

But let us not think for a moment that this is anything new. Since the time of the ancient Sumerians, specific groups of peoples with common language, customs, religious practices, and beliefs have been villanizing peoples different than them—effortlessly inflicting pain and destruction—in order to achieve a goal, basically to steal all of their victims' material goods. Look at how we characterized the "Japs" as inhuman machines during World

War II so that it became easy to drop nuclear bombs on two of their cities and instantly incinerate several hundred thousand of their defenseless men, women, and children.

One pattern that is clear from both history and clinical psychiatry is that violence begets violence. The maxim of the Bible—"He who lives by the sword shall die by the sword"—is true. Cultures and societies that are victimized by others or under threat from others are more likely to use violence against others. In fact, the last half of the 20th century was unusual in the Western world in that there weren't any major military conflicts between nations. This is largely the result of increased feelings of security between nations and the lack of a recent history of violence to act as stimulants for future conflicts. An alternative viewpoint is that the Americans have dominated the world scene and suppressed any potential upstarts.

A similar pattern can be seen at the level of the individual in the cycle of violence that begets repeated patterns of childhood abuse. It is well established that perpetrators of childhood abuse usually had a history of abuse in their own childhood. There has been a great deal of questioning about the causes and possible prevention of this "circle of violence." However, a significant portion of the cause of this phenomenon may best be understood on a psychological level. It's what I call the "dark side" of the trauma response. A psychotherapy supervisor of mine once described it as the horrible nature of having your darkest and most repressed fantasies come to life before your eyes. You then must live the rest of your life with the knowledge that you have crossed a boundary that separates you from everyone else in your community, for whom these events exist only in nightmares. Having seen the truth you are wise, but your wisdom separates you from your family, culture, and community. You know the truth, but instead of the truth setting you free, the truth makes you unable to function socially or at work. You are wise, but your wisdom is a disease.

I am reminded of the movie *Blue Velvet*, directed by David Lynch. The movie starts out with a typical American scene: a suburban street, well-cut green lawns, a sprinkler spraying against the blue sky. A young man is mowing his lawn and notices something strange out of the corner of his eye. He looks more closely, and the object really is strange: a human ear, lying on the grass. This is the start of a truly peculiar movie, about a nightclub singer who is kept hostage by an evil man who has cut off the ear of her boyfriend. He loves to hear her sing "Blue Velvet," and he makes her perform it again and again. The evil man has complete control over the singer.

Domination of another human being is a compelling force. In the face of victimization, many victims of trauma feel powerless, worthless, like nothing. These feelings don't go away when the trauma stops, even when the perpetrator dies. Sometimes the only way to overcome that feeling of powerlessness is to dominate another human being. That is why many victims of violence and trauma must resist the compulsion to victimize others. Many choose never to have children for that reason. In other cases, the violence and abuse is all they have known, and that is the only way they have learned to relate to others, the only behavior in their repertoire.

We have gone a long way toward reducing the ongoing warfare and violence between cities and nations over the past 12 millennia. Intraspecies violence is a problem that has plagued us since we first walked out of the forests (or savannah), planted crops, domesticated animals for our use, and began to build cities and nations. However, in the United States, we continue to be plagued by an epidemic of violence that makes our nation seem sometimes like we have more in common with ancient barbarian societies than with modern civilization. As noted in the first chapter of this book, we cannot open the newspaper or turn on the television set without hearing and seeing news of some recent tragedy. Whether it is killings in a high school in Colorado, or a racist who enters a Jewish day care center to shoot children because of their religious affiliation, or anthrax spread through the mail, a week does not go by in our current society where there is not a violent tragedy to fill the newspapers and television. What is even scarier is that the massive diffusion of information in our modern "age of information" appears to be stimulating a series of copycat incidents, not to mention the potential for an entire country to be traumatized by watching a traumatic event occur live on television.

A particularly frightening recent development is the series of shootings by children in school settings. The so-called citizen's "right to bear arms" (which in fact is a distortion of history, where our founding fathers outlined the right of the *militia* to bear arms—there happened to be a volunteer militia in the early days of our country) has been promoted as a justification for an extensive diffusion of firearms throughout society. Children who are not old enough to appreciate the difference between right and wrong are being taught how to use firearms, putting in their hands the ability to end a life with a simple movement of a finger that can be stimulated by whatever random emotion happens to be stirring in their adolescent minds at the moment. Adolescents have an imperfectly formed view of their own mortality and that of others, thinking of themselves as immortal and not always considering what impact their actions may have. The period of adolescence is also a turbulent time often plagued by crises of personality and identity, with associated depression, anxiety, hostility, and paranoia. These children are not people we want bringing weapons into the classroom; and yet children in our society have widespread access to firearms.

The United States seems to have a type of cultural blind spot for recognizing the absurdity of the current situation related to firearms. We are deadlocked in the great "gun debate," as if some arbitrary judge will one day declare one group or the other most eloquent and that will resolve the "question" once and for all. I was reminded of the absurdity of this situation when I was watching the "breaking news" television coverage of a recent massacre, the shooting of little children in a Jewish day care center in Los Angeles by a member of the Aryan Nation racist group. One of California's senators, Barbara Boxer, was being interviewed on television shortly after the event occurred, and she pointed out that there were several gun control laws currently stalled in Congress that could have prevented the incident, including one requiring background checks on guns sold in fairs (which is where the day care center assailant purchased his gun, because he had a criminal and psychiatric record and could have been easily identified by a background check). The interviewer commented that he appreciated her opinion, but that they didn't have anyone on the other side of the gun control debate available to speak so he didn't want to pursue the topic any further. The absurdity is that by making the question a "debate" it turns it into a question that can never be resolved, because there will always be someone with opinions on both sides of the issue, and since verbal arguments will never have an impact on the question until there is a major sea change in the way our society views the issue. Unfortunately, it looks like the only way that will come about is by a continuation of the increase in the public outrage accompanying the crescendo of murder being documented on nightly television, to counteract the vast sums of money that are being funneled to the nation's politicians to maintain the status quo of gun-related violence.

Gun-related violence has taken a major toll on our society and is an important cause of psychological trauma in our cities and, increasingly, in the suburbs as well. Data from the Center for Disease Control in Atlanta show that between 1986 and 1992 guns were the cause of 523,864 deaths in the United States— including 107,119 homicide-related deaths, 397,371 suicide-related deaths, 16,585 accidental deaths, and 2,789 deaths of unknown cause. That means that about 75,000 people are dying each year from gun-related violence. This figure is incredible compared to, for example, European countries, where only a few hundred people die each year from gun-related violence. Arguments that deaths would occur from other causes if guns were eliminated are fallacious, as evidenced by the drop in homicide rates in Vancouver, British Columbia (Canada), after guns were illegalized, and by the much lower homicide rates in European countries with very strict gun control laws.

The impact of gun-related violence on our society is hard to calculate. We must add to the 75,000 deaths per year from gun-related violence the larger number of individuals who are injured, often seriously, but survive, as well as those who are traumatized by witnessing violence, or having a family member or friend affected in some way. For children growing up in the inner city, it is impossible to avoid the effects of violence. The problem is so severe in New Haven that the Yale Child Study Center has formed a partnership with the New Haven Police Department to intervene with children at the site of violence to protect them from the harmful effects of witnessing or in other ways being affected by violence.

Exposure to violence can not only increase the risk to the individual of later becoming a perpetrator of violence, it can also have a rippling psychological effect on others close to you, an effect known as "secondary traumatization." In 1991, when I was the Medical Director of a specialized inpatient treatment unit for Vietnam veterans with PTSD, the most recent conflict in the Balkans erupted. This region has seen repeated conflicts between disparate ethnic and religious groups over the past 100 years or so, and many of the antagonisms are rooted in deep-seated conflicts that extend back over centuries. At that time, Serbian "paramilitary forces" were going into Muslim villages and burning people out of their houses. From extensive and focused experience through psychotherapy with my Vietnam combat veterans with PTSD, I knew the terrible realities of warfare, especially in situations where the boundaries between civilian and combatant become blurred, as happened with the Viet Cong and later in the Balkans. When soldiers go into a village and don't know who is the enemy and who is the friend, they sometimes lose their heads and kill indiscriminately. If the problem of friend versus foe becomes chronic, indiscriminate killing can be habit forming. Also, the feeling of power and control over the lives of others can stimulate soldiers to do things they wouldn't otherwise do. Again and again, as a psychiatrist treating ex-soldiers who had been psychologically scarred by the trauma of war, I saw ordinary American boys who had taken the rage, fear, and horror that came along with their experience and vented it on anyone who was around them.

In the course of writing this book, I realized that I, too, am coping with my responses to the overwhelming horror of these people, trying to handle the horror of the stories that I myself have heard. While working on the book, I saw a patient with PTSD who had finally come to the end of his rope and came in asking for treatment. Jeff had been a cop in the Bridgeport police force for 20 years. When I saw him, he had reached a crisis point where he couldn't cope with his daily memories of a traumatic event that had happened 15 years before. His wife told him he had to get counseling right away. The morning of the incident, he took a call at 5 o'clock concerning a suicide attempt. It was only four blocks away. He entered the house and a woman was screaming, "My son hurt himself, he didn't mean it, you've got to help him." The father was very silent. A 5-year-old girl was crying and saying, "Help my brother, he's hurt." Jeff entered the room of what had been a 17-year-old boy. He was lying on his bed with a shotgun on his chest. His face looked normal but the top of his head was a cavity. He had literally blown his brains out. As Jeff stood there, some of the brains that had been sticking to the ceiling fell on his shoulder. The boy's body was making a gasping sound as if he were breathing.

My police officer gained some measure of relief from telling me his story, but had I taken on some of the toxic burden? When the most recent war in the Balkans broke out, I read in the papers fragmented accounts of villages being burned. In my dreams I filled in the details. With the knowledge gleaned from my interactions with war veterans about what is possible in war, I saw civilians being burned alive in their homes and shot if they tried to run. It is amazing, but at the time there was no general knowledge that such things were happening in the Balkans, but now we know that these things were all too common. It is the knowledge of the reality of existence that comes with one who has experienced trauma, or been a witness, that gave me the prescience to know the real truth about what terrible things were happening at the time in the Balkans. However, that knowledge was too much for me, and was part of the reason why at the time I began to focus more on research of trauma rather than psychological treatment of trauma survivors.

These effects are known as *secondary traumatization*. The effects of trauma can ramify from the trauma victims to friends, family, and therapists, yielding significant effects that can resonate through generations. Perhaps this is what Shakespeare intuitively comprehended when he wrote of the curse of the House of Capulet in *Romeo and Juliet* ("the sins of the fathers will be visited upon their sons"). There are entire institutes that deal with the effects of secondary traumatization in psychotherapists who see trauma victims. The International Society for Traumatic Stress Studies— a society of psychiatrists, psychologists, social workers, and researchers, as well as trauma victims—has a "debriefing" session at the end of each day of their annual meeting; so that participants can unload the trauma of listening to scientific and clinical presentations about the effects of trauma on the individual.

This chapter has reviewed the far-reaching consequences of traumatic stress, the high magnitude of traumatic stressors in our society, and some of the factors that may increase vulnerability to psychopathology. In the next chapter, we review the diagnostic schemas currently used for disorders related to traumatic stress, and how those schemas can be improved by thinking about trauma-related psychiatric disorders as diseases of the brain. The current chapter has lighted upon several areas, including the causes and manifestations of trauma-related pathology, the impact of trauma on the sense of meaning, and effects of trauma on the brain. I have commented on the potential to prevent trauma-related disorders by eliminating violence in our society. As the poem by T.S. Eliot states, our end is our beginning; that is, if we could stop the circle of violence from emerging, we could arrive at the hoped-for end of the road, where the victims become freed from their eternal misery of mental anguish by virtue of the fact that they never experienced the psychological trauma in the first place. As we await this brave new world, let us pray for those less fortunate than some of us, who have been exposed to a close-up view of the lower circles of Hell.

CHAPTER SIX

A Brief History of the Classification of Stress-Induced Psychiatric Illness

And some cease feeling
Even themselves or for themselves.
Dullness best solves
The tease and doubt of shelling . . .
Happy are these who lose imagination:
They have enough to carry with ammunition . . .

—From "Insensibility,"
by Wilfred Owen

Early Psychiatric Concepts of Traumatic Stress

Psychological trauma has a wide range of effects on the individual. One of the most widely recognized effects relates to the development of psychiatric disorders. These disorders range from PTSD to depression, personality disorders, alcohol and substance abuse, and somatic disorders. Our current approach to looking at trauma-related illnesses is based on the *Diagnostic and Statistical Manual* in its current version (*DSM–IV*). The development of the *DSM* from its inception after World War II has led to a progressive "splitting" of psychiatric disorders into finer and finer categories, from the initial broad psychoanalytical categorization of "neurosis" versus "psychosis." This pattern of progressive splitting may have run against the realities of psychiatric nosology. Namely, psychiatric disorders may be closer to the "neurosis-psychosis" dichotomy of the analysts than the fine-tuned subcategorization of the current experts on psychiatric diagnosis. I would argue that the old "neurosis" of the psychoanalysts is the domain of the current breed of trauma-focused psychiatrists, viewed as being primarily an environmental disorder, whereas the old "psychosis" belongs to the schizophrenia specialists and may have more of a groundwork in genetic predisposition. According to this framework, neurosis encompasses depression, anxiety disorders (including panic disorder, generalized anxiety disorder, and PTSD), personality disorders (including borderline personality disorder), the somatic disorders, and to a certain extent alcohol and substance abuse disorders. The old neurosis concept would correspond to trauma-spectrum disorders that I have described in more detail earlier in this book.

In order to appreciate how we have gotten to our current state of diagnosis, it is helpful to understand the history of the development of psychiatric diagnoses. Our current psychiatric diagnoses are not absolute entities but instead are the products of a long process of modification based on changes in medical opinions.

The diagnosis of trauma-related disorders goes back to a time even before the psychoanalysts. During the American Civil War, DaCosta (1871) first described a syndrome involving symptoms of exhaustion and increased physiological responsivity ("Soldier's Heart" or "DaCosta's Syndrome") seen in soldiers exposed to the stress of war. DaCosta felt that this syndrome was a physical disorder involving the cardiovascular system that was caused by the extreme stress of war. DaCosta's approach was similar to theories of the time advanced by Kraepelin (1919), who also believed that schizophrenia had its basis in the constitution, leading to abnormalities in the brain and physiology.

Brain-based explanations of psychiatric disorders left the scene at the turn of the century with Sigmund Freud. Freud originally believed that his famous patient Anna O. was a victim of exposure to traumatic sexual experiences in childhood, and only later changed his views to the theory that fantasies, and not the reality, of childhood sexuality led to mental illness (Nemiah, 1998). His final formulation of psychodynamic theory did not incorporate environmental events such as traumatic stress in the development of mental disorders.

With the advent of World War I, the large number of psychiatric casualties of combat forced attention on the effects of the stress of war and led to the description of "combat fatigue" (Saigh & Bremner, 1999a). Psychiatrists described phenomena such as amnesia on the battlefield, where soldiers forgot their name or who they were. After the war, however, the effects of combat stress on the mind were soon forgotten. With World War II, interest in the mental health effects of the stress of war was revived. Again, psychiatrists described amnesia and other dissociative responses to trauma (Sargent & Slater, 1941; Torrie, 1944). Internment in German concentration camps was noted to result in symptoms among survivors including recurrent memories of the camps, feelings of detachment and estrangement from others, sleep disturbance and hyperarousal, as well as problems with memory and concentration (Thygesen et al., 1970).

The experience of World War II was still fresh in the minds of psychiatrists when the first edition of the *DSM* was formulated in 1952, which led to the addition of gross stress reaction. Gross stress reaction described a series of stress-related symptoms in response to an extreme stressor that would be traumatic for almost anyone. This may have stemmed from the experience of military psychiatrists in WWII, who observed during the war that many normal men were having mental breakdowns in the face of combat. However, gross stress reaction specified that the individual must have a normal prestressor personality, and that the symptoms should naturally resolve with time. This disorder did not take into account the fact that individuals with a preexisting psychiatric disorder may develop a new disorder that is specifically related to the stressor, or that acute responses to stress can translate into long-term pathology. Embodied in gross stress reaction was the ambivalence that has pervaded psychiatry until the current time about whether stress has merely transient effects, or whether it can lead to permanent psychopathology.

It was perhaps forgetting the horrors of WWII that resulted in gross stress reaction being dropped from the *DSM–II* in 1968. It wasn't until another major conflict, the Vietnam War, that mental disorders related to traumatic stress were once again recognized by psychiatrists. This time, however, there was a greater acknowledgment for the lasting effects of traumatic stress on the mind. Also, researchers such as Charles Figley (1978) argued that the stress of war in and of itself led to psychopathology, as opposed to factors such as "bad character" (preceding the war). This was the background leading to the inclusion of PTSD (with both acute and chronic types) as a disorder in the *DSM–III* in 1980. In the *DSM–III* criteria for PTSD there fortunately was a resistance by Nancy Andreasen (1985) and others to those who argued for the uniqueness of individual traumas or the experience of different cultures or ethnic groups in the face of trauma. For example, at the time some advocated for a "Vietnam syndrome" that would describe a constellation of symptoms unique to Vietnam veterans, whereas others have argued for "postrape syndrome" or specific childhood sexual abuse syndromes (ideas for which there is little empirical evidence). This resistance was indispensable to the scientific advancement of the study of traumatic stress. With *DSM–III*–based PTSD we finally had a diagnosis that recognized the lasting pathological effects of traumatic stress. Because of the specific way in which PTSD develops, it is unique amongst psychiatric disorders in requiring exposure to an extreme stressor.

The recent history of psychiatric diagnosis related to stress has been dominated by the development of the major stress-related diagnoses that require exposure to a major stressor for the diagnosis, including PTSD and acute stress disorder (ASD). Other disorders that have been linked to stress (but that do not require exposure to a traumatic stressor for the diagnosis) have been developed in successive editions of the DSM, including unipolar depression, somatization disorder, borderline personality disorder, adjustment disorder, alcohol and substance abuse, and the anxiety disorders (generalized anxiety disorder, panic disorder, and obsessive-compulsive disorder).

Acute stress disorder (ASD) was introduced as part of *DSM–IV* in 1994. This reversed the trend of *DSM–IIIR*, which did not include acute PTSD or any acute stress response diagnosis, and harkened back to the acute PTSD in *DSM–III*. ASD is of duration of less than one month, and (like PTSD) requires exposure to an acute threat to life with accompanying fear, helplessness, or horror. In addition, a diagnosis of ASD requires three of five dissociative symptoms (numbing, derealization, depersonalization, amnesia, or being "in a daze"); one or more of each of the PTSD reexperiencing, avoidance, and hyperarousal symptoms; and functional disturbance (as in *DSM–IV* PTSD). Studies have shown that ASD diagnosis predicts 83% of cases at one year (Brewin et al., 1999). Reexperiencing and hyperarousal (but not avoidance) were equally adept at predicting development of chronic PTSD. These findings indicate that perhaps there are two subtypes of acute trauma response—one primarily dissociative and the other intrusive/hyperarousal—that both can lead to chronic PTSD. The weak predictive value of avoidance raises questions about this symptom cluster. The current intrusion and avoidance clusters were originally based on the influential theory of alternating waves of intrusions and avoidance proposed in 1976 by Mardi Horowitz in *Stress Response Syndromes* (Horowitz, 1976). This theory has survived as dogma in the PTSD field for many years, although there has not been supportive empirical data. In a retrospective longitudinal study of the course of symptoms in PTSD patients, we found no evidence for the theory of alternating intrusions and avoidance, or for another popular but unsupported theory, that of delayed onset. Rather, symptoms increased soon after the trauma, then plateaued and remained largely unchanged over time (Bremner, Southwick, et al., 1996).

Trauma results in a broad array of symptom outcomes that are not limited to those contained within the symptom criteria for PTSD. These symptoms include PTSD, depressive, somatization, dissociative, anxiety, borderline personality disorder, and substance abuse symptoms. In a similar vein, van der Kolk, Herman, and others have argued for a "complex PTSD" diagnosis that includes PTSD symptoms as well as dissociative and personality disorder symptoms. Some authors have argued for the recognition of other stress-related disorders not encompassed in the spirit of PTSD; for example, traumatic grief (Prigerson et al., 1998). This disorder involves symptoms similar to PTSD, including those specific to grieving for the lost loved one that lasted for a longer period than normal grieving and with a more intense effect on social and work function.

There are a number of other traumas besides combat that can lead to long-term symptoms of PTSD. In fact, civilian traumas are probably 10 times more common as causes of PTSD than is combat stress. As mentioned above, 8% of the people in the United States have a history of PTSD, related to a wide range of traumas, including childhood abuse, rape, assault, car accidents, natural disasters, and other traumas (Kessler et al., 1995). The scope of the problem may be even greater in our inner cities. For instance, one study found that 9.2% of urban youths in Detroit's inner city suffer from PTSD (Breslau et al., 1991). One of the more troubling psychological traumas is childhood abuse, an invisible epidemic that is plaguing our society. For example, 16% of women are sexually abused before their 18th birthdays, and about half as many men, which means that about 50 million individuals in this country were severely abused in childhood. This doesn't count victims of severe physical or emotional abuse or neglect. Our research suggests, surprisingly, that emotional abuse and neglect may be as damaging as sexual abuse (Bremner,

Vermetten, & Mazure, 2000). As many as 15% of individuals who are abused may develop symptoms of PTSD. PTSD is twice as common in women as in men, partially related to higher rates of sexual abuse in women. These figures add up to the startling fact that about 30 million people in this country have a history of PTSD, making it one of the most common illnesses in our country that are associated with significant impairment in function.

Assessment of Traumatic Stress

An essential component of treating psychological trauma is appropriate diagnosis and assessment. It is important to screen for the possible presence of PTSD, dissociative disorders, alcohol or substance abuse, and other related disorders such as personality disorders and anxiety or somatic disorders. Patients who are actively abusing alcohol or substances (with the past two months) should undergo treatment of these disorders first. It is not uncommon for PTSD symptoms to be "unmasked" when patients go through detoxification, especially from opiates, which serve to dampen hyperarousal and other PTSD symptoms. A number of treatment programs have evolved in recent years to help patients with comorbid PTSD and substance abuse that specifically target exacerbations of substance abuse related to traumatic cues.

Accurate diagnosis of PTSD and dissociative disorders in the trauma survivor is critical. It is important to specifically ask about symptoms as listed in the *DSM–IV*. A large number of trauma survivors do not get appropriate diagnosis and treatment due to a lack of careful history taking. The possibility of acute stress disorder in a retraumatized patient should be considered. In patients with depression, it is useful to determine whether their symptoms of depression are secondary, or came in the aftermath, of PTSD. It is also helpful to understand whether depression is a stand-alone diagnosis or is comorbid with PTSD, because this can affect treatment response.

Appropriate assessment of trauma survivors includes a detailed assessment of trauma. A number of instruments have been created to assess the occurrence of childhood trauma. Some have focused on reports of specific traumas, such as parental physical or sexual abuse, and most have not undergone rigorous testing to establish whether or not they are reliable and valid. We developed the Early Trauma Inventory (ETI), a 56-item interview that assesses traumatic experiences before the age of 18 in four domains: physical abuse, emotional abuse, sexual abuse, and general traumas. The ETI takes about 45 minutes to administer and can be used for clinical and research purposes. Questions regarding physical abuse range from items that more commonly occur, such as "Were you ever spanked with a hand?" to less common events, such as "Were you ever locked in a closet?" Sexual abuse items range from questions such as "Were you exposed to someone flashing?" to "Were you ever forced to have anal sex against your will?" Emotional abuse items range from "Were you often shouted at?" to "Did your parents or caretakers fail to understand your needs?" The general trauma component assesses occurrence of events ranging from parental loss to natural disaster to criminal victimization. Items for which a positive response is obtained are followed up with questions regarding frequency, duration, and perpetrator. An index of severity of trauma exposure was developed based on assessment with the ETI, which we refer to as the ETI Childhood Trauma Severity Index. These indexes were shown to be reliable and valid measures of childhood trauma (Bremner, Vermetten, & Mazure, 2000). Bernstein and colleagues (1994) also developed a measure of childhood trauma that has been shown to be reliable and valid.

Several measures have been developed to measure PTSD and related symptoms in children and adults. The most standardized measure of PTSD symptoms in adults is the Clinician Administered PTSD Scale (CAPS). This instrument has been shown to be reliable and valid, and provides a measure of the severity of current PTSD symptoms. The CAPS can also be used to follow change in symptoms of PTSD over time; for example, after treatment (Blake et al., 1995). The Mississippi Scale provides a continuous measure of PTSD symptoms. This instrument has also been shown to be reliable and valid (Keane, Caddell, & Taylor, 1988). For measurement of general dissociative symptom level (a common outcome of trauma), the Dissociative Experiences Scale is a reliable and valid measure that has been widely applied, and provides a general measure of dissociative symptoms on a daily basis (Bernstein & Putnam, 1986), whereas the Clinician Administered Dissociative States Scale is a reliable and valid measure that measures dissociative states and change over time (Bremner, Krystal et al., 1998). A variety of measures have been developed for children; however, the Children's PTSD Inventory is the PTSD symptom measure that has been most comprehensively assessed in terms of psychometric properties (Saigh & Bremner, 1999b).

These measures provide assessments of psychiatric symptomatology. Although symptom evaluations can give some idea of the severity of symptoms and their change over time, they cannot be used to determine psychiatric diagnosis. Such determination can be performed with the Structured Clinical Interview for DSMIV (SCID). The SCID is a structured interview that provides psychiatric diagnosis based on the *DSM–IV*. Nevertheless, symptom measures like the CAPS provide supplementary information to the SCID, in that two different patients who meet criteria for PTSD based on the SCID may nevertheless have very different levels of PTSD symptomatology, which can be accurately assessed with a symptom measure like the CAPS.

As I've stated before, I became interested in PTSD based on my work as a trainee on a specialized inpatient unit for patients with combat-related PTSD. This program was established by the U.S. Congress to provide treatment and conduct research on the effects of the Vietnam War on veterans. However, in the course of working with these veterans, I realized that there are at least 10 times as many individuals in the United States who suffer from PTSD related to nonmilitary causes, such as childhood abuse, as there are military-related PTSD sufferers. I asked some of my more experienced psychiatric colleagues at Yale whether or not they felt that childhood abuse was an important topic for research study for a psychiatrist. They gave me their opinions that childhood abuse was not very common, and in any case was not an important topic for a psychiatric physician researcher to tackle. I next asked my father, a country psychiatrist with 30 years of clinical experience. His response was, "Of course it's important, and it's probably a critical factor in the development of psychiatric illness in at least a quarter of my patients." I then asked the other psychiatrists and social workers in the psychiatric clinic at the VA if they would be willing to screen their patients for a history of childhood abuse, in order to participate in my studies using brain imaging to examine the effects of abuse on the brain. They felt that they couldn't ask their patients about anything in their childhoods, because if their patients had been abused that subject would make them much more upset, and then the psychiatrists and social workers would have trouble dealing with them. I offered to screen everyone coming into the clinic for abuse myself, and to take on as my personal patients anyone who became extremely upset as a result of this screening.

Fascinatingly, the results of the screening procedure were the opposite of my colleagues' fears. The patients who did have abuse histories were extremely appreciative that at last their psychiatrists were finally figuring out how to properly assess them as patients. I and a nurse clinician who had herself been sexually abused as a child started a group for adult survivors of childhood abuse. One of the members of the group told his story of abuse to me for the first time in one of these 15-minute screenings. He grew up in Boston in a violent and chaotic home. In one episode, he was stabbed by his sister during a fight. He said his sister was "a whore" and the boys in the neighborhood would often come over to his house to take sexual advantage of her. In order to keep the boys away from her, he would instead offer himself as a substitute. In this way, he was sexually abused by the boys in the neighborhood starting when he was 12 years old. Another member of the group was the son of alcoholic parents who frequently fought when they were intoxicated. His father would come home late at night, and everyone would hide as he searched the house looking for anyone he could find to beat. He usually found the patient's mother, whom he would beat and then rape. Often, when his parents were intoxicated, they would have intercourse on the living room floor in the middle of the day, and the children of the neighborhood would come over to watch. When the patient finally reached an age where he was old enough he beat up his father, something he had waited his whole childhood for, and then he left home.

Tom was a group member who had been sexually abused by his father as a child. He told me:

> My father was known as a prominent member of the community. He was rich and had a lot of power in community. No one would believe me if I told them what he was really like. He used to come into my room and force me to perform oral sex on him. Even today, I dream every night about performing oral sex on my father, then I wake up sweating and so filled with fear that I cannot go to sleep at night. During the day I have the sensation, like daydreams, of having his penis in my mouth. It makes me sick, like I am choking, and I want to vomit. The only time I feel OK is when I am high or drunk. I go down to an island off the coast and bring a six-pack of beer and just sit there alone. I feel safe there because there is no one else around. I like to go to the beach. It gives me a feeling of being safe.

Roxanne was a 30-year-old woman who had been sexually abused by her schizophrenic father. Her days were filled with recurrent physical sensations, like hallucinations, of her father lying on top of her. She would hear his voice saying disgusting things to her. Sometimes when these visions came to her she would revert into a 4-year-old identity she called "Little Missy." Little Missy would silently sit in the group and suck her thumb. Sometimes she asked for crayons and would draw childish pictures on paper, or would ask for juice or milk.

The members of our little group found an incredible sense of solidarity with each other. For the first time in their lives, they had the feeling that they were not alone. For a year after the group ended, the members would continue to congregate at the hospital at the usual group meeting time.

The Mental Health Consequences of Traumatic Stress: Posttraumatic Stress Disorder, Depression, Somatization, Substance Abuse

One of the lessons I drew from this experience is the difficulty of accurate assessment of trauma: Victims of trauma do not spontaneously divulge their dark secrets. In order to learn about trauma, it is important to have a structured approach to the topic. Early on, I and other colleagues at the National Center for PTSD formed a work group to devise a questionnaire for the assessment of childhood trauma, called the Early Trauma Inventory (Bremner, Vermetten, & Mazure, 2000). We found that patients who were traumatized were more likely to report their trauma experiences in an anonymous questionnaire than to confess them in a more public forum. Later in my career, I moved to the Yale Psychiatric Institute to establish the Yale Trauma Research Program, a research and treatment program for women who had been abused as children. In the course of working with patients in our program, I learned more about the long-term effects of childhood abuse from patients such as Lucy.

Lucy came from an upper-class family in Rhode Island. Although on the surface everything seemed fine, her family life was like a nightmare. She told me:

My father was drunk and an abuser. He never used to talk to us. He didn't think my brother was a man, and he would never talk to him. My brother had colitis, and my father never accepted him because of that. My brother went into the hospital when he was 7 and I was 10. My father wouldn't go see him in the hospital. When he got out, I was so upset I was out of my body looking down on me and my brother. I touched his arm but he just stared at the ceiling. The priest told us that he was suicidal, but he was only 10 years old.

When I was a child, my mother grabbed me by the hair and swung me around the kitchen. I was like a mop. We never were allowed to talk during dinner. My parents controlled everything about my life. It was always very tense, like a knife. One time we were sitting at the dinner table and my mother started screaming. I couldn't figure out why. I later discovered when I went to college that people actually talk at the dinner table. I asked my friend, Why do you want to go home to your family for the holiday?" and she said, "Because it's fun." And I said, "Why?" She said, "because we talk about what we did that day, and tell jokes." I'd never heard about something like that. I knew I never wanted to go home, ever.

I left the house when I was 17 years old. I got pregnant, which was the sin of all sins. I knew she didn't approve of that, so she went one way, I went the other.

I met my husband and looked into his eyes and knew that I was in love. Sounds strange, later I realized that it was strange, but I didn't know that at the time. I fell in love with him when he was drunk, although I didn't know that at the time. He assaulted me and threw me around like a rag doll. He would go after me. I didn't understand that his throwing me around was abuse. I ended up marrying my father, who was drunk and an abuser.

When Lucy came to participate in our treatment program she was living a life of fear. She believed that she could never get away from her husband, that he dominated her life and had connections with everyone in the state of Rhode Island so that he would always get the best of her. She felt that if she went to an emergency room for help with her suicidal impulses, her husband would have the power to influence the doctors in a way that would harm her, so she sought out our treatment program in Connecticut as an alternative. However, she was so afraid to take the train to Connecticut, or even go out of her house, that she was unable to follow through with treatment.

Cynthia was another patient in our program. She grew up in a small town in Kentucky with her parents. She remembers her parents constantly fighting in her early childhood. She would go into her room to get away from their constant fighting. She would try and "blot everything out" in her room. She told me:

I learned as a child to separate myself from what was going on around me. I had like an autistic mind. I would do things automatically but I wouldn't be aware of what was going on. I need to be in my own world, when things enter that world it disrupts my thinking. I developed this like a technique for survival.

Lately my autistic technique has been breaking down. I keep going over and over things trying to figure out the bad things that happened to me in the past. I cant function, because I keep getting these thoughts that pop into my head, then I have to think about them and figure it out, then another bad memory pops into my head, and I spend my whole day like that, paralyzed.

My family was always very physical. My father would walk around half naked. They would say things sexually inappropriate. There would always be me and my father against my mother, or me and my mother against my father. My mother would say things to me like my father didn't sexually satisfy her. I didn't need to hear these things as a child.

When my family moved to Connecticut when I was a child I was left for the day with my uncle. My uncle wanted me to lie near him in bed. I remember my mother and her sister coming home and I was standing there in his pajama top with no bottom, and he was going to wash the sheets in the washing machine. I can't remember anything else except that he molested me, but I don't remember the details. I just went up to my mother and said "I don't ever want to see him again." My mother said I didn't have to but she kept asking me what had happened. I just screamed at her "I don't know." I didn't even want to think about it. I later found out that he had also molested my cousin. That's all I remember about that.

My mother was always so close to me that I couldn't tell her anything bad because she became so upset that it would make me more upset. I hated my mother for leaving me with my uncle like that.

Wendy was a young woman who had been molested by her father as well as an uncle and several cousins. Her mother died when she was 8 years old. She said that:

My father brought me home from the funeral and told me that I would have to take the place of my mother now. The same day that my mother died I had to deal with my father having sex with me at the age of 8 years old. I felt an incredible sense of betrayal. He said I was to sleep with him in his bed from now on. I got into bed with him and turned my back to him. I was very afraid and I wanted to cry, but I just lay there and my whole body become numb, like it didn't exist anymore. He was touching me and kissing me from behind. I felt him pushing his penis against my back. I cried and said, "No, Daddy, stop it, stop it" over and over, but he just kept saying, "it's OK, it's OK" over and over, and kept pushing himself against my back and trying to push himself inside of me. Finally I just gave up and separated myself from what was happening like I was a million miles away. In that way I could separate myself from the pain. Afterward he told me how I was his special girl and he loved me, but I just cried and cried. After that when he pushed himself into me I went to that faraway place. Now if anything touches my back I feel like I am back there at the time, feeling his heavy breathing, and having that intense fear.

Wendy continued to have recurrent thoughts of her father molesting her in his bed. Often during the day she would have the physical feeling of something pushing into her back. These bodily sensations would fill her with a sensation of intense fear; she would go into a daze and not be aware of what was going on around her. She stayed awake late into the night talking with others on an Internet chat group for abuse survivors. She felt cut off from the world and was unable to have caring feelings for others. She was unable to have intimate relationships with others because whenever she became sexual she was filled with intense feelings of fear and was unable to relax enough to perform intercourse.

Symptoms of PTSD are often very disabling and can last a lifetime. The symptoms of PTSD encompass a broad range of effects on memory, thinking, and behavior. First and foremost is the requirement for a psychological trauma, currently defined as a threat to one's life or that of others close to one, accompanied by intense fear, hopelessness, or terror. The diagnosis also requires one symptom in an intrusive memories category, including intrusive memories of the event, nightmares, feeling worse or increased physiological reactivity with reminders of the trauma, and flashbacks. Three symptoms are required from the avoidant category, including avoiding thinking of the event or reminders of the event, amnesia for the event, decreased interest in things, feeling cut off from others, feeling emotionally numb, or experiencing a sense of foreshortened future. Two symptoms are also required from a hyperarousal category, including increased startle, hypervigilance, irritability, decreased concentration, and decreased sleep. These symptoms must last a month and are associated with significant disturbance or distress in work, family, or social functioning.

One of the hallmarks of PTSD is an inability to recognize what is a true threat from what is a benign and nonthreatening event, which we describe as *pathological conditioned responding*. For instance, one of my patients, who had been raped and molested in childhood, views someone touching her as a threat, related to her experiences of being raped and molested. Someone accidentally brushing up against her, or putting an arm on her shoulder in a friendly gesture, is not necessarily a true threat; however, her fear alarm systems are now oversensitized and cannot discriminate between everyday events and what is truly dangerous. To use another example, a rape victim who was raped in a dark alley will continue to have fear reactions to dark alleys for many years after the original event, as well as fear reactions to similar settings, like dark elevators.

I myself was pickpocketed on Bourbon Street when I was at a scientific conference in New Orleans. The next day, when I walked down to Bourbon Street to meet a friend for dinner, I had a sense of fearfulness as I approached that den of iniquity. However, if I went back now I am sure I would have no fear reaction whatsoever. My fear response to the environment of Bourbon Street has been cancelled out over time, or to use a more technical term, there has been an *extinction of fear*. We know from studies in rats reviewed in prior chapters that the "extinguished" fear response is not removed from the brain but is merely suppressed and ready to come right back if a similar situation is encountered. We know this because reexposure to the stressful event results in the fear response coming right back as if it had never left. These responses are probably related to changes in higher cortical brain areas, like frontal cortex, that are responsible for canceling out fear memories in more primitive brain areas in the center of the brain, so that these fear responses remain just as strong throughout life as when the traumatic event first occurred. In my situation, not having continued fear responses to Bourbon Street is adaptive. As an academic who travels to four or five scientific conventions a year, I am doomed to return again and again to New Orleans (since it is one of the few cities with a convention center sizable enough for large meetings). There I will be condemned to repeatedly wander the streets of Bourbon Street in the evenings with my scientific colleagues, like Virgil in one of the upper levels of Dante's *Inferno*. However, it should also be pointed out that I did not develop PTSD as a result of my misadventure. If I were violently attacked on Bourbon Street it is possible that I would develop PTSD, and never be able to return to the place without intense feelings of fear. The critical point here (as reviewed in Chapter 3 and elsewhere in this book) is that a failure to cancel out, or extinguish, fearful responses to situations that remind one of the original trauma is highly characteristic of the PTSD response.

PTSD is also characterized by intrusive traumatic memories over which the individual has no control. I talked to a journalist shortly after the terrorist attack on the World Trade Center. The journalist had a friend who had run to the scene of the attack to try and help out. He saw an arm holding a cell phone sticking out of the rubble. He pulled on the arm to try and help the person out, but all that was there was an arm severed from the body, still holding a cell phone. For days after the event, this person continued to have images in his mind of the severed arm.

This type of experience is common to all types of trauma. I mentioned earlier the case of one of my patients with sexual abuse-related PTSD who had recurrent memories of being forced to give oral sex to his father. These memories came throughout the day, but they were triggered by situations that reminded him of the event, such as having something large in his mouth. I also had a patient who had been assaulted by a person who had been drinking Coca-Cola. During the attack, her hair had been grabbed from behind. Following the attack, she had recurrent intrusive memories of the assailant that were particularly triggered by the smell of Coca-Cola. Vivid memories of the attack were also triggered by something pulling on her hair. These memories were accompanied by increased physiological arousal and feelings of upset, also characteristic symptoms of PTSD. The key feature of these intrusive traumatic memories is that they are not stimulated by free association, but rather by specific objects or sensations in the environment that are physically similar to the original event. Therefore, a PTSD patient may encounter something in the environment at any time that will trigger extremely upsetting memories of the trauma. This drives patients to isolate themselves in a vain attempt to avoid anything that will remind them of the original trauma. A stroll though the streets of the city that for most of us would be a pleasant and relaxing experience becomes a voyage of terror beset with hidden dangers for the patient with PTSD. These patients strive in vain to push intrusive traumatic memories from their minds, and to avoid situations that will remind them of the trauma. Patients become increasingly isolated, not wanting to go out of their homes, answer their telephones, or have relationships with others that may introduce some new element of uncertainty and have the potential to trigger their traumatic memories.

A symptom that indicates a high level of PTSD problems is flashbacks, which are memories of traumatic events that come over the individual suddenly, without any warning, and are experienced like a movie that is playing in front of the person's eyes, as if the event were actually happening in the present. Flashbacks are experienced in a dissociative state, with the patient feeling that colors are very bright or diminished, there is a slowing of time, or things seem unreal. A good example of that is when Tom Cruise, in a scene from the movie *Born on the Fourth of July* (in which he plays Ron Kovic, a real-life traumatized and disabled Vietnam veteran), is sitting at a bar in Mexico and sees the scene of coming up over a dune in Vietnam as if it were a movie playing in front of his eyes.

Reminders of the traumatic event lead patients with PTSD to feel worse. In the aftermath of the terrorist attack on New York, people had to go back to their jobs in lower Manhattan. In addition to the sights of the destruction, there was a terrible smell associated with the tragedy that was described as a combination of smoke and burned rubber. This smell decreased with time, but one Friday afternoon shortly after the attack the wind kicked it back up, which led to feelings of panic, nausea, and terror in many people working in lower Manhattan. Many of these people left work early in a panicked attempt to get off of the island. Smells are detected by the olfactory cortex, located just above the nose, where they enter the brain directly through a perforated piece of bone called the *cribiform plate*. There they have a direct pathway to a part of the brain, called the *amygdala*, (described in detail in Chapters 3 and 4), that triggers the fear response. Smells, therefore, have a direct pathway to the primitive fear responses without conscious control. They represent a direct link to primitive emotional responses to threat. I was very interested to hear about the response to smells among workers and residents of New York, because we have found that smells of reminders such as diesel (reminder of helicopters in Vietnam) have a similar direct emotional effect in combat veterans with PTSD. As well, similar effects are seen from trauma-specific smells in PTSD patients having other types of trauma.

I have referred briefly to avoidance of thinking about the trauma, or things that would remind one of the trauma, as symptoms of PTSD. In the *Diagnostic and Statistical Manual* there is a grouping of symptoms referred to as "Avoidance" that are really a hodgepodge of symptoms of avoidance with symptoms of dissociation and cognitive disturbance. This grouping is reflective of the imperfections of our psychiatric diagnostic schema. Amnesia for reminders of the trauma is frequently seen in PTSD patients (Loewenstein, 1995). In the case of my patient, Cynthia, described earlier in this chapter, she had an isolated memory of her mother returning home and surprising her uncle in the act of washing sheets. It is pretty clear from the details that this patient had been sexually abused, but she had no consciously available memory of what had actually occurred. This type of amnesia for traumatic events is very common. I have another patient who has a feeling that her father sexually abused her. The details of the abuse, however, are not clear. With these patients, it is important to allow them to remember their traumatic experiences at their own pace, and not push them or coerce them into remembering such events before they are ready.

Even more extreme examples of amnesia for traumatic events can occur. For instance, one patient in our specialized inpatient unit for Vietnam veterans with PTSD had no memory of anything that had happened to him during the 12 months he was in Vietnam. However, he had all of the symptoms of PTSD that are described here. Amnesia for traumatic events is theoretically related to dissociative amnesia, which is a diagnostic category in the dissociative disorders, defined as gaps in memory that can last from minutes to hours or days and are not due to ordinary forgetfulness (dissociative amnesia is described in more detail below). I had another patient in our specialized inpatient unit for the treatment of PTSD in West Haven, Connecticut, one day, and the next day, found himself in combat fatigues in the woods in Ohio in the middle of the night, with no idea how he had gotten there. Another patient whom I treated as an outpatient was walking down the streets of Boston, and the next thing he knew he was in a motel in Texas. These patients obviously had major gaps in their normal day-to-day memory, which we feel are related to amnestic events in the aftermath of trauma.

Disturbances of cognition involving concentration and memory are also currently classified as part of the avoidance symptoms of PTSD. Problems with concentration have almost become a national malady in the aftermath of the terrorist attacks on the World Trade Center and the Pentagon. I've mentioned that I first became interested in disturbances in memory in my PTSD patients when I was Chief Resident on the specialized inpatient PTSD unit at the West Haven, Connecticut, Veterans Hospital, and I noticed that my patients had trouble with memory. My colleagues and I administered tests of memory, such as remembering a story or a list of words. We found that PTSD patients had specific problems with this type of memory, but no changes in intelligence or other types of memory (such as memory for pictures). We also saw similar findings in individuals who had PTSD related to severe physical or sexual abuse in childhood. This led us to the conclusion that stress may have resulted in damage to the hippocampus in PTSD patients, which could explain the memory problems we had observed. PTSD patients have problems remembering things, such as what to buy at the grocery store or what they had for breakfast that morning. I still distinctly remember one of my patients with combat-related PTSD who participated in one of our early studies of memory function in PTSD. He asked about the results of the study, and when I told him that we had found that patients with PTSD had problems with memory based on our measurements, his response was the opposite of what I had expected. Rather than feel discouraged by the results and the implications for his own condition, he felt a sense of relief, knowing that the problems he had been having with memory were related to his combat experiences and PTSD. I was able to help him by counseling him to not pursue additional education in accounting, but rather seek a career in something that did not require memorization of factual details.

The third group of PTSD symptoms is hyperarousal. These symptoms include hyperarousal, feeling on guard and hypervigilant, increased startle, and sleep disturbance. When we asked Vietnam veteran PTSD patients about their PTSD symptoms since the time of the war up until the present, they reported that symptoms of hyperarousal were the first to develop, followed later by intrusions and avoidance (Bremner, Southwick, Darnell, & Charney, 1996). This makes sense, since the hyperarousal responses have survival value, especially if the individual is in a situation of continued threat (e.g., a veteran who continues to be in a combat situation). These responses can increase the response to threat and facilitate survival. Obviously, the organism has a mechanism to decrease the threshold for responsiveness in these types of situations. Normally, when the threatening period has passed, these responses are "turned off." Pathology enters into the picture if responses cannot be turned off when the individual is no longer threatened; for example, when a soldier returns to peacetime. When reminders of the trauma continue to be present—as they do for those residents and workers in New York who have to pass the sights and smells of Ground Zero every day—it can be difficult to turn off the stress response. One factor that is known to turn acute stress responses into chronic PTSD is a history of prior stress exposure. For example, as indicated elsewhere in this book, we have found that a history of childhood abuse increased the risk for developing PTSD in soldiers who went to Vietnam (Bremner et al., 1993), and women who were sexually abused in childhood were more likely to develop PTSD if they were raped as adults. This phenomenon is known as *stress sensitization*, and can be modeled in animals. One way to think about it is that if an individual is exposed to stress repeatedly, then at some point the body may conclude that this state of threat is pretty much a permanent condition, and may turn the fight-or-flight response on permanently.

However, this state is not necessarily an adaptive one. As mentioned previously, PTSD patients can often lose the ability to discriminate between true threat and secure situations. It is as if their fear-alarm systems are on overdrive, so that their ability to discriminate a real signal from background is impaired. For example, rape victims often have excessive fear responding to all situations, including intimate relationships that may lead to normal and possibly satisfying sexual experiences. As well, they may be unable to discriminate benign from threatening situations due to pathological hyperarousal with any type of touching or intimacy. In a vain attempt to "force normality," they may take the plunge and force themselves to have intimate contact with men

DOES STRESS DAMAGE THE BRAIN?

even if they find it terrifying. However, the male predators of the world take advantage of traumatized women, who have difficulty regulating boundaries and judging social situations, and thus increase their vulnerability. This leads to situations in which they are repeatedly victimized, which increases their pathology and leads to a vicious cycle of vulnerability to revictimization.

Some authors have explained this behavior as novelty seeking or excessive risk taking that is related to an "addiction to trauma." However, I believe that there is a simpler answer: Changes in fear response systems in PTSD patients underlie the ability to correctly identify threat, as if excessive temperatures have broken a thermometer and it can no longer measure the true temperature. Studies based on identical twins with and without PTSD can identify the genetic and environmental contributions to both the development of PTSD and the risk that individuals will place themselves in a situation in which they are likely to be traumatized. I use the term "the walking disaster" to describe these individuals. There also may be families of "accidents waiting to happen," in which all family members are at increased risk for traumatization. This phenomenon may be related to either a genetically based vulnerability to trauma mediated through inherited characteristics, such as excessive risk taking. It may be secondary to acquired behaviors related to, for example, a chaotic family life that leads to subtle changes in behaviors that put the individual at risk. The relationship between home life and risk-taking behavior may be more overt as well, as in the example of the boy who joins the Navy at an early age in order to escape from an alcoholic and abusive father (out of the frying pan, into the fire).

The hyperarousal associated with PTSD is related at least in part to excessive activity of the noradrenergic system, which mediates the fight-or-flight response associated with stress, as described in Chapter 4. PTSD patients are often on guard, which is related to their perception of the world as an unsafe place. Many patients will insist on sitting with their back to the wall and always having the doorway visible to them. Female victims of rape or sexual abuse may feel extremely uncomfortable with men, especially authority figures, even male therapists or physicians who are there to help them. This is an unconscious response over which they have little control. I had one memorable patient with PTSD from the Vietnam War who set booby traps up around his house. He spent the night "on patrol" to keep unwanted intruders from coming onto his property. These types of responses can approach a psychotic level of thinking. The startle response is characterized by jumping or startling at loud noises or sudden events. The norepinephrine system and the amygdala, as described in Chapter 4, play important roles in the startle response.

The experience of the traumatized patient has created the impression that the world is not a safe place for them. We all live our lives assuming that someone will not suddenly jump out from behind a building and force us at gunpoint into a car, or that a bomb will not suddenly explode in the office building where we work. We go to work every day assuming that our babysitters will not sexually molest our children, or that our children's schoolbus will not drive over a cliff. We need to create these myths of invulnerability in order to be able to feel some sense of happiness and peace, and so that we don't become too distracted to be productive. However, anyone who has experienced any of these catastrophic events will never again have this false sense of security; they walk through life with the heavy knowledge that the world is not a safe place. The fact that no one else they encounter feels this way adds to their sense of isolation and makes them feel cut off from others. They have the feeling that only they understand the truly threatening nature of the world. It is a terrible burden to feel that they are responsible for protecting the family and keeping away the true threat that exists in the world. This can lead to feelings of hopelessness and, sometimes, suicide. Witness the mother of a young girl who was paralyzed by children who opened fire in Columbine High School. She became overwhelmed by depression in the aftermath of the shooting, walked into a gun store, asked to look at a handgun, and then shot herself on the spot.

Men and women have different responses to extreme stressors. I view this as being related to the different responses that men and women have to threats, which is determined by genetic factors. The most important factor in genetics is the ability to survive long enough to pass your genes on to the next generation for preservation of the gene pool. This can mean either maintaining your own preservation long enough to reproduce yourself, or successfully preserving your children so that they can live long enough to reach a reproductive stage. If you think back to the period that encompassed 99.9% of the history of *Homo sapiens*—when there were roving bands of hunter-gatherers—the responses to acute threat that were most effective for males were angry and violent displays of counterattack. Females did not have the strength to physically resist, and were reliant on the males for physical defense. If there was a threat to the group, nurturing behavior toward the children helped them survive the threat so that they could grow up and pass their genes on to the next generation. In that respect, nurturing behavior during times of threat is more likely to result in the passing on of female genes, whereas aggression and violence are more likely to result in the passing on of male genes. This explains why males exposed to stress are likely to respond with anger and aggression, whereas women respond with behaviors such as expression of emotion and talking with others. I was called by a journalist in the immediate aftermath of the terrorist attack on the World Trade Center who asked me about gender differences in the response to the attack. He said that a group of his friends walked by Ground Zero and the women were tearful while the men became angry and had thoughts of revenge. The women commented that the men were "militaristic" and argued with them about that. My response is that biologically it should not be expected that men and women would have a similar response, because of the considerations outlined above.

Psychological trauma, especially when it occurs early in life, can have lasting effects on one's sense of self. Our sense of self does not exist from the time of birth; rather, it is the result of an accumulation of a lifetime of experiences and relationships with others. For example, a particularly positive experience with a basketball coach will allow the individual to "take away" an aspect of that role model's personality, incorporate it into the sense of self, and strengthen his or her personality. A more fundamental interaction is between parent and child. Trauma perpetuated on the child by parents can have particularly devastating effects that last throughout life.

Depression is another psychiatric outcome commonly seen in individuals exposed to psychological trauma. Symptoms of depression include depressed mood most of the day, decreased interest or pleasure in things, irritability, decreased appetite, decreased concentration and energy, sleep disturbance, increased agitation, feeling worthless, and recurrent ideas of suicide. If these symptoms last two weeks or more and are associated with significant impairment, they meet criteria for major depressive disorder. It is obvious that there is a great deal of overlap between symptoms of depression and symptoms of PTSD. In fact, most clinicians specializing in trauma feel that depression seen in the aftermath of trauma is similar to PTSD and is different from the more typical type of depression that is not related to trauma.

The risk for other anxiety disorders in addition to PTSD is also greater following trauma. Panic attacks can be increased, characterized by episodes of panic anxiety in which people feel they are going to die or go crazy, accompanied by sweating, rapid heart rate, stomach in knots, feelings of choking, increased muscle tension, hyperventilation, chest pain, palpitations, and feeling unreal. Many panic patients have *agoraphobia*, or the fear of going into public places like the supermarket, driving over bridges, or just going out of the house.

Psychological trauma also increases the risk for personality disorders. In the *Diagnostic and Statistical Manual*, the personality disorders are not classified with the "major" psychiatric disorders, which are listed on "Axis I"; instead, they are listed separately on "Axis II." However, I believe that some personality disorders, such as borderline personality disorder, should be listed on Axis I. Borderline personality disorder (BPD) is defined as a pattern of instability in personal relationships, self-image and affect, and marked impulsivity, as shown by at least five of the following: efforts to avoid abandonment, unstable interpersonal relationships, identity disturbance, self-damaging, self-destructive behavior (e.g., reckless driving, substance abuse), suicidal behavior, mood swings, feelings of emptiness, inappropriate anger, and stress-related paranoia or dissociative symptoms. BPD captures the profound effects that trauma can have on the development of personality. In the majority of cases, BPD has been linked to exposure to early trauma, and many theorist have postulated that this disorder is related to a disruption in the connection between caregivers and the individual in early infancy, whether related to stressors like childhood abuse or neglect, or to other factors.

Trauma patients also have an increased use of alcohol and drugs. This is partially related to increases in hyperarousal and hypervigilance, as well as an attempt to overcome sleep disturbance and cancel out intrusive memories and pathological emotions. As is repeatedly shown in movies and books, whenever anyone has a sudden shock the preferred response is a quick shot of brandy, whiskey, or some other strong spirit. As so often happens, this popular wisdom has an element of truth. Studies in animals have shown that alcohol can prevent the long-term negative behavioral consequences of traumatic stress, as valium, opiates, and antidepressant medication. These effects are at least partially mediated through the noradrenergic (adrenaline) system. The medications act in the brainstem to decrease activity of this system. This has led to the hypothesis that some substances may be used by PTSD patients as an attempt to self-medicate their own symptoms of PTSD. Based on this knowledge, we hypothesized that substances such as alcohol, valium, and heroin would be felt to improve symptoms of PTSD, especially those symptoms in the hyperarousal category. We asked patients with PTSD about the effects of each of these substances on their symptoms of PTSD. As we had hypothesized, all three—alcohol, heroin, and Valium—made symptoms in the hyperarousal and intrusion categories better (Bremner, Southwick, et al., 1996). Other substances that tend to stimulate the noradrenergic system, such as cocaine, actually had a negative effect on PTSD symptoms. In addition, patterns of alcohol and substance abuse began soon after the trauma, and increased in parallel with symptoms of PTSD. These findings were consistent with theory that traumatized patients use alcohol and drugs to medicate their own symptoms of PTSD.

Trauma and Dissociation

One particularly troubling outcome of exposure to psychological trauma involves symptoms of dissociation (Kluft, 1984; Lewis & Putnam, 1996; Guroff, Silberman, Barban, & Post, 1986; Putnam, Spiegel, & Cardena, 1991; Ross, Joshie, & Currie, 1990; Spiegel, Hunt, & Dondershine, 1988). As defined in *DSM–IV*, dissociation is a breakdown in memory, identity, and consciousness. Dissociative symptoms in traumatized patients include *amnesia* (gaps in memory not due to ordinary forgetting), *depersonalization* (out-of-body experiences and other distortions of the sense of one's own body, such as feelings that your arms are like toothpicks or your body is very large), *derealization* (distortions in visual perception, such as seeing things as if they are in a tunnel, in black and white or in colors very bright, or distortions in time, like the feeling that time stands still or is moving very fast), and

DOES STRESS DAMAGE THE BRAIN?

identity disturbance (fragmentation of the sense of the self). These symptoms typically occur together, suggesting that they are all part of the same group of symptoms.

Dissociative symptoms are often linked with exposure to traumatic stressors. For instance, following a car accident, many individuals report looking down on the scene from above, feeling emotionally numb, or that time stood still.

Symptoms of dissociation have often been portrayed in the popular media. Many of Alfred Hitchcock's films have provided a very good depiction of dissociative amnesia and its relationship to psychological trauma. For instance, in *Spellbound*, for the early part of his life the main protagonist has amnesia related to a traumatic event that he experienced. This amnesia is overcome by returning to the scenes of his earlier life, with the assistance of an attractive female psychoanalyst (it *is* a movie).

The past decade has seen a rapid expansion of research in the field of dissociation (Bremner & Marmar, 1998). The development of instruments, including the Dissociative Experiences Scale (DES; Bernstein & Putnam, 1986), Structured Clinical Interview for DSMIIIR-Dissociative Disorders (SCID-D; Steinberg, Rounsaville, & Cicchetti, 1990), Dissociative Disorders Interview Schedule (DDIS; Ross et al., 1990), Peritraumatic Dissociation Questionnaire (Marmar et al., 1994), and Clinician Administered Dissociative States Scale (CADSS; Bremner et al., 1998), has facilitated research in this field.

There has been some controversy about whether dissociation is a normal psychological response or a pathological symptom seen only in trauma survivors (Kluft, 1984, 1990). Part of this controversy relates to overlap of dissociation with other constructs, like hypnotizability and absorption. Both hypnotizability and absorption (e.g., the capacity to become absorbed in a movie) are normal personality features that vary in the general population. Some of the questions asked on scales to measure dissociation include absorption-type questions, which may identify a normal personality trait instead of a pathological response. In my opinion, dissociative symptoms—such as repeatedly seeing things as if you were in a tunnel—are indicators of psychopathology and are primarily found in patients with pathological responses to trauma.

Following this line of thinking, there is evidence that dissociation at the time of trauma is a marker for long-term psychopathology. The French psychiatrist Pierre Janet, working in Paris at the end of the 19th century, was the first to describe symptoms of dissociation in the aftermath of psychological trauma (Nemiah, 1998). He hypothesized that individuals who had a dissociative response to trauma developed a type of "neurophysiological breakdown" that made them more vulnerable to have subsequent dissociative reactions to minor stressors, as well as to display long-term chronic psychiatric symptoms.

My colleagues and I tested this hypothesis by asking Vietnam veterans about dissociative symptoms at the time of combat trauma. We found that Vietnam veterans who dissociated at the time of combat trauma were more likely to later develop PTSD and continued to have dissociative responses to subsequent stressors (Bremner et al., 1992; Bremner & Brett, 1997). We found that Vietnam combat veterans with PTSD had increased dissociative symptom levels compared to combat veterans without PTSD (Bremner et al., 1992; Bremner, Steinberg, et al., 1993), and that individuals with dissociative responses to trauma are at increased risk for PTSD (Bremner et al., 1992) and continue to have dissociative responses to subsequent stressors (Bremner & Brett, 1997). These studies showed a close relationship between the diagnosis of PTSD and dissociative disorders. For example, 86% of a PTSD sample met criteria for a comorbid dissociative disorder (Bremner & Brett, 1997), whereas essentially 100% of patients with dissociative identity disorder (DID) met criteria for PTSD (R. Loewenstein, personal communication, 11/1/98). Marmar and colleagues (1994) found that dissociative responses to trauma predict long-term PTSD in emergency personnel, whereas more recent prospective studies have documented the association between dissociative states at the time of trauma and the development of chronic PTSD (Koopman, Classen, & Spiegel, 1994; Shalev, Peri, Canetti, & Schreiber, 1996). One recent study showed that dissociative symptoms in the first 24 hours after a trauma were not predictive, rather dissociative symptoms at about one week after trauma were (McFarlane, 2000). It may be that immediate dissociative responses are nonspecific responses to trauma, and that continued dissociation in a situation of chronic stress is the best predictor of pathology. The natural course of dissociation is outlined in Figure 6.1. Based on these findings and others, I have argued for inclusion of PTSD and dissociative disorders in a common "trauma spectrum disorders" cluster of psychiatric diagnoses (Bremner, 1999a; Ross, 2000).

In order to conduct studies of treatment and neurobiology of dissociation, we developed a scale for use as a repeated measure

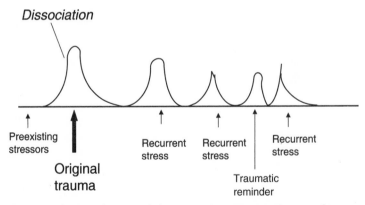

Figure 6.1 The natural course of dissocation. Dissociation at the time of trauma may be a marker for an increased risk of psychological problems in later life. Individuals who dissociate at the time of trauma have an increased propensity to dissociate following exposure to minor stressors later in their lives. Dissociation, described as part of the trauma-spectrum disorders, is hypothesized to be related to stress-induced deficits in hippocampal function.

of dissociative states (mentioned above), the Clinician Administered Dissociative States Scale (CADSS; Bremner et al., 1998). The CADSS is a 27-item scale with 19 subject-rated items and 8 items scored by an observer. The subjective component consists of 19 items that are administered by a clinician who begins each question with the phrase "at this time" and then reads the item to the subject (Table 6.1, pages 208–209). The subject then endorses one of a range of possible responses: 0 not at all, 1 slightly, 2 moderately, 3 considerably, 4 extremely. The subject's response on this 0 to 4 scale is recorded, and the clinician moves on to the next item. Some of the dissociative symptoms measured with the CADSS that were most commonly endorsed in traumatized patients included "Did things seem to be moving in slow motion?" "Did sounds change, so that they became very soft or very loud?" and "Did it seem as if you were looking at things as an observer or a spectator?" We found that these symptoms increased when PTSD patients were reexposed to reminders of their original trauma during a traumatic memories group I conducted at the inpatient PTSD program at the VA hospital.

Tests of reliability and validity of the CADSS were performed in both normal individuals and patients with psychiatric disorders. The CADSS was found to be a reliable and valid measure for the assessment of childhood trauma. PTSD patients with high dissociative disorder comorbidity were compared to other patient groups and control subjects. Scores on the CADSS were significantly different for patients with PTSD versus patients with schizophrenia, depression, normal individuals and Vietnam combat veterans without PTSD (Bremner et al., 1998) (Figure 6.2). A group of patients with PTSD were assessed before and after exposure to a traumatic memories group. They showed a significant increase in dissociative symptomatology in comparison to baseline, during exposure to a traumatic memories group.

In the course of conducting research on dissociation, I realized that many of my patients with PTSD dissociate when they are in

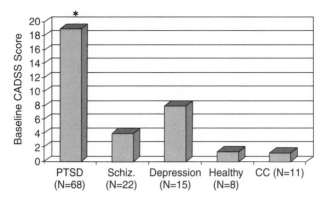

*p<.05; greater CADSS score in PTSD vs other groups

Figure 6.2 Dissociative symptom level as measured with a scale for the measurement of dissociative states (CADSS) in patients with PTSD, patients with other psychiatric disorders, and normal individuals. Patients with PTSD have higher dissociative symptom levels than other groups, consistent with the idea that PTSD and dissociative disorders are part of a common group of *trauma-spectrum disorders*.

a situation that reminds them of their original trauma. In most cases, this dissociation is not under conscious control, but instead happens automatically, which suggests to us that automatic fear-related brain circuits mediate these responses. One of my patients with PTSD from combat in Vietnam, whom I will call David, had recurrent dissociative responses that made it hard for him to function in day-to-day life. When he was in Vietnam, David drove a "track"—a mobile artillery unit that fired rounds at the enemy—during his frequent combat missions into enemy territory. He became good friends during his tour with a man named Bobby, and they would help each other out during times of need. One day, David's unit was on a patrol. Bobby was driving his track just in front of David, when the unit was suddenly ambushed by the Viet Cong. An artillery round hit Bobby's track, and Bobby started screaming for help. David jumped out of his track and ran to help Bobby. As David pulled him out of the track, Bobby emitted a chilling moan, and David realized that the

Table 6.1. Correlation of individual items with total score and frequency of endorsement of items on the CADSS in PTSD patients at baseline (N = 68)

Subjective Items	r	No. Endorsed (%)
(At this time, in this room)		
1. Do things seem to be moving in slow motion?	.55***	33 (48%)
2. Do things seem to be unreal to you, as if you are in a dream?	.70***	28 (41%)
3. Do you have some experience that separates you from what is happening? For instance, do you feel as if you are in a movie or a play, or as if you are a robot?	.61***	32 (47%)
4. Do you feel as if you are looking at things from outside of your body?	.77***	24 (35%)
5. Do you feel as if you are watching the situation as an observer or spectator?	.53***	36 (53%)
6. Do you feel disconnected from your own body?	.57***	24 (35%)
7. Does your sense of your own body feel changed? For instance, does your own body feel unusually large or unusually small?	.61***	20 (29%)
8. Do people seem motionless, dead, or mechanical?	.62***	23 (34%)
9. Do objects look different than you would expect?	.71***	15 (22%)
10. Do colors seem to be diminished in intensity?	.71***	23 (34%)
11. Do you see things as if you were in a tunnel, or looking through a wide angle photographic lense?	.81***	28 (41%)
12. Does this experience seem to take much longer than you would have expected?	.49***	29 (43%)
13. Do things seem to be happening very quickly, as if there is a lifetime in a moment?	.61***	21 (31%)
14. Do things happen that you later cannot account for?	.85***	22 (32%)
15. Do you space out, or in some other way lose track of what is going on?	.74***	37 (54%)
16. Do sounds almost disappear or become much stronger than you would have expected?	.71***	33 (48%)

Table 6.1. (*Continued*)

Subjective Items	r	No. Endorsed† (%)
17. Do things seem to be very real, as if there is a special sense of clarity?	.45***	34 (50%)
18. Does it seem as if you are looking at the world through a fog, so that people and objects appear far away or unclear?	.74***	25 (37%)
19. Do colors seem much brighter than you would have expected?	.61***	18 (26%)
Observer Items		
20. Did the subject seem eery or strange, or in some other way give you an uncomfortable feeling?	.52***	17 (25%)
21. Did the subject blank out or space out, or in some other way appear to have lost track of what was going on?	.59***	20 (29%)
22. Did the subject appear to be separated or detached from what was going on, as if not a part of the experience or not responding in a way that you would expect?	.54***	23 (34%)
23. Did the subject say something bizarre or out of context, or not speak when you would have expected it?	.25*	8 (12%)
24. Did the subject behave in a bizarre, unexpected manner, or show no movement at all, being stiff and wooden?	.35**	7 (10%)
25. Did the subject have to be put back on track, or grounded in the here and now, during or soon after the experience?	.38***	8 (12%)
26. Did the subject show any unusual twitching or grimacing in the facial musculature?	.09	2 (3%)
27. Did the subject show any unusual rolling of the eyes upward or fluttering of the eyelids?	.10	2 (3%)

*$p < 0.05$, **$p < 0.01$, ***$p < 0.00185$ (significant with adjustment for multiple comparisons); $df = 66$ for all items
†Number (%) of subjects who endorsed that item as being moderate in severity or greater

lower part of Bobby's body was missing. Suddenly, it seemed to David as if everything around him was slowing down. Sounds were disappearing, even though the battle continued, and David's perception of the world around him changed. Everything seemed foggy, as if it were far away, and it seemed as if he were looking through a tunnel, with the periphery of his vision gone.

The world seemed strange or foreign, and David couldn't recognize his friends or his surroundings. He felt like he had no idea who he was. After the battle, David sat immobile and was unresponsive to others. Some of his friends protected him by hiding him in a Vietnamese hootch (straw house) for two days. He sat on the floor, not knowing who he was or being able to recognize his surroundings, only looking at the glint coming off a knife that he held in his lap.

After his discharge from the army, David returned to his home town where he married, started working at the local factory, and later had a son. David continued to have discrete episodes, usually during times of stress, of suddenly being unable to recognize familiar surroundings or people close to him, such as his wife and son. David said that during these episodes he would look at his wife and be able to recognize her facial features, but be completely without the sensation of familiarity. During one episode, David was on a family vacation in Florida, and he, his wife, and son were walking through a crowded Disney World. He suddenly had the sensation that all of the people around him were strange or foreign. Looking at his family, it seemed as if he did not know who they were. Colors in the environment seemed blurred, and his surroundings seemed foreign or strange. He said that his wife had to lead him out of Disney World by the hand, and they could not spend any more time there during their vacation.

Another patient of mine with Vietnam combat-related PTSD, Bill, served in the army from 1963 to 1966. He was a jokester in high school who was everybody's friend. After graduation, a group of his friends went down to the army recruiter to get information about enlisting, and he went along. He enlisted to have the opportunity of being with his friends.

Soon after his enlistment, the United States became involved in the Vietnam War. Bill was sent over as a combat infantryman. One time Bill was killing the enemy wounded with a bayonet instead of a gun, to prevent the gunfire from revealing their position to enemy reinforcements. Bill described the experience in this way:

> As I was bayoneting the wounded, I had the sensation of separating from myself, and looking down from a distance at the "killer" who was bayoneting the enemy soldiers. I first had this feeling when I noticed some pleasure within myself at killing the enemy, which filled me with horror and disgust, and which seemed unconnected with my conception of myself and of what I felt I was capable of doing. From that time on, in combat situations I would separate from myself and watch while the "killer" would carry out combat missions. The killer was better able to do the job, as he was without concern for others or fear, unlike myself.

After his discharge from the army in 1966, Bill reported continued episodes of separating from his body in times of stress, usually when he became angry or felt physically threatened. These episodes occurred during situations such as barroom brawls, which recreated the experience of being in combat. Bill presented for treatment with the chief complaint of "blackouts" that were increasing in frequency and over which he felt he had no control. A seizure disorder had been ruled out with electroencephalogram and computed tomography of the head. After a careful history, it was discovered that these "blackouts" were actually episodes in which he would separate from his body and watch while the "killer" would do something harmful or destructive that would get him into trouble. During the most recent episode, Bill had become angry at someone during the course of an argument, and ran home to get a knife. While running back to the site of the dispute, Bill separated from his body and watched with consternation the activity of the "killer." Bill ran up to the other person and put the knife to his throat, while Bill tried to urge the "killer" not to do anything that would get him into trouble. Bill was eventually able to get control of himself (or the other side of himself) and the other person was not hurt.

Paul was born and raised in a small town in Connecticut. At the age of 18, he joined the Marines and was sent to Vietnam for active combat duty. He was a member of the 101st cavalry, General Custer's division.

In 1969, while on patrol in Vietnam, Paul's unit was ambushed and his best friends—Johny, Willy and Mack—were killed. Willy walked into a claymore mine which blew his legs off and blew his body into Paul, knocking him down. Then the Viet Cong opened fire. They shot Mack in the face. Paul saw it happen as if in slow motion. He saw his arm moving and the glitter of his watch. Then he saw Johny with a bullet in his head. He had a strange look, his eye blown out of the socket. Paul related the event in the following way:

> Johny was screaming. I held him in my arms, rocking him. He told me to tell his mother he was sorry, and that it hurt real bad.
>
> I felt like the experience was drawn out over a long period of time. I had moments of losing track of what was happening, and things happened during the event that I later couldn't account for. At first things became extremely bright, like under the floodlights at night in a baseball field, and then suddenly colors became very dull, as if I were looking at the world through a fog. It seemed like I was looking at things through a tunnel, or as if there were a pair of binoculars turned backwards. I could hear the moaning of my dying friends, but it sounded long and drawn out. Things seemed unreal, as if I were in a dream, or as if I were watching the situation as a spectator. I felt disconnected from my own body, like I could look back at myself and see my own reaction. My own body felt

much larger than normal, like a giant, and I thought that I would get hit by a bullet. I felt like I was in shock.

After describing the above account, Paul looked out the window of my office in West Haven and said, "It looks like a toy city. They broke me. I broke myself."

The first time Paul saw his dead buddies was in 1974. He used to think about them, and see them in his mind. He had built his house next to a mountain. It was dusk, and he was sitting on his porch. There was a field out behind the house. They were out there, on patrol, walking in full combat gear. He started calling them. His sister asked, "Who are you calling?" He said, "Call, you can get them back." He remembered her calling for them there on the porch, even though she couldn't see them.

Paul said, "I usually see them at Christmastime. They'd come in and see me and ask me how their families were doing. I'd say I didn't know. It would ruin my Christmas." Paul would sit at the bar in his basement and drink with his dead buddies. He walked into the house one day, and they were sitting there at the bar. They drank beer together. They told him to go back to Vietnam with them, that they'd be together again. They'd fight together again, but this time they'd win the war. They had the smell of the Mekong delta, a damp smell. They said if Paul didn't go they'd kill his wife and child. He didn't want to go, but they convinced him. Paul took a large amount of cocaine in an attempt to kill himself. He thought he'd be joining them. Then he woke up alone.

Paul was at his sister's house, walking through a field in the backyard. It looked like a landing zone. He had the sensation of walking through a bubble. He heard a fleet of helicopters. His daughter came, hugged him, and asked what was wrong, did he hear helicopters? He said, "Yeah, can't you hear them?" She replied, "Let them land, don't go with them." He went out and got in his car. Then he saw his dead buddies. Johny was sitting next to him. He was young and had freckles, he was only 18. Paul started driving. Willy and Mack were in the backseat. They didn't say anything. They were like zombies. They were wearing combat fatigues, and their faces were very white. Paul could see their freckles as if they were glowing. Paul said to himself, "It's not real, it's in my mind." They weren't talking, but he felt he could read their minds. He felt scared. They had been with him a long time, and he was becoming frightened of them. Then Johny grabbed the wheel and yanked it. The car drove off the road onto someone's lawn. Paul felt lightheaded and was having a hard time breathing. He drove home, parked the car, and ran up to see his wife. He said, "Get them out of my car." She went down and looked, and said that there was no one there.

These dissociative symptoms are similar to psychotic symptoms in many ways. Paying attention to some specific clinical characteristics can aid in differing dissociative from psychotic symptomatology. First of all, dissociative symptomatology is invariably related to a traumatic event, whereas psychotic symptomatology does not show such a specific connection with trauma. Second, auditory hallucinations are a recognized clinical feature of PTSD that many patients experience, and should not be considered to be indicative only of psychosis. Auditory hallucinations in PTSD are related to the traumatic event, and often consist of a dead buddy talking to the patient, voices crying out in pain, or other actual traumatic memories. Psychotic auditory hallucinations, on the other hand, commonly consist of an unrecognized foreign voice with specific types of content, such as making disparaging comments about the individual. Finally, visual hallucinations in PTSD are related to the traumatic memory and involve the perception of normal "intact" scenes, whereas psychotic visual hallucinations have bizarre content and often involve a breakdown of the scenario of the scene.

In the cases outlined above, specific dissociative responses that occurred during the original trauma were replicated in dissociative responses to later traumatic events. These dissociative responses retained the same form over time, as in the case of David, who experienced prominent derealization symptoms during his traumatic combat-related event, such as things slowing down, feeling as if he were in a fog, and not being able to recognize people around him, and later experienced similar symptoms during his trip to Disney World, which he described vividly as the sensation that people around him seemed strange or foreign. The conservation of specific dissociative responses suggests that memory processes may play a role in dissociative responses. Traumatic events are reexperienced as flashbacks and intrusive memories over which affected patients have no control and that appear to flood their consciousness at will.

Symptoms of dissociation also occur during exposure to natural disasters or sudden tragedies. I recently heard about a veteran who was in Lower Manhattan when terrorists flew a commercial airliner into the World Trade Center on September 11. He stood transfixed by the scene, literally frozen at the site and unable to move. He was still standing in the same site when the second plane flew into the second tower. At that point a policeman forced him to move from the site. He wandered in a daze for 24 hours and eventually ended up on Staten Island, not knowing how he had gotten there or what had happened in the meantime. This vignette illustrates that in individuals with a prior history of trauma, dissociative responses may be more pronounced than in individuals with no prior history of trauma.

A particularly troubling dissociative disorder that has received extensive media attention (e.g., the movies *The Three Faces of Eve* and *Sybil*) is dissociative identity disorder. This disorder was previously termed "multiple personality disorder" but the name was changed by the American Psychiatric Association in order to emphasize the identity fragmentation that occurs with the disorder. The name change is also in response to extensive media attention, which has focused on the "either/or" aspect of whether an individual has one personality or more than one. In my clinical work, I have not found this type of dichotomous thinking to be helpful in traumatized patients with identity disturbances. Typically, patients describe identity fragments to which they may have attached a name label, and which may have different levels of development but are not completely formed into distinct personalities in the same way that we would think of normal personality. Some of the identity fragments may be associated with painful memories (e.g., a 6-year-old fragment who was sexually abused, is very angry, and carries the feelings of fear and shame), whereas others are protected from these painful memories (a 10-year-old "good girl" who is happy and polite). However, these identity fragments are all part of the same person, and ultimately it is not possible to have "multiple personalities"; rather, it is the perception of traumatized patients that they have distinct identity fragments within themselves. These identity fragments may play a role in avoiding painful memories of trauma that can incapacitate the individual in his or her daily life. However, ultimately patients need to come to terms with their painful memories and realize that all of the identity fragments are part of just one person.

In order to understand dissociative identity disorder, it is important to have an understanding of normal personality development. Almost all cases of dissociative identity disorder are related to early childhood abuse (Putnam et al., 1986). Childhood abuse can have lasting effects on the sense of self. Our sense of self does not exist from the time of birth; rather, it is the result of an accumulation of a lifetime's experiences and positive relationships with others. For example, a particularly positive experience with a math teacher will allow the individual to "take away" an aspect of that role model's personality, incorporate it into the sense of self, and lead to a strengthening of the personality. A more fundamental example of this phenomenon is the interaction between infant and mother. This is what Winnicott (1988) and others who wrote about object relations theory called the phenomenon of the "good enough mother." In abusive families, the mother may not only be not "good enough," but may actually be a source of threat. This has an important impact on the child's development of the sense of self, leading to a fragmentation of identity and a walling-off of aspects of memory and the self. Childhood abuse can also be associated with lasting feelings of shame (related to a common process of self-blame) and rage against the perpetrator and others in the family who did not provide protection. A sense of powerlessness in the face of the aggressor can put abuse victims at risk for becoming perpetrators themselves when they become adults, in an attempt to have the feeling of power over another that they could not have as children.

Toward a Development of a Trauma-Spectrum Group of Psychiatric Disorders

The current diagnostic schema do not appropriately address the experiences of clinicians who take care of patients with stress-related psychiatric disorders on a daily basis (Ross, 2000). In my opinion, this is an artifact of the continuing drive to create categories and classifications of psychiatric diagnoses that contain discrete disorders that are unrelated to one another and not based on any particular theoretical foundation or view of etiology. This is largely a byproduct of the domination of psychiatric diagnosis by the field of psychoanalysis for the better part of the 20th century and the subsequent reaction to this domination. For psychoanalysis, theories of etiology were central to diagnosis; for example, anxiety neurosis was related to repressed conflicts that were made manifest only in symptoms where the relationship to the disorder was not immediately obvious. The development of the *Diagnostic and Statistical Manual* represented a gradual removal of psychiatric diagnosis from the psychoanalysts under the mantel of "science" and "objective diagnosis." A major objective of the move to make psychiatric diagnosis empirical was to remove any etiological underpinning for these diagnoses. However, what is not appreciated is that there often was little or no empirical basis for these new psychiatric diagnoses, which were often determined by a committee of "experts." The new diagnoses were also felt to represent separate and distinct entities that, by definition, would have unique biological, psychological, and social etiologies. This sent many young researchers running to show unique biological "fingerprints" for the disorders, and when they were unable to show specificity they felt compelled to explain the "failure" of their research investigations. However, often it was not understood that there was no empirical basis for these disorders as separate diagnoses, for the reasons outlined earlier. Also, many academic psychiatrists had particular biases toward the development of specific diagnoses, or used the development of new diagnoses to fuel a productive academic career of publication in academic journals that led to increased attention, notoriety, and promotion within their academic institutions. In addition, there was an unstated hostility toward psychoanalysis that led the generations of younger psychiatrists to seek to expunge any remnant of the hated profession from their schemas, much as the Catholics of Rome sought to exterminate any memory of the hated "heretic" Albigensians in the Middle Ages.

The billions of dollars to be gained by the pharmaceutical industry also played an important part in solidifying the Brave New World of psychiatric diagnosis. When drug companies could argue for a single drug for a single psychiatric diagnosis, they could expand their markets and profitability. The last decade has seen an intense effort by the pharmaceutical industry to "train" psychiatrists to identify a single disorder and target a specific medication to that disorder. Needless to say, this energy did not necessarily lead to a productive diagnostic schema that could stand the test of time, adequately represent the phenomena that were encountered in clinical practice, and form a solid basis for hypothesis testing in science. This has led us to our sorry state

DOES STRESS DAMAGE THE BRAIN?

of current affairs, where clinicians and researchers alike essentially ignore the current diagnostic schema, although sometimes with a modicum of guilt for not "following the line" of their profession.

Based on the close relationship among dissociation, PTSD and trauma, I have argued for a reorganization of the current diagnostic criteria for the anxiety disorders (which currently includes PTSD) and dissociative disorders (Bremner, 1999a). Currently in the diagnostic criteria of the American Psychiatric Association, there is the diagnosis acute stress disorder (ASD), which describes dissociative and PTSD symptoms in the first month after psychological trauma. Recent research indicates that ASD and PTSD are closely related disorders. Their criteria should therefore be made to be consistent with one another. Considering the important role of dissociation in the acute stress response, and the relationship between ASD as currently configured and PTSD, inclusion of dissociative symptoms in the diagnosis of PTSD should be considered. In addition, based on the propensity of PTSD patients to have dissociative responses to subsequent traumas and even minor stressors (i.e., amnesia, depersonalization, and derealization), it makes sense to create a similar dissociative cluster for chronic PTSD. This cluster would also include symptoms such as emotional numbing. With incorporation of amnesia, depersonalization, and derealization into chronic PTSD, these could be dropped as separate diagnoses in the dissociative disorders that are theoretically unconnected to trauma. Dissociative identity disorder, a more extreme response to stress, could be maintained as a separate disorder.

A major theme of this book is the concept of psychiatric disorders with a common basis in exposure to trauma. To allow the clinical realities to fit with our diagnostic schema, I have proposed the development of a new category of trauma-spectrum disorders (Bremner, 1999a). This would include both acute PTSD (the current ASD) and chronic PTSD (using revised criteria to be in line with ASD), dissociative identity disorder, conversion disorder, and adjustment disorders. A diagnosis to capture pathological responses to bereavement (traumatic grief) has been proposed as a separate diagnosis (Prigerson et al., 1998). If traumatic grief is introduced as a diagnosis in subsequent editions of DSM, it should be included in the trauma-spectrum disorders. PTSD and ASD would be dropped from the anxiety disorders—several of which (e.g., obsessive compulsive disorder) they have little relationship with— and dissociative disorders would be dropped as a category (with the non-DID diagnoses absorbed by PTSD). Other disorders that are highly correlated with an exposure to psychological trauma, such as borderline personality disorder and possibly somatization disorder, may appropriately be included in the trauma-spectrum disorders. We should also consider the relationship between trauma and depression. It is clear that there are some types of depression linked with exposure to trauma that would be appropriately grouped with trauma disorders. However, there are also some patients with a strong family history of depression who may not have a history of psychological trauma but nevertheless develop recurrent episodes of depression. These "familial type" depression patients may be different than patients with stress-related depression, and would not appropriately be included in a group of trauma-spectrum disorders.

Up until now, we have focused on the effects of psychological trauma on the development of psychiatric disorders that are generally recognized by psychiatrists. However, psychological trauma can have effects on our sense of meaning, identity, and place in the community that don't easily fit into our psychiatric pigeonholes. These effects are described at greater length in the next chapter.

CHAPTER SEVEN

**PTSD and Other
Stress-Related
Psychiatric Disorders
as Diseases of the
Brain Caused
by Stress**

*A problem was clearing the land [in the Washington Territory in the region
of present-day Lynden, Washington] of the massive, centuries old Douglas fir
and cedar to create farmland and pasture. Once the trees were cut down the
trunks and stumps still got in the way of plowing. This problem was circum-
vented by rolling the trees to lower ground and burning the stumps, a project
for which the whole family was enlisted. One day, while clearing the land,
Winifred's clothes caught on fire and she was severely burned. A daughter of
Enoch Hawley described a visit to the Bremner homestead after her accident:
"Winifred was suffering dreadfully with her burns and required two women to
care for her. Her most severe burns were on her back and they would keep trying to change her position so she would be more comfortable. Women in the
vicinity had been taking turns helping Mrs. Bremner. Mother wanted to help
but it was impossible for her to remain so long away from the store. She suggested that Winifred be taken to our house, and a bed was made on a
stretcher. Four men carried her the entire distance over wet, muddy roads.
Winifred remained with us many months before she was able to walk again."
It took many months for Winifred to recover. She must have developed com-
passion for burn victims during her ordeal, for she later adopted an orphan
(Bill Norton) who had been burned in a fire where he lost his mother.*

—From *A History of the Bremner Family*,
by J. Douglas Bremner

PTSD as a Neurological Disorder

This book has described psychiatric symptoms related to stress—including symptoms of PTSD, dissociation, anxiety, and depression—and has outlined a hypothesis for how these symptoms are related to neurological disturbances brought on by exposure to stress. As reviewed in detail in previous chapters, stress has effects on brain areas that play a critical role in learning and memory, including the hippocampus and prefrontal cortex. Other brain areas that are connected with these regions, including the amygdala and cingulate, are hypothesized to play a role in stress-related psychiatric symptoms. Stress also results in long-term dysregulation of stress hormones like cortisol and norepinephrine, that in turn modulate the laying down and recall of memory traces at the level of the hippocampus and other brain structures. We have developed a model in the previous chapters for how stress results in long-term changes in these brain structures and systems that lead to symptoms of stress-related psychiatric disorders, including PTSD and dissociative disorders.

The picture that emerges from this book following a review of all of the case histories and scientific studies is that stress results in long-term problems with learning and memory that have a neurological basis. Stress patients start to look like patients with organic memory problems or early dementia. In fact, PTSD has been described as a disorder in which there is accelerated aging, which may include both an acceleration of the memory deficits that are seen in a subgroup of the elderly, as well as increased risk for atherosclerotic diseases like stroke or heart disease, and metabolic diseases like diabetes (which are reviewed in more detail in the last chapter of this book). One of my patients who had been sexually abused and had PTSD reported that she had chronic problems with memory that interfered with her ability to function on a day-to-day basis. She said: "Lately I feel like my mind is degenerating, like I have Alzheimer's, or some horrible dementing illness. I can't remember anything or think about anything normally, I forget things easily, so I can't use my automatic thinking mode for survival. I have gaps in memory [dissociative amnesia], I walk into a room and I see something I've never seen before, like a cup or a towel. I say to myself, 'I've never seen that before, where did that come from?' I feel like I am falling apart." This patient shows how PTSD is associated with broad-based problems in learning and memory. We have hypothesized that these problems are due to the negative effects of stress on the hippocampus, a brain area that plays a critical role in learning and memory.

Hippocampal dysfunction may also play a role in dissociative symptoms related to trauma. The hippocampus has an important role in integrating or binding together different aspects of a memory at the time of recollection (Squire & Zola-Morgan, 1991). It is felt to be responsible for locating the memory of an event in time, place, and context. *Dissociation* is defined as a breakdown in normal memory, consciousness, or identity. Hippocampal damage may be responsible for this breakdown, as reviewed in Chapter 4. In addition, as noted earlier, dissociation at the time of trauma is associated with long-term psychopathology. This dissociation may represent not a risk factor for later pathology, but instead the initial onset of a PTSD-dissociative spectrum disorder. Dissociation at the time of trauma may represent the subjective sensation of hippocampal damage at the time of stress, given the critical role the hippocampus plays in the integration of both memory encoding and retrieval. According to this model, fragmentation of memory and dissociation would not be expected to occur in all individuals who were exposed to traumatic stress, but only in those who developed psychopathology (PTSD) with associated hippocampal atrophy and dysfunction. Finally, our group and Stein and colleagues found a relationship between hippocampal atrophy measured with MRI and increased dissociative symptoms in PTSD. These studies suggest that hippocampal damage related to stress may be linked to an increase in dissociative symptoms.

Stress-related symptoms that have an underlying neurological basis can lead to severely debilitating disabilities. During my early research and clinical experience with combat veterans, I was struck by the degree to which combat veterans with PTSD had major difficulties with even minor aspects of daily living. These veterans could not remember where they had to go during the day, were unable to keep appointments, and had significant impairments in relating to others. Unfortunately, the Veterans Administration at that time was focused on rehabilitation models that involved sending disabled veterans back to school for retraining. The retraining of combat veterans with PTSD typically involved schooling to learn a skill such as accounting, which was completely incompatible with their limitations in new learning and memory. Many of my patients were relieved to learn that their difficulties in school may have been related to a stress-induced neurological deficit. I believe, based on the research studies outlined in prior chapters, that stress-induced hippocampal deficits make it difficult for PTSD patients to engage in tasks that require new learning and memory. In any case, these patients' lives were much more fulfilled when I redirected them from careers such as accounting to jobs that did not rely to the same degree on new learning and memory.

Another difficulty that trauma patients have is trouble relating to others and fitting into society, which I believe is related at least in part to problems with the frontal cortex. As discussed in prior chapters of this book, the medial prefrontal cortex has been shown to play a critical role in emotion. This includes both emotional responses in a social situation and relating to others, as well as the modulation of fear-related emotions that may be recalled during a life-threatening event, and which are felt to be mediated by a part of the brain called the *amygdala*. This brings to mind the case of Phineas Gage, who had a railroad spike driven through those parts of his frontal cortex. Although he was able to reason and converse normally, he was completely disabled, in that he was unable to work or have social relationships because he was unable to read the social cues of others and respond in an appropriate way. In a similar way, PTSD patients are unable to respond normally to others and to read social cues. This results in a situation in which they feel misunderstood and cut off from others, and society is unable to integrate them in the larger whole. Because of this, we have thousands of veterans who live in the woods and won't come out for treatment or to see their families, or women who were abused in childhood who seek the anonymity of prostitution or marginal careers such as exotic dancing, where they won't need to have any real intimate contact with others.

Psychological trauma has lasting effects on the individual that are not easily captured in our psychiatric diagnostic categories. These include the effects of trauma on the individual's perception of society, the world, and the meaning of their relationship with the world and with others. The psychiatric disorder PTSD is perhaps unique in representing an interplay between psychiatric and neurological disease, and a profound alteration in the individual's existential view of the world and their place in it. For trauma survivors' their relationships with the dead are often as important or perhaps more so than their relationships with the living.

The Central Role of Memory in PTSD and the Trauma Response

Central to the effects of trauma on the individual are the effects on memory and the resultant collection of memories that unfold over the life of the trauma survivor. These memories include both traumatic and nontraumatic memories, and collectively make up trauma survivors' view of who they are as people. Thus, the trauma victim may feel that he or she is defined as an individual who has experienced severe psychological trauma. Ironically, treatment of psychological trauma would involve removing traumatic memories that cause symptoms, or alternatively diminishing their forcefulness. Removing traumatic memories, however, may eliminate an individual's sense of who he or she is as a person. Treatment must take this fact into account, and help the individual build a sense of who he or she is are as a person apart from the psychological trauma.

Removing traumatic memories is fraught with meaning for the survivor of psychological trauma. Engraved over the doorway of the Holocaust Museum in New York City are the words "Never Forget." In these two words are both the pride and the curse of not only the Jewish people, but in fact all groups of peoples who have been subjected to the terrible injustice of genocide and victimization. We all have a compelling need to feel that the world makes sense and that there is a purpose behind what happens to us. Survivors of torture or concentration camps believe that they need to bear witness, to always remember what happened to them so that they can tell others in order to prevent it from happening again. They feel a moral responsibility to "set the record straight," to give the correct version of history, so that their perpetrators don't write the history books and cancel out the atrocities that they committed. Victims also feel a need to act on behalf of those who did not survive. In cases in which almost everyone in a camp was killed, this pressure can be overwhelming. In some instances, there were last-minute promises—for instance, to take care of the children of another internee—that were impossible to keep, or other unfulfilled obligations that the individual could not maintain for one reason or another.

Trauma victims frequently suffer from "survival guilt," the feeling that the individual should not have survived when so many others died. The bare fact that the person survived when so many others perished adds to the feeling that the world is meaningless and nothing makes sense. Victims believe that they do not deserve to "leave all of this behind them" and "get on with their life" when only a fluke of chance has led to the fact that they survived and so few—perhaps no one else—did. They may feel that they have more in common with the dead victims from their past than the people in their current life, who are less understanding of how they feel, and might be completely alien to the victim. Primo Levi, an Italian writer who survived the Nazi concentration camps, poignantly wrote about these feelings in the aftermath of the war in Italy. His sense of alienation and despair deepened over the years, in spite of the fact that he became a celebrated writer. He eventually committed suicide. Many trauma survivors feel that they can only relate to other individuals who survived similar psychological traumas. After the Holocaust, many survivors immigrated to the United States, where they found themselves in a completely alien culture, in which the majority of the people differed in ethnicity, race, and language. Many Holocaust survivors gravitated toward other individuals who had had experiences similar to their own.

Trauma survivors may feel that to forget the traumatic memories of the past involves a betrayal of those who died. They may think that to forget about those who died is being disloyal to those who gave the ultimate sacrifice. Forgetting about those who died also involves losing those to whom the victim feels closest, especially if secondary to PTSD the victim is unable to feel close to anyone else (meaning someone still living). However, by keeping these memories, by standing by the credo "Never Forget," trauma survivors sentence themselves to a lifetime of traumatic memories over which they may never have control.

Memory is a funny thing. As mentioned above, over the door of the Holocaust Museum in New York is a sign that says "Never Forget." The survivors of the most terrible calamity of the 20th century pledged themselves to be living memorials to the horror and sacrifice of those who did not share their good fortune, to survive. These survivors will go on and fill in the forms of a semblance of a normal life, like rainwater will eventually fill in the craters left by the explosion of a volcano. The survivors will never forget, and shine into the future like a beacon against violence and corruption, fascism, and evil. And yet here lies both their pride and their curse: By never forgetting, they will keep alive the memory of those who have died. Their memories will compensate for the fact that those who sacrificed were ambiguous, because doesn't sacrifice imply that something was gained? By preserving the memory of the dead they are fighting against the nagging reality that many died for no reason, that it did not fit into any grand scheme, and there was no meaning to their deaths. The survivors keep the memory, and keep the dead alive. But the memories keep them sick.

I've always felt that this is "the rub" for individuals who have experienced extremely stressful events in their lives. There is a moral imperative to preserve the memory of those who are lost; especially if one feels that there is a lack of justice in the events surrounding their loss. Victims of the Holocaust feel that they must continue to remember their stories and tell others, to honor the memory of the dead, and to ensure that similar things will not happen again. If they forget, then those who died in the gas chambers will have died in vain, and evil will have triumphed. However, by preserving the memory of the dead, those who survived preserve troubling memories and feelings of anger that interfere with their ability to live in the world as they find it now. Giving up memories and images of the dead also means giving them up as people to whom they are close.

My own mother died, suddenly, when I was 4 years old. She had developed nausea and confusion, and had been taken to the local hospital where she was diagnosed with spinal meningitis. They raced her to a larger hospital in Seattle, but she died on the way there. She was only 30 years old. I cried that day when my father told me the news. Later in the week, I wandered into a room in our house where my brother and sisters and our father

DOES STRESS DAMAGE THE BRAIN?

were crying together. I must have been happily playing, because I remember that my siblings were very angry with me for not showing any grief. I couldn't understand, because I had already cried and was done with that. In my childish understanding, I really didn't understand that her absence was permanent. I had cried because she was gone at that time, but I thought she was just somewhere else and would come back eventually.

My memories for that time are strange. I have an intensely vivid recollection of sitting in our gravel driveway in our house on Puget Sound and watching the wind blow through the red-barked madrona trees. I also remember sitting in the garden and feeling a sense of mastery because I had realized that if I sat completely still, I would not be stung by a bee that was buzzing around me (for which I held the characteristic horror of a young child). I've always felt certain that the first two memories are connected with the "stressor" of my mother's death, because they both had a strange and emotional quality to them. Other memories of that time are especially strong, much stronger than memories for the years immediately following that time. For instance, I have a strong memory of driving north up Interstate 5 from Olympia to Lynden with my grandparents, and seeing the airplanes taking off from the Seattle-Tacoma Airport.

"Your father and your new mother are on one of those planes, on their way to their honeymoon in Hawaii," said my grandmother. I peered out the window, and thought that they were in the plane I saw taking off.

Throughout the early part of my childhood, I continued to hold to my mother's memory through a visual image. In sleep, I would see her in a recurrent dream I had at that time. I would be traveling through a forest where every leaf on every tree, and every branch, was something that I knew intimately well, for which I had personal knowledge. Sometimes I would be flying over the tops of the trees in the forest. There were houses in the forest, and I would explore them. I walked up onto the porch of one of the houses and opened the door. My mother was standing there before me, silent. This dream gave me the feeling that I dreamed it repetitively, every night, although I don't know if I really did dream it that often, or if this was just the feeling I got from the dream. At the time, I had the sensation of directly communicating with someone from beyond the thin veil of the living. I was in direct communication with the dead, with the afterworld.

The struggle to find meaning in the face of psychological trauma is at the core of our western civilization. One of the most poignant stories in the Bible is that of Job. Job was considered to be one of the most blessed and favored children of God, and was prosperous in family and the fruits of the field. In appreciation of these gifts, Job gave daily prayer of thanks to God. However, Satan told God that Job was appreciative to Him only as long as things were going well for him. A better test of his faith would be to see if Job still worshipped God if things were not going his way. Therefore, God was persuaded to test Job's faith by sending a series of plagues and pestilences that destroyed his crops, killed his family, and covered him with hideous sores. Even then, Job continued to give praise to God, a confirmation of his faith. However, in this story is a central dilemma: Why would God visit calamity on Job for no apparent reason, other than to play with him and test his faith? Does this rationale justify what he did to Job? Not really. The whole story has a hollow tone. It is established religion's vain attempt to provide meaning for something that may not actually have any meaning. This is a struggle that trauma survivors face every day. To the degree that they can assign meaning to their experiences, they have the possibility of regaining a foothold in a productive and satisfying life. However, for many survivors, the attempt to find meaning (as in the story of Job) does not ring true.

The quest to find meaning, however, seems to be a part of the human experience that is not easily quenchable and can sometimes take people to extraordinary lengths. I was recently at a scientific congress of researchers in the field of traumatic stress. I and the speakers at the congress were invited to a special lunch during the midday break. Our conversation turned to strange events such as alien abductions and the supernatural. One of my colleagues related his experience as someone who had been called to Oklahoma City in the aftermath of the bombing of the Murrah Federal Building. He related how there was a common belief that an angel had been spotted in photographs of the bombed-out building, someone who was facilitating the transfer of the spirits of the dead to the otherworld. He described it as a possible example of a psychotic reaction that was shared by the community. To me, however, it did not seem so strange. I am a fan of the television program "Unsolved Mysteries" (or I was, at least, before it was taken off the air). Beneath the veneer of supernatural and strange phenomena this show is all about the dispossessed, the inconsolable grieving, the separated infant—in short, the victim. One of the most popular scenes on this show was about people who receive messages from the Great Beyond; for instance, individuals who see an image of the deceased, or someone (like an angel) intervening on their behalf, to send a message to the living, or in some other way have an impact on the living. The fact is that about half of Americans believe that the government is withholding information about UFOs (and at times in my life I have been among them), and a significant proportion of the American population believes that some people have been abducted by aliens from another planet. The experience of visitation from beyond the grave is a common one that I myself have experienced in a certain way, related to my own mother's death.

Thirty years after my mother's death, a group of Japanese journalists came to Yale to do a story on our research. For some reason, the Japanese are fascinated by the phenomenon of dissociative identity disorder (DID; formerly termed multiple personality disorder), and had been visiting various experts in the area to do a story on the topic for Japanese Public Television. Essentially, DID is always related to a history of childhood abuse, and the journalists came to Yale to understand the effects of psychological trauma on memory and the brain. As detailed earlier in this book, we had found that the trauma of childhood abuse leads to shrinkage of a part of the brain, the hippocampus, that plays an important role in memory, and that victims of childhood abuse predictably had severe deficits in the ability to remember. At one point, while we were having dinner together in New Haven, I tried to explain how the stressful nature of an event can influence how it is stored in the brain, sometimes making the memory very strong, and in other situations making it more difficult to retrieve. The Japanese film crew seemed to have trouble understanding how that could be the case, even after I gave several examples, so I decided to take a different tack.

"What was the most stressful event you remember from your childhood?" I asked the leader of the group.

He seemed a little startled by the question, and then paused to reflect. It seemed that no one had ever asked him a question like that before. "When I was 3 years old, I fell into a well, and was down there for many hours before someone found me and was able to get me out."

I was stunned by his answer. Now that was a traumatic event that even a trauma psychiatrist could appreciate. "Do you remember that event better than, for example, what you had for breakfast that morning?" I asked.

"Of course," he replied. I saw that by putting it into a personal context, he had finally understood the scientific point I was trying to make.

There is controversy over whether traumatic memories are distinct from other memories, or whether they are just another type of memory that differs from normal memory only by their content. Scientists in the field of cognitive psychology, which deals

DOES STRESS DAMAGE THE BRAIN?

with how our minds work in memory and thinking, have debated back and forth whether traumatic memories are really special or whether we are making much ado about nothing by trying to give them a special category. The stakes in this debate are whether different rules apply to remembrance of traumatic events from childhood, such as childhood abuse, and whether the "forgetting" of childhood abuse (with later delayed recall) is related to the specific traumatic nature of the memory, or whether the memory of abuse should be held to the same standards as any other type of memory. The obvious stakes are related to litigation in which individuals allege that they retrieved memories of abuse many years after the fact.

The role of emotion in memory has not been thoroughly examined in the scientific world. Most cognitive psychologists view memory as being uniform and not divided into separate types of memory, such as neutral memories and traumatic memories. As mentioned in prior chapters of this book, emotional situations can affect the way that memory is laid down, related to increased release of stress hormones that affect the way brain areas involved in memory lay down memory. In my own research using imaging of brain function with positron emission tomography, my colleagues and I found that different brain areas activated in women during remembrance of emotional word pairs such as "rape–mutilate" compared to neutral words like "apple–horse." It is clear that the emotional context of a memory is important, and that more research is needed to understand the effects of emotion on memory.

The recreation, recollection, or reassemblage of traumatic memory has implications for the recovery from a traumatic event. I know from my own experience of losing my mother at an early age, that the memories of the event seemed to change and transform in multiple ways over time. Family-shared unspoken agreements of silence helped to amplify the distortion process. The dependent status of being a child inhibited any assertive attempts to learn more about the past or to put things into an assemblance of meaning. For me, it really took years to get over that trauma in at least a partial way, or to have a sense of understanding. That did not happen until I returned to my home as a medical student and spent a year within a research laboratory in Seattle. In my mind, I felt I had to go home in order to see my grandfather, to whom I am very close, before he passed away. I decided to write down as much as I could about our family's history, and about the reflections of my grandfather growing up in Washington State during the early part of the 20th century.

After finishing the book, however, I didn't feel like I had finished. There was one half of my family, my mother, about which I knew hardly anything. Her life history was not a favorite topic at the dinner table, and soon after her death we lost all contact with her family. To make matters worse, her "family" wasn't even her biological family, as she had been adopted at birth.

Nevertheless, this type of journal therapy was ultimately beneficial to me. I felt that I was able to let things go and move forward in my own life, with my own career and my own family. I think that all trauma survivors need to go through a "logotherapy" of the type I experienced, or something like it, in order to heal and move forward. Unfortunately, I also know from my own experience that, for many individuals, such a move toward health can also mean an abandonment of loyalty toward the dead. Maybe if the dead come to us in dreams and give us permission to let them go . . .

Childhood Abuse and Delayed Recall of Trauma

One of the most common and debilitating forms of trauma in our society today is childhood abuse (Finkelhor, 1986). As mentioned in earlier chapters, childhood sexual abuse affects 16% of women at some time before their 18th birthday. At least one million new cases of childhood abuse are documented and verified each year.

With these types of statistics it is clear that we are suffering from what I have called a silent epidemic of childhood abuse.

Childhood abuse and other traumas may be particularly relevant to our inner cities. With rates of childhood abuse as common as what I outlined above, and possibly higher in impoverished families, it can be seen that childhood trauma is an important factor in our inner cities. Add to this the traumatization related witnessing of injury, assault, and death on the streets, as well as increased exposure to adults having problems with alcohol and substance abuse, and we can see that our children in the inner cities are especially at risk. The multiple potential traumas of childhood abuse, chaotic family life related to poverty, family violence, and witnessing violence on inner-city streets may put these children at increased risk for traumatization. We have reviewed the potential effects of stress on the capacity for new learning and memory. These studies raise the possibility that the extreme stress of the inner city may impair inner-city children's capacity for learning, acting through impairment of hippocampal function or other mechanisms. These factors may play a critical role in the difficulty of inner-city children to use education to help them to improve their situation in life.

Another area relevant to the effects of stress on memory is the controversial topic of possible delayed recall of trauma (Bremner, 1998, Brewin, 1996; Fivush, Haden, & Adam, 1995; Freyd, 1997; Freyd & Gleaves, 1996; Kihlstrom, 1995; Lindsey & Read, 1994; Loftus, 1993; Loftus, Garry, & Feldman, 1994, 1996; Loftus & Loftus, 1980; Schacter, Coyle, Fischbach, Mesulam, & Sullivan, 1995; Schooler, 1994). This has received the most attention in the area of childhood abuse, because of the litigation associated with the topic. However, it is relevant to all types of traumas. PTSD patients report deficits in declarative memory (remembering facts or lists), fragmentation of memories (both autobiographical and trauma-related), memory distortions, and dissociative amnesia (gaps in memory that can occur for min utes or even days, and are not due to ordinary forgetting (Brewin et al., 1996; Williams, 1994; Williams & Banyard, 1996). Many trauma victims claim to remember only certain aspects of the abuse event, a phenomenon related to dissociative amnesia (Bremner, Steinberg, et al., 1993). The wide range of effects that traumatic stress has on memory complicates questions related to delayed recall of trauma.

There is a limited amount of research on delayed recall of childhood abuse and other traumas. Cases of individuals who have no memory of childhood sexual abuse, and then suddenly remember an abuse event years after the fact, have been widely publicized in the popular literature. For example, one man who was listening to a report about a priest who had been arrested for molesting children 20 years before suddenly had a memory of being molested by that particular priest. The validity of this type of delayed recall of childhood abuse has been hotly debated in the scientific literature, as reviewed elsewhere in this volume. Studies show that memories are in fact be susceptible to insertions, deletions, and distortions, often resulting in a situation in which an individual remains convinced of the validity of the memory as experienced in its altered form (Kihlstrom, 1987). A variety of experimental paradigms have demonstrated the capacity for false recall (Loftus et al., 1978; Pezdek & Banks, 1996; Roediger & McDermott, 1995). Findings from these studies have led to criticism of clinical reports of delayed recall of childhood abuse. The clinical and scientific literature related to delayed recall of childhood abuse has become polarized, with two conflicting viewpoints related to whether or not delayed recall of childhood abuse is valid.

One of the primary criticisms of the viewpoint that delayed recall represents valid memories is the apparent illogical act of forgetting events that most people would consider impossible to forget. However, studies of animals reviewed in prior chapters in this book have demonstrated that stress can impair memory function in some circumstances, acting through stress hormones and brain chemicals that affect the way memories are laid down. In addition, stress can result in lasting changes in structure and function of brain areas involved in memory. We don't have good research data on the proportion of PTSD patients who experience delayed recall of abuse; however, clinical experience dictates that fragmentations and alterations in memory for traumatic events are more common in patients with PTSD, and include memories for some events that are continuous, memories for other events that are delayed or fragmented, and other memories that are never retrieved at all.

Stress-induced hippocampal damage represents one possible mechanism for delayed recall of trauma. As discussed before, the hippocampus is a brain area involved in learning and memory (Squire & Zola-Morgan, 1991) that is particularly sensitive to stress (Bremner, 1999b; McEwen et al., 1992; Sapolsky, 1996). This function is critical to the stress response; for example, in assessing potential threat during a life-threatening situation, as occurs with exposure to a predator. I have reviewed in prior chapters the research evidence showing that stress results in long-term changes in the hippocampus, and the hypothesis that stress-induced hippocampal deficits underlie deficits in verbal declarative memory in PTSD patients. These patients cannot remember simple things on a daily basis, and for that reason are often unable to hold regular jobs. We found a magnitude of memory impairment on the order of a 40% reduction on neuropsychological tests relative to normal that is equivalent to patients with epilepsy who have had their hippocampus surgically resected (Lencz et al., 1992). My patients often describe the debilitating effects of their memory impairments on how they function socially and at work. For instance, one of my abuse-related PTSD patients complained that she felt like she had an early dementia. I frequently counsel my patients not to pursue a career or training that requires memorization.

Hippocampal dysfunction may also lead to distortion and fragmentation of memories of childhood abuse (Bremner, Krystal, Charney, & Southwick, 1996). There is also evidence that the mind has the capacity to actively inhibit certain aspects of memory, especially if there are memories too terrible to recall, representing another possible mechanism for delayed recall of abuse (Anderson, Bjork, & Bjork, 1994; Anderson & Spellman, 1995). Modulation of memory function by cortisol and norepinephrine may represent a mechanism of delayed recall of childhood abuse. As mentioned elsewhere in this book, cortisol acts over the period of hours to weaken the laying down of memory traces, whereas norepinephrine has a rapid effect to strengthen memory traces (McGaugh, 1989). Long-term dysregulation of these systems may result in chronic changes in the way memories are retrieved in abuse survivors with PTSD. For example, exaggerated cortisol release during stress in PTSD may result in an inhibition of memory retrieval. This may account for the finding that rape victims report that memories for the rape trauma are actually less clear than those for neutral memories (Koss, Figueredo, Bell, Tharan, & Tromp, 1996). Exaggerated release of norepinephrine with stress in PTSD would actually be expected to facilitate recall based on the animal studies cited above. Such a mechanism may be responsible for the sudden eruption into consciousness of long-lost memories of childhood abuse during adult stressors that some PTSD patients claim to experience. Both acute and chronic responses of these neurochemical systems to stress must be considered in order to understand alterations in memory encoding and retrieval that we propose underlie delayed recall of childhood abuse.

Abnormalities of frontal lobe function may also underlie delayed recall of childhood abuse. The medial prefrontal cortex is of particular interest because of the role it plays in emotion, social behavior, and inhibition of responses. Human subjects with lesions of medial prefrontal cortical areas have deficits in interpretation of emotional situations and impairments in social relatedness (e.g., the famous case of Phineas Gage; Damasio et al., 1994). Other aspects of prefrontal cortical function may be relevant to PTSD. The prefrontal cortex is involved in selecting responses and planning for execution of action. Patients with lesions of the prefrontal cortex exhibit a variety of abnormalities of cognition, including impairments in ability to select a correct response, as well as insertion, distortions, and confabulations of memory.

These types of memory alterations are seen in patients with abuse-related PTSD. We (Bremner, Shobe, & Kihlstrom, 2000) used a paradigm to assess capacity for false memory as reported by Roediger and McDermott (1995). This paradigm evaluated free recall using lists of words that are all highly associated with a single primary associate ("critical lure"). During free recall, about 40% of normal subjects falsely recalled the "critical lure" word. We used this paradigm to assess the propensity for false memory recall in 63 subjects, including women with a self-reported history of early childhood sexual abuse (with and without the diagnosis of PTSD), and healthy men and women without a history of childhood abuse. Women with abuse-related PTSD had a higher frequency of false recognition recall of critical lures (95%) than did women with abuse histories without PTSD (76%), and non abused non-PTSD women (79%). There were no differences between normal men and normal women. PTSD women also showed a pattern of poorer recall of previously studied words, consistent with previous findings of declarative memory deficits in PTSD, and a larger number of intrusions on nonstudied words other than critical lures. These findings are consistent with a greater propensity for distortions in memory in women with self-reported childhood sexual abuse and PTSD. As noted earlier, prefrontal cortical dysfunction in abuse-related PTSD is a possible reason for these phenomena, which would explain the increase in capacity for distortion and source amnesia effects.

Medial prefrontal cortical dysfunction in abuse-related PTSD could explain both cognitive deficits (insertions and distortions) as well as problems regulating mood and emotion. Medial prefrontal cortical areas modulate emotional responsiveness through inhibition of amygdala function, and we have hypothesized that dysfunction in these regions may underlie pathological emotional responses in patients with PTSD (Bremner, Narayan, et al., 1999). The development of conditioned fear responses—as in the pairing of a neutral stimulus (bright light, the conditioned stimulus) with a fear-inducing stimulus (electric shock, the unconditioned stimulus), which leads to fear responses to the light alone—is mediated by the amygdala (Davis, 1992; LeDoux, 1993). Repeated exposure to the conditioned stimulus alone normally results in the gradual loss of fear responding. The phenomenon, described elsewhere in this book, is known as *extinction to conditioned fear responses*, and has been hypothesized to be secondary to the formation of new memories that mask the original conditioned fear memory (Bouton & Swartzentruber, 1991). The extinguished memory is rapidly reversible following reexposure to the conditioned–unconditioned stimulus pairing, even up to one year after the original period of fear conditioning (McAllister & McAllister, 1988) This suggests that the fear response did not disappear, but was merely inhibited. Such inhibition may take place through connections between medial prefrontal cortex and amygdala (Carmichael & Price, 1995; Devinsky et al., 1995; Vogt et al., 1992).

Imaging studies of brain function in PTSD are consistent with dysfunction of the medial prefrontal cortex in PTSD. Failure of activation in this area and/or decreased blood flow in adjacent medial prefrontal cortex in PTSD may lead to increased fearfulness that is not appropriate for the context, a behavioral response that is highly characteristic of patients with PTSD. If abuse-related PTSD patients are unable to regulate emotional responses to exposure to cues of the original trauma, they may develop behaviors in which they avoid reminders in order to protect themselves. This, in turn, could lead to "amnesia" that is only overcome in unusual circumstances that are later identified as "delayed recall." Consistent with this idea, studies do show that PTSD symptoms increase after delayed recall of childhood abuse.

Medial prefrontal cortical dysfunction may also play a role in the increase in intrusions, distortions, and source amnesia seen in patients with PTSD. In addition, considering the role of medial prefrontal cortex in inhibition of responses, dysfunction in this area may underlie the dysregulation of memory inhibition and access (including childhood abuse memories) in PTSD, further facilitating delayed recall of childhood abuse.

The model for the effects of traumatic stress on brain systems and structures involved in memory may have clinical relevance for psychotherapy of childhood abuse survivors. Psychotherapy may influence delayed recall of childhood abuse; because it naturally involves the facilitation of recall through encouraging the investigation of feelings related to traumatic events. The psychotherapist may provide a supportive environment that allows the patient to experience strong emotions that he or she may be afraid to experience outside of the therapeutic setting. This may lead to a mood state similar to that experienced at the time of the trauma. It has been shown that memory recall is facilitated when moods are the same as during the original laying down of the memory trace, a phenomenon known as *state-dependent recall* (Bower, 1981).

If brain systems and structures that mediate memory are dysfunctional in patients with abuse-related PTSD, then recall of childhood abuse may only occur in the context of special situations, such as psychotherapy sessions. Psychotherapy may therefore facilitate remembrance in ways other than providing false suggestions or promoting insertions of memories that never in fact took place. This may explain why some traumatic events are fully recalled for the first time during psychotherapy, which has fueled the controversy about whether these recalled events are true or false. The fact that traumatic events are recalled during therapy does not necessarily imply that they represent a false memory. Nevertheless, many therapists are concerned about how to proceed with psychotherapy in light of the recent controversy concerning the engendering of false memories of abuse. These therapists feel that if they ask directly about abuse, they may be accused of suggesting to their patients abuse events that did not in fact take place. Patients should be allowed to tell their own story, not one inspired by their therapists. Considering the evidence in support of the potential for suggestion to facilitate false memory illusions, as a therapist it is important to avoid imposing one's own ideas on the patient regarding a past history of abuse. Patients with PTSD may be even more susceptible to suggestion than are normal persons. However, due to issues of shame and other reasons, they may not report abuse unless asked directly.

Trauma Type and Trauma Outcomes: Similarities and Differences

There has long been a debate about whether different types of traumas lead to similar or diverse outcomes. Much of the history of the field of traumatic stress has been driven by a focus on specific traumas. For example, there are some groups who have focused on the effects of the Holocaust on its victims, or the role of World War II, rape trauma, car accidents, and so on. Different countries and cultures have placed a special emphasis on their own traumas as well. For instance, Armenia had a destructive earthquake, the British had the war in the Falkland Islands, and other countries have had their own unique traumas. I've found that each country or culture has to have its own trauma in order to be able to put the general field of trauma into perspective. For instance, several years ago I gave a lecture in England that was part of an all-day symposium on traumatic stress. Until the English had their own identifiable national trauma in the form of the Falkland Islands War with Argentina, they couldn't "relate" to the discussions of the effects of psychological trauma that had been going on in the United States. Their attitude prior to that time had been that the United States was special because of the Vietnam War, and for a variety of reasons the trauma experienced by Vietnam veterans was not really relevant to them. Over the years, I have encountered a number of similar "not in my neighborhood" reactions, in which people from countries outside of the United States have denied that psychological trauma is a significant problem in their own country, or has significant effects, until something happens in their own culture and context to which they can relate.

Another issue is related to whether different types of trauma have different effects. We have seen a number of different trauma types identified as different syndromes, including "rape trauma syndrome," "battered wife syndrome," "battered child syndrome," "shell shock" (from combat), and many others over the years. Both clinical experience and research studies indicate that patients exposed to different types of traumas have more in common than they have differences. Traumas from a wide variety of situations, in different cultural contexts and countries, show a surprisingly similar pattern of intrusive memories, nightmares, flashbacks, avoidance, sleep disturbances, problems relating to others, dissociation, startle responses, and hyperarousal. In my experience, the most important factor that influences differences in outcomes between different patients is the age at which the trauma occurred. Patients who are traumatized early in life, such as abuse survivors, have an increase in personality problems, as well as dissociative responses and depression. When patients with no prior history of major traumatic stressors or psychiatric disorders, are traumatized in adulthood they tend to develop more of a "pure" PTSD picture, with hyperarousal and intrusions empha-sized to a greater degree than are problems with personality.

One important factor that influences the degree of dysfunction in PTSD patients is the chronicity of exposure to stressors in life and how that relates to the development of chronic symptoms of PTSD. We all are exposed to stressors of varying degrees through-out our lives, and sometimes these stressors reach such a level of severity that they produce a mild stress response. For example, if you are in a car accident, you may have difficulty approaching the car, or driving without experiencing some anxiety or fear responsiveness. However, after a few days of driving, this fear responsiveness will diminish. You can imagine that if you got into a car accident every other time you drove, the fear responses would not diminish as quickly, and could even develop into a chronic response. Also, the fear responses would make it difficult for you to function in a normal way. Therefore, excessive jumpi-ness behind the wheel would increase the likelihood of another accident, creating a vicious cycle. One can even take the analogy further and note that due to the excessive level of background fear, the traumatized motorist would be overresponding to every-thing in the environment, and therefore would not be able to appropriately respond to something that was truly threatening, such as a large truck approaching from an intersecting street. The PTSD patients I have treated in my clinical work are very similar to the hypothetical driver I just described: They tend to have multiple traumas over time, and their behavior puts them at risk for further traumatization. This was exemplified by one of my patients, Alice, a woman with a history of childhood sexual abuse and PTSD who suffers from chronic symptoms of deperson-alization and derealization. She said:

> When I was 10 I had a pelvic exam (for a physical illness). My mother was so freaked out but I didn't care. I just blot every-thing out, leave my body, and go somewhere else. Dentists say

I am the best patient they have ever had. Sometimes I play a trick with my mind and I imagine myself flipping backwards and floating to the center of the earth. That's a good place for me to be, I like it there. I lose track of what is happening to me. Then I wake up and say, "What are these people doing to me, where am I?" That makes me more vulnerable to be raped, because I don't even know what is happening, I don't know what they are doing to my body. I lose feeling in my body. One part of my body takes over feeling for the whole body, like if I have a cut on my finger then my whole body is that cut on the finger. I am just a little nothing. When I am a whole person it makes me scared.

If someone wants to pursue sex with me my whole body shuts down. I become very afraid and I say, "uh-oh, here it goes again, this guy is going to hurt me." If I am attracted to someone I feel it is evil, like I am a molester, and I think, "What if this person knows what I am thinking?"

When I was in college, someone got into my dorm room and raped me. I don't know how he got in there, I don't remember. I blacked out, I didn't know what was happening to me. He became violent and I was all bruised. When it happened I wasn't there mentally there, I felt my body didn't exist, I floated off somewhere. My body wasn't there but my mind was protesting, saying, "what is happening to me?" After that, if something happened like that, I just became a rag doll, so they didn't hurt me. I thought everyone in the dorm conspired against me. I had to keep seeing this guy in the hall, because his room was just down the hall. I thought that if this is my life I want to die. I was a victimized female. I shut myself in my room and wouldn't come out.

Now if someone wants to massage me or something I don't know what they are doing to me. Once someone was massaging me and I didn't even know what they were doing. I felt aroused and then I freaked out, and I realized he was molesting me. I don't know what is happening to me so I can't stop people when they cross my boundaries. I went to a rape crisis center

and they said, "why don't you tell him to take a step back?"
But I don't even know what they are doing, so how can I do
that?

The Neurological Viewpoint of the Effects of Stress
on the Individual, and Implications for a Trauma-Spectrum
Model of Stress-Related Psychiatric Disorders

A central theme of this book is that stress results in long-standing
changes in neurological function that underlie symptoms of
stress-related psychiatric disorders. This idea can be helpful in
explaining many of the phenomena that are described in this
book. A common neurological deficit following stress would help
to explain the common symptoms that are seen in the aftermath
of trauma. There is no reason to believe that an Armenian
trauma is qualitatively different than a British trauma, or that
the Palestinian response to stress is different than the Israeli response to stress. Physiologically, stress is stress. That is why the
responses to different types of stressors in different cultures and
different countries are so similar.

When we think about specific aspects of the response of traumatized patients, understanding neurological function can help
to elucidate what we are seeing. In traumatized patients, there is
an inability to cancel out fear responses even when there is no
true threat. We have hypothesized that this is related to an inability of cortical areas, such as the frontal cortex, to inhibit fear
responses embedded in primitive brain areas such as the amygdala. PTSD patients cannot properly regulate cortical inhibition
of the amygdala; therefore, they are unable to turn it off when
there is a true threat. It is like the story of Peter who cried,
"Wolf." The cortical areas are constantly crying wolf, so when a
true wolf comes along, the amygdala does not turn on like it is
supposed to.

A common neurological response to stress may also explain
why there is such overlap among what we call trauma-spectrum

psychiatric disorders. A common neurological deficit would explain why these disorders, which have been considered in psychiatric diagnostic schemas as being separate, represent overlapping disorders that have their common basis in neurological changes in the brain. Then the question becomes why there is a difference in presentation among disorders such as PTSD, borderline personality disorder, and dissociative disorders when they all share in common a neurological deficit. Do these disorders merely represent different points along a continuum? Do the differences in symptoms represent other factors, such as differences in developmental epoch at the time of the trauma? Or are there other factors that we currently do not appreciate that account for the subtle differences in symptomatology among these disorders?

This hypothesis of a common neurological deficit could explain why there is such overlap among many disorders, and why clinicians are frustrated with the current diagnostic schema. The past half-century of psychiatry has been largely absorbed with an attempt to force clinicians to accept a "splitters" approach to psychiatric diagnosis, which has led to finer and finer splitting of psychiatric diagnoses with successive versions of the *DSM*. An important foundation of this evolution of psychiatric diagnosis is the absence of any theoretical foundation for diagnosis. This was largely a reaction to the previous era, in which psychoanalysis dominated psychiatric diagnosis and imbued a heavily dogmatic and theoretical foundation for it. However, cutting ourselves off from any theoretical foundations has had its price. It has led us into our currently absurd position of trying to justify why multiple psychiatric diagnoses—all spawned from the back of the *DSM* like the heads of the Hydra that sprouted out after the single head called "anxiety neurosis" was lopped off by the so-called biological psychiatrists—are actually distinct entities when all of the evidence points to the contrary. This situation has led us close to a grassroots revolution, in which the clinicians who actually see the patients are ready to assassinate the number crunchers who developed this idiotic scheme, and are forcing the clinicians to comply with it in the name of "consistency of diagnosis" or "research protocol." In fact, these clinicians started ignoring the *DSM* years ago. However, if queried, they will spout the dogma like Protestants challenged by Catholic inquisitors in Spain during the 14th century. The fact is that it is time for us all to wake up and realize the truth—that these disorders are not truly distinct, that they have a common basis in neurology, and that we need to take a more enlightened approach to their evaluation and treatment.

Of course, the most relevant rationale to straighten ourselves in terms of diagnosis is so that we can appropriately treat patients with trauma-related psychiatric disorders. If we can properly diagnosis trauma patients, we can apply the correct treatments for these disorders. We are starting to learn more about treatments for trauma-related disorders, and the good news is that some treatments we have learned about in the past few years show considerable promise for disorders such as PTSD.

CHAPTER EIGHT

Treatments for PTSD and Other Stress-Related Disorders May Act Through the Brain

William Clark was attacked by a party of Indians, March 12, 1676 [in Plymouth, Massachusetts], and 11 members of the family, including his wife and several children, were killed. He himself being absent at meeting escaped. His son was tomahawked, who ever after wore a silver plate on his head, from which he was called silver head Tom.

—From *A History of the Bremner Family,*
by J. Douglas Bremner

The Comprehensive Approach to Treating Traumatic Stress

In this book, we have formulated the potentially devastating effects of traumatic stress on the individual. Obviously, the best way to block the effects of traumatic events would be to eliminate traumatic events in the first place (Gabriel, 1987). Until that time comes, we will have to think about ways to reverse or reduce the effects after the fact. However, the consequences of traumatic stress are not completely without any potential for hope. There are now several studies of psychotherapy and medication treatment of PTSD. These studies indicate that there is hope for reversal of symptoms of PTSD, provided by the use of psychotherapy treatments such as cognitive-behavioral treatment or medications such as selective serotonin reuptake inhibitors (SSRIs) or mood-stabilizing agents like valproic acid or carbamazepine. Both behavioral and medication treatments are hypothesized to act on the brain to reverse some of the neurological changes that are believed to underlie trauma-related psychiatric disorders like PTSD.

As mentioned above, I want to emphasize that one of the most important ways to handle the consequences of traumatic stress is to prevent traumatic stress from happening in the first place. I will never forget one of my first PTSD patients, who gave me an important lesson about the treatment of the consequences of psychological trauma. I was a young psychiatric resident working on a recently established specialized inpatient unit for the treatment of Vietnam combat-related PTSD at the National Center for PTSD at the West Haven Veterans Administration Hospital in West Haven, Connecticut. Part of my job was to screen prospective "candidates" for our inpatient treatment program, a process that involved assessment of the presence of PTSD, history of substance abuse, and motivation for treatment. At the time, I was highly convinced of the great potential benefits of our treatment program for chronic combat-related PTSD. One of the veterans with combat-related PTSD, after hearing my spiel about the wonderful potential benefits of treatment, gave me a book whose subject was essentially that if we eliminate war we will no longer have PTSD. This was an important lesson that I never forgot. However, until we succeed in preventing traumatic stressors, we need to think about how to treat victims of traumatic stress. The two types of treatment that have been shown to have some usefulness are medication treatment and psychotherapies (specifically, behavioral treatment).

Medication Treatments for PTSD

There are a limited number of controlled studies of medication treatment in PTSD (Sutherland & Davidson, 1999). The best type of research studies of medications involve comparing the medication of choice to a sugar pill, or something that is called a *placebo*. Placebos have no physiological effect, but research studies have shown that about a third of patients taking placebos experience an improvement. It is not known why this takes place. Some feel that a placebo's success is due to suggestibility; however, there may be something about the nonspecific effects of treatment that have some type of neurological-spiritual effect that may transcend our ability to understand the effects of treatments as we know them. When we talk about placebo-controlled trials, we refer to a comparison of the treatment of choice to a placebo. In these studies, neither the patient nor the doctor knows what type of treatment is being administered.

The first placebo-controlled trial of medication for treatment of PTSD was conducted at the West Haven VA and compared the antidepressants imipramine and phenylzine to a placebo in combat veterans with PTSD (Frank, Kosten, Giller, & Dan, 1988). Both medications showed improvement in treatment for PTSD symptoms—especially those in the area of intrusions, including nightmares, flashbacks, and intrusive memories—but the placebo did not. A four-week trial of the antidepressant desipramine showed improvement only for patients with PTSD and comorbid depression (reviewed in Sutherland & Davidson, 1999). This study may have been limited by too short of a treatment duration. Davidson and colleagues compared amitriptyline to a placebo, and found modest improvement in PTSD symptoms, as well as symptoms of depression and anxiety, in combat-related PTSD (Davidson et al., 1990).

In the past decade, there has been an increased focus on treatment of PTSD with the selective serotonin reuptake inhibitor (SSRI) medications. These medications—which include fluoxetine (Prozac), paroxetine (Paxil), and sertraline (Zoloft)—act by blocking the transporter that brings the serotonin back from the space between the neurons (synapse) into the neuron, effectively increasing the levels of serotonin in the synapse.

Because alterations in serotonergic function have been found in animal models of stress, there is a rationale for the use of the medications in the treatment of PTSD (reviewed in Sutherland & Davidson, 1999). In one controlled trial, fluoxetine (Prozac) at doses of 40 mg or higher was shown to be efficacious in a mixed sample of patients with civilian-related PTSD, but not those suffering from combat-related PTSD (van der Kolk et al., 1994). At least two additional studies (published and unpublished) have shown no efficacy of fluoxetine in combat-related PTSD. In addition, Wellbutrin was not shown to be efficacious for combat-related PTSD. In a large multicenter trial, sertraline (Zoloft) was shown to be efficacious in women, with more modest effects in men (Brady et al., 2000). A large multisite study of paroxetine (Paxil) showed improvement in PTSD symptoms in both men and women with PTSD. A multisite study of nefazodone (Serzone) did not show improvement of symptoms; however, another single-site study of it with combat veterans with PTSD did show an improvement in PTSD symptoms. A controlled trial of alprazolam (Xanax) showed efficacy for anxiety but not for PTSD symptoms. Mood-stabilizing agents such as valproic acid (Valproate) and carbamazepine (Tegretol) are commonly used in clinical practice, often in combination with SSRI medications. These medications have been shown to be helpful in noncontrolled studies of PTSD. A panel of experts recommended SSRIs as first-line treatment of PTSD, and also endorsed combination therapies with mood-stabilizing agents (Foa et al., 1999).

SSRI medications like Paxil and Prozac may actually act on the brain to reverse the effects of traumatic stress on the brain. Studies by Ron Duman at Yale and others found that SSRIs increase branching of neurons in the hippocampus, which, as mentioned previously in this book, is a brain area that plays a critical role in learning and memory that is very sensitive to stress. These scientists also found that SSRIs promote some of processes within the neuronal cells that are beneficial for the development of neurons. It has also been shown that the hippocampus has the capacity to grow neurons in adulthood, an act known as *neurogenesis* (Gould et al., 1998). Duman and his group found that SSRIs promote neurogenesis in the hippocampus.

Based on these findings, we wanted to see if hippocampal volume reductions in patients with PTSD were reversible. Someone who at the time was a postdoctoral fellow in my laboratory named Eric Vermetten and myself treated PTSD patients with Paxil for a year, and found a 5% increase in hippocampal volume measured with MRI. We also found a 35% improvement in hippocampal-based memory function as measured with neuropsychological testing, for example the ability to remember a paragraph or a list of words (Vermetten et al., personal communication, November 11, 2001). The patients in this study found that treatment with paxil led to a significant improvement in their ability to work and function in their lives. They were able to concentrate and remember things much better than before treatment with medication. Based on this study, we speculated that Paxil had a beneficial effect on neurons within the hippocampus.

We also found that Paxil had an important effect on symptoms of PTSD. Treatment with Paxil resulted in a 40-point drop in the Clinician Administered PTSD Scale, a measure of PTSD symptoms. In addition, we found that individual patients had significant improvements in their lives following treatment with Paxil. Earlier in this book I described the case of Jeff, one of my patients who was a young police officer disturbed on a daily basis by intrusive memories of arriving on the scene of suicide.

He said, "I drift from one thing to another. Nothing seems to have any meaning anymore. I feel as if my life will end tomorrow, but I don't care." Jeff would think over and over about how this thing had happened, how it could have been prevented. The boy was depressed because he had acne, and thought a girl he liked wouldn't like him in turn. Jeff would ruminate about how this could be his own son. He was tormented by his thoughts. Sometimes, when he was reliving the event, he wasn't aware of anything around him. He tried to talk about it, he tried to be a tough cop and hold it in, but nothing relieved his anguish.

We started Jeff on Paxil at a variable dose. Within six weeks, Jeff showed an improvement in a number of PTSD symptoms, including intrusive symptoms like recurrent mental images of his trauma. Jeff appeared to have an almost complete resolution of the symptoms that were causing him so much distress.

Another medication, called Dilantin (phenytoin), also has a beneficial effect related to the effects of stress on the hippocampus. This medication, which is commonly used for the treatment of epilepsy, was shown by McEwen and colleagues to block the negative effects of excitatory amino acids on the hippocampus (Watanabe et al., 1992). In most patients, epilepsy is in fact caused by hippocampal damage that leads to scarring in this brain region. The scar is the site of an abnormal discharge of neurons, which spreads throughout the brain, causing all of the neurons to discharge abnormally, and producing a seizure. Excitatory amino acids are highly concentrated in the hippocampus, and the hippocampus is quite sensitive to the negative effects of excitatory amino acids on neurons. In seizures there is actually an increased release of excitatory amino acids, which leads to further scarring in the hippocampus and thus to a vicious cycle of seizures with increasing hippocampal injury. In a similar way, stress results in an increased release of excitatory amino acids, causing hippocampal injury. Dilantin acts for both seizures and stress to decrease excitatory amino acids, preventing further neuronal injury. Dilantin has actually been shown to block the negative effects of stress on the hippocampus in studies in animals. The prominent stockbroker Jack Dreyfus took Dilantin and found it to be helpful for the depression he was suffering from. Based on this, he established a foundation for research of the effects of Dilantin on behavior. We are currently conducting a study of the effects of Dilantin on symptoms of PTSD and hippocampus and memory in patients with PTSD.

Psychotherapy Treatments of PTSD

In addition to medication treatments, psychotherapies have been found useful in the treatment of PTSD (Shay & Munroe, 1999). Although a number of psychotherapy treatments have been applied to survivors of psychological trauma, the cognitive-behavioral treatments have been most thoroughly evaluated. A number of studies have shown that exposure therapies (systematic desensitization, imaginal exposure, and in-vivo exposure) performed by trained clinicians are effective in treating PTSD (Meadows & Foa, 1999). These treatments involve gradual exposure to memories of the traumatic event with self-report ratings of subjective distress. Over the course of treatments, there is a gradual diminution of symptoms associated with the traumatic memory.

In systematic desensitization, there is pairing of imaginal exposure to the trauma with relaxation, so that the anxiety associated with thinking about the traumatic event is inhibited by relaxation. When the individual becomes anxious, he or she is instructed to erase the scene, relax, and then imagine the scenario again. This is repeated until anxiety is no longer associated with the imagination. In imaginal exposure therapy, to enhance the vividness of the memory, individuals are asked to imagine the event in their minds and focus on their thoughts and emotions as if the event were happening now. As described by Meadows and Foa (1999, p. 378), instructions for imaginal therapy are given as follows: "I want you to close your eyes and begin to talk about the assault. Talk about it in the first person, as if it is happening to you right now. As you're talking, picture the story in your mind, and describe what is happening. Describe it in as much detail as possible, including what you're doing, what he's doing, what you're thinking and feeling. Try not to let go of the image, even if it's upsetting to you, and we will talk about it after the exposure is finished." In-vivo exposure consists of confronting fear-evoking situations associated with the trauma; for example, a rape victim who was assaulted in a dark alley might return to a dark alley over several sessions until she becomes desensitized.

Controlled trials have demonstrated the usefulness of these three therapy techniques, with better results being obtained when treatment is applied as soon as possible after exposure to the trauma (Meadows & Foa, 1999). Other treatments that are effective for PTSD fall into the category of anxiety management. The most studied anxiety management technique in PTSD is stress inoculation training (SIT). SIT involves several anxiety-management techniques, including psychoeducation, muscle relaxation training, breathing retraining, role playing, covert modeling, guided self-dialogue, and thought stopping. This treatment program has been shown to be effective in the treatment of PTSD.

Relationship among Therapy, Extinction, and Brain Mechanisms

Cognitive-behavioral treatments such as exposure therapies may counteract the neurological consequences of exposure to traumatic stress. As mentioned in earlier chapters, one of the hallmarks of PTSD is an inability to extinguish or wipe out fear responses with reminders of the trauma. In PTSD patients this can become very disabling, to the point at which it interferes with daily activities. Using the laboratory model of conditioned fear responses, pairing an unconditioned stimulus (e.g., an electric shock) with a conditioned stimulus (e.g., bright light) leads to a fear reaction to the conditioned stimulus ("bright light") alone. With repeated exposure to the conditioned stimulus there

DOES STRESS DAMAGE THE BRAIN?

is a decrease in fear responding, which may be related to an inhibition of the amygdala (which plays a critical role in acquisition of fear responses) by areas such as the medial prefrontal cortex. In a similar way in normal individuals, fear responses to reminders of the trauma normally become extinguished with repeated exposure to reminders of the trauma. However, for PTSD patients, we hypothesize that dysfunction in the medial prefrontal cortex leads to an inability to extinguish traumatic memories through inhibition of activity in the amygdala. One of the roles of behavioral therapies may be to facilitate the ability of the brain to inhibit or extinguish traumatic memories, through techniques such as gradual exposure to traumatic reminders, in the supportive context of a therapeutic environment.

Role of Hypnosis in Trauma Diagnosis and Treatment

Although hypnosis has had a controversial place in the treatment of stress-related psychiatric disorders, in the hands of competent and trained professionals it does serve a potentially useful role (Spiegel, Hunt, & Dondershine, 1988). Much of the controversy related to the use of hypnosis is related to the fact that information obtained during the course of a hypnotic session has been used in court, or that suggestions were offered to patients during the course of hypnotic sessions that led to false ideas related to events from childhood. However, experts in the field of hypnosis, such as the psychiatrist Dr. David Spiegel of Stanford, are quick to point out that the hypnotic process has the potential to lead to suggestion, and that the technique must be used with both caution and an understanding of the potential limitations (1994).

These same experts also do not support the use of hypnosis in the court setting. The psychologist Dr. John Kihlstrom of Berkeley and others have shown that memory processes occur below the level of conscious awareness, and that these unconscious memories occur outside of our normal awareness (1987). The modern idea of unconscious memory processes based on experimental results from cognitive psychology is similar in many ways to the ideas of Sigmund Freud—that unconscious memory processes form the basis and motivation of much of human behavior. However, we now have more empirical evidence to support such ideas. In the psychiatric field of traumatic stress disorders, we also have clinical evidence for many trauma-related memories occurring outside of conscious awareness. These gaps in memory can generalize and include many aspects of normal, everyday experience, and are described in the DSM as "dissociative amnesia." Freud originally described dissociative amnesia as "psychogenic amnesia," and attributed it to a walling off of painful or unacceptable thoughts or memories. Many authors since Freud's time have conceived of dissociative amnesia as a protective mechanism against traumatic stress, although the evidence is more consistent with the idea that individuals who dissociate are more likely to have long-term psychopathology.

When applied in the proper way, hypnosis does have a potential utility in the treatment of stress-related psychiatric disorders. Memories that are not available to consciousness due to processes such as dissociative amnesia may be accessed through techniques such as hypnosis. David Spiegel has shown that sessions involving the use of hypnosis may lead to an improvement in PTSD symptoms (1994). When memories that were not previously fully available are brought into consciousness, they can be processed for the emotional and cognitive content and gradually integrated into the patient's normal storehouse of memories. This process must be performed with caution, because the reintroduction of traumatic memories into consciousness may be associated with a feeling of upset and an increase in psychiatric symptoms. Some authors have advocated for obtaining written informed consent from patients who are to undergo hypnosis, so that these patients can recognize the potential limitations and pitfalls.

Eye Movement Desensitization and Reprocessing (EMDR) Therapy

Another type of treatment that has received increasing usage is eye movement desensitization and reprocessing (EMDR) therapy. EMDR involves bilateral stimulation while traumatic memories and images are allowed to play through one's consciousness. The originator of EMDR, Francine Shapiro, suggests that the eye movements in conjunction with the replay of traumatic images lead to a change in brain function that has a positive effect on patients with PTSD. Several research studies have shown positive effects of treatment with EMDR (reviewed in Sutherland & Davidson, 1999). However, these studies are limited by the fact that it is very difficult to control for the effects of EMDR on patients. Typically in studies of treatment effects, whether it is a medication or psychotherapy treatment, we compare the treatment of choice to some other "control" condition that is very similar but does not have all of the beneficial components of the treatment itself. The reason why this is done is to assess whether patients are improving due to a placebo effect, (i.e., an improvement related to hope in the cure), or the positive relationship with the doctor, or other factors. We know from studies in PTSD that many medication treatments studied in an "open label" way (i.e., without any placebo control condition to compare to) were very positive, leading to unrealistic expectations about the potential benefit of that particular treatment. However, with more careful and controlled studies involving a placebo condition, it was found that the treatment offered no specific benefit. It also should be noted that we have no information about the effects of EMDR on brain function.

The use of a control treatment is relevant to evaluating the effects of EMDR in the treatment of PTSD. Many of the elements of EMDR include treatments that have been previously utilized in PTSD, such as hypnosis and exposure therapies. The movement of a finger, hand, light, or other object in front of the subject's eyes is a technique that has often been used in hypnosis. As mentioned above, hypnosis has been applied to the treatment of PTSD, although its use is controversial and needs to be applied with caution and under expert hands. Also, the exposure to images running through a patient's mind is similarly related to the techniques utilized by behavioral therapies involving flooding. In my opinion, we don't have enough data to evaluate some of the claims that EMDR is having specific neurological effects that lead to an improvement in symptoms. However, I believe that all treatments that have a positive effect are working through neurological changes; it is only a question of establishing exactly what those changes are.

Central to the effects of trauma on the individual are the effects on memory and the resultant collection of memories that unfold over the life of the trauma survivor. These memories include both traumatic and nontraumatic memories, and collectively make up the trauma survivor's view of who he or she is as a person. Thus, trauma victims may feel that they are defined as individuals who have experienced severe psychological trauma. Ironically, treatment of psychological trauma would involve removing traumatic memories that cause symptoms, or alternatively diminishing their forcefulness. Doing so, however, may eliminate an individual's sense of who he or she is as a person. Treatment must take this fact into account, and help the individual build a sense of self apart from the psychological trauma.

Similarities and Differences in Treatment Approaches for Different Traumas and Different Patients

Trauma affects a wide range of people and can take a variety of forms. It is important to consider the context in which it occurs when thinking about treatments for trauma. When I approach a patient with psychological trauma, I consider all aspects of the context in which his or her trauma occurred. The developmental age at which the trauma began, and whether it continued into the current time, is one important aspect to consider. Early childhood is a significant time for the development of identity. Stressful events or disruptions in the maternal–infant bond can lead to problems with the development of a stable and secure self-identity. For these reasons, trauma that occurs early in life leads to more problems with identity as the child matures. This can contribute to identity confusion in adulthood, and, at its most extreme, personality disorders and dissociative identity disorder. Patients with early trauma also develop multifactorial psychiatric disorders, which can include depression, somatic disorders, and alcohol and substance abuse. As I have discussed elsewhere in this book, I have referred to this range of psychiatric disorders as trauma-spectrum disorders. It is important to identify all of the disorders from which a trauma patient is suffering, and to identify treatments for all aspects of these disorders.

Patients without a history of childhood trauma who are traumatized in adulthood, whether it is from a car accident, natural disaster, or the events of September 11, look similar, regardless of the trauma type. These patients typically have a more "pure" presentation of PTSD symptoms, with increased arousal and vigilance, but fewer of the depression and personality symptoms that early trauma patients develop. These adult trauma patients respond well to cognitive behavioral therapies that concentrate on processing of the actual traumatic event, with a desensitization to aspects of the event that increase arousal and intrusive memories. With time, the traumatic event is processed both emotionally and cognitively, and negative cognitions and other unhelpful cognitive processes are corrected while the event is placed in a proper context and integrated into the patient's catalogue of life experiences. These patients can also benefit from medication treatment in conjunction with behavioral treatments, such as SSRI.

Early trauma patients, on the other hand, have a more complicated presentation and do not always benefit from traditional cognitive behavioral therapies. For these patients, the reintroduction of traumatic memories may be associated with an increase in negative affects and emotions or identify confusions and crises that the patient cannot control. In such situations, retrieving traumatic memories for attempted therapeutic benefit is not always helpful. Early trauma patients need long-term therapies aimed at psychological support, supplemented with medications where appropriate. Many early trauma patients who have disabling psychiatric symptoms are treated with multiple medications, which may include SSRI and a mood-stabilizing agent like valproic acid or carbamazepine.

Although patients who have their first traumatic event in adulthood look very similar in their presentation regardless of trauma type, there are some aspects of trauma that influence a patient's presentation. This is largely related to different trauma types leading to different types of fear reactions. For example, women who are victims of sexual assault will be more likely to have problems with sexual intimacy, related to fear responses associated to sexual activity. Conversely, motor vehicle accident victims may have fear responses related to approaching an automobile.

The response to trauma is also influenced by factors such as the meaning the event had for the individual, and social and cultural factors related to the event. A child who is sexually abused by a biological parent whom they trust and rely on for caregiving and support will have a different response than will someone who is victimized by a stranger. Dr. Jennifer Freyd (1997) of the University of Oregon has written about the negative consequences of being abused by a biological parent, and the profound feelings of betrayal and confusion that this act may engender. Also, patients who are not able to talk about their trauma in a supportive environment and social context may have additional suffering. This happened to many veterans of the Vietnam War who, upon returning to the United States, did not find their country to be supportive of the sacrifices they had made. Similarly, in

Muslim countries there is great shame for women to admit that they have been victims of sexual assault. Therefore, in countries such as Bosnia where there was systematic rape of the female population, many families do not want to talk about their traumatic experiences. Thus, the cultural and societal traditions surrounding traumatic events must be understood and respected in order for there to be a successful treatment intervention.

Rapid Interventions for Trauma Treatment

Appropriate treatment of trauma victims may require rapid interventions soon after the trauma. We know from animal studies that memories are not immediately engraved in the mind—it can take a month or more before they become indelible. For instance, animals that undergo lesions of the hippocampus within the first month after an aversive memory lose all recall of what had happened. During this time period, the memories continue to be susceptible to modification; this time period is known as *memory consolidation*. However, if you wait too long, a month or more, it is no longer possible to erase the negative memory simply by lesioning the hippocampus. At that point, the memory becomes engraved in the long-term memory storage areas in the cerebral cortex, the outermost part of the brain. After the memory has become engraved in long-term memory storage, it is indelible and no longer easily amenable to modification. This may represent the case of, for example, combat veterans with longstanding PTSD, for whom no amount of treatment is able to erase the traumatic memories of their combat experiences. That is why it is important to intervene early, before the traumatic memories become indelible.

Based on these animal studies, we have developed the hypothesis that early interventions will be beneficial before traumatic memories become firmly engraved in the mind. We know from animal studies that medications given before exposure to trauma—including Valium-type medications, antidepressants, opiates, and alcohol—can diminish or prevent the long-term behavioral effects of stressors. Clinical studies also suggest that these types of medications can prevent long-term psychopathology. For example, in a study of people exposed to a hotel fire, individuals who were intoxicated with alcohol at the time of the fire had a better psychiatric outcome than did those who were not. Also, there is some evidence from studies performed by Roger Pitman and colleagues at Harvard and the Manchester (NH) VA Medical Center that when the beta noradrenergic receptor blocker propanolol was given immediately after exposure to rape trauma the development of long-term psychiatric symptomatology in victims was reduced. This may mean that it is better to get treatment before you are even diagnosed with having a psychiatric disorder, which often requires having symptoms for at least a month.

A lot has been learned about the effects of stress on the brain and about the potential mechanisms by which treatments may lead to a reduction or prevention of symptoms. This increase in knowledge has highlighted the fact that psychological trauma has effects on the entire physical organism and all physical organ systems. As we have become more aware of this phenomenon, we have started to enlarge our perspective from being focused on psychiatry and psychology, and things of the mind, to considering the entire organism and considering the consequences of psychological trauma as a multiorgan disease. This viewpoint is dealt with in more detail in the next chapter.

CHAPTER NINE **The Whole-Body**
Approach to
Understanding
Traumatic Stress

Leaving John's River [Alaska] he dropped down to the Dolby River, and at or
near the mouth he stopped for lunch. His fire attracted two natives, one an
old medicine man and the other a native of about twenty-six years old. They
came to his camp, and although John [Bremner] had but a scant outfit, he fed
them. After they had eaten, John started to pack the grub box down to the
boat, leaving his rifle loaded in camp. When he got within a few feet of the
boat, the old medicine man told the young Indian to shoot John and they
would have his boat, gun and grub and no one would ever know what became
of the old man as the white men were few and the Indians were many in num-
ber. The young Indian did as he was told, through fear of the medicine man,
and shot poor old John twice but didn't kill him. Then the old medicine man
took the gun and shot him three more times before he was dead. They sank
his body in the river and went on their way with the boat and supplies.

In due time, when John didn't show up, Pete Johnson and John Minook
made another boat and dropped downriver to look for him. It was through
John Minook that the murder was discovered.

With John Minook as interpreter, the party of twenty-two men went up
the Koyukuk River to the camp where the two murderers were living. It was
some distance up the Dolby River and the exact location was not known. As
this was the first steamboat to navigate the Koyukuk the natives were very
much frightened before they realized what was happening. The only two to try
and get away were the murderers. They were captured and the Chief was told
that he too would be taken if he did not give up all the men who killed John
Bremner and that they were going to hang by the neck until they were dead.
He was also told that if the Indians killed another white man these same men
would come back and take him and his family and hang them too.

Upon reaching the mouth of the Koyukuk, where the two natives were to
be hanged, a dispute arose over the hanging as the young Indian, when asked

if the old man had shot John, had said no. The party did not realize that he was more afraid of the old medicine man than of death by hanging.

To settle the dispute a line was drawn by the spokesman of the party, who said. "All in favor of hanging both Indians step on this side of this line." Only seven of the twenty-two crossed the line. So the old man was turned loose and the party dispersed.

The young man was hanged on a cottonwood tree on the tipper end of the seven mile island at the mouth of the Koyukuk River. The old medicine man returned to the village on the Dolby River, and the relatives of the young Indian tried to kill the old man by cutting him up, but he recovered to make his way to the Yukon River, where he died two years later. The feud between the two Indian families lasted for three years and caused the death of six Indians.

—From *Sourdough Sagas,*
by H. Heller

Physical and Health Effects of Traumatic Stress

A unifying theme of this book is that stress has far-reaching effects on an individual's mind, brain, and body. It should be clear at this point that the same physiological systems involved in the stress response also have effects on other organ systems in the body. For example, cortisol, which is released during times of stress, has effects on mood, memory, and behavior; neurological effects on the brain; as well as effects on other physical systems such as the cardiovascular system, accelerating the process of atherosclerosis. The stress response is like a fire alarm that rings throughout the body. A flood of hormones and neurochemicals activate the fight-or-flight response and prepare the individual to cope with the life-threatening situation. However, as in any emergency, sometimes parts of the infrastructure become damaged in the rush to save the whole. With repeated episodes of stress, this damage can accumulate. The parts of the body that are most sensitive to the wear-and-tear effects of stress over time are (logically enough) those areas that are mobilized during the stress response (Sapolsky, 1996).

There are a number of bodily systems that could potentially play a role in the stress response. These systems include the immunologic, metabolic, cardiovascular, and neurological. We are only recently realizing the impact of stress on these multiple systems and what they mean for health.

Indeed, it is only recently that in the field of science we have begun to appreciate the far-reaching effects of stress on the entire body organism. From this perspective, it is clear that there has been a false dichotomy among mind, brain, and body. Previous generations of mental health scientists and practitioners often focused on psychology as an end in itself, without considering the possibility that psychological processes had a foundation in brain physiology. However, with advanced research it has become clear that, as stated above, the effects of stress on psychology are mediated through the neurological consequences of the stress response, and that the stress response has effects not only on neurological systems but also on a variety of other organ systems, including cardiovascular, metabolic, and immunologic. Therefore, it is artificial to consider the psychological consequences as entities in and of themselves, in isolation from the neurological and general physical effects.

The nature of the stress response is not focused on mental or even neurological processes specifically, but by its very nature has a broad and nonspecific effect on all aspects of the physical organism. The immediate response of the body to stress is critical in mobilizing the organism for survival. Consider the situation where you are attacked in a dark alley. Adrenaline (epinephrine) and the related norepinephrine are released throughout the body, acting like a rapid response fire alarm system. Adrenaline has a number of actions in the body, including stimulation of the heart to beat more rapidly and squeeze harder with each contraction, while norepinephrine acting in the brain helps to sharpen focus and stimulate memory. Blood pressure increases to stimulate blood flow and delivery of oxygen and glucose, necessary energy stores for the cells of the body to cope with the increased demand. There is a shifting of blood flow away from the gut (digestion of the pasta salad you had for lunch can wait) and toward the brain and the muscles of the arms and legs (you need to think fast and/or run hard to get away from the threat). The spleen increases the release of red blood cells, which allows the body to send more oxygen to the muscles. The liver converts glycogen to glucose, the type of sugar that can be immediately used. Breathing becomes heavy, so that extra oxygen can get to the lungs, and the pupils dilate for better vision. Release of endogenous opiates acts on the brain to dull our sense of pain, so that the pain of a physical injury incurred during an attack does not impair our ability to escape from the situation. More delayed stress responses include release of cortisol, which dampens the immune system (we are less likely to die immediately from an infection than from our attacker), and conversion of fat to glucose in the liver.

Although the body's stress response plays a critical role in short-term survival, this is often at the expense of long-term function. Elevated levels of cortisol can lead to hippocampal damage with associated deficits in memory, specifically the ability to learn new information (Sapolsky, 1996). Chronically elevated levels of cortisol may also affect mood, leading to depression and feelings of fatigue. Stress also impairs the immune system, which can lead to an increase in infections and possibly even increased rates of cancer. Chronic stress with decreased blood flow to the intestines can result in chronic ulcers. As reviewed in the beginning of this book, it seems paradoxical that the systems of the body designed to respond to stressors and save the body, can also have long-term detrimental effects on the very body they were supposed to protect. The answer may lie in the fact that surviving long enough to pass your genes into the next generation was the most important thing from the standpoint of evolution. Most of the negative consequences of stress involved disorders like heart disease, cancer, and memory problems, that are diseases of late life, not really relevant to primitive populations that had much shorter life expectancies than we do today.

A complex interplay between the stress response systems (cortisol and adrenaline) that mediate the body's response to threat underlie the harmful effects of stress on the individual (McEwen & Stellar, 1993; Seeman et al., 1997). These systems are all interrelated and regulate one another in mediating the response of the organism to stress. For instance, the adrenaline (norepinephrine) system activates the cortisol response, and vice versa—the cortisol system (through corticotrophin-releasing factor, or CRF) activates the adrenaline (norepinephrine) system. Both the cortisol and adrenaline systems have the ability to brake themselves. Cortisol released during stress (Seeman et al., 1995) acts directly on a broad array of physical functions, including blood pressure, heart rate, serum lipid levels, immune function, and plasma norepinephrine and epinephrine. Stress-related release of cortisol and other metabolic and endocrine stress-related changes may increase susceptibility to a number of physical disorders, including cardiovascular disease and diabetes (Brindley & Rolland, 1989). Work by the Yale neurologist Larry Brass, MD, showed that the stress of the WWII POW experience was associated with an increase in cerebrovascular disease. POWs had a 7.7-fold greater relative risk of developing stroke than did non-POW military controls (Brass & Page, 1996). This study suggested that stress has effects on the blood vessels in the brain that can increase the risk for diseases such as stroke.

Stress also has effects on the cardiovascular system that increases the risk for heart disease. Patients with depression (which is related to stress in many cases) and heart disease are about five times as likely to have a sudden death than are patients with heart disease without depression (Musselman et al., 1998; Rozanski et al., 1999). PTSD has also been associated with an increased risk for cardiovascular disease. There has been surprisingly little research on the direct link between stress and cardiovascular disease, but other psychosocial factors—such as stress, anxiety, personality, and education—have been connected to increased risk of heart disease (Berkman, Vaccarino, & Seeman, 1993; Krumholz et al., 1998; Mendes de Leon et al., 1998; reviewed in Musselman et al., 1998; Soufer et al., 1998; reviewed in Rozanski et al., 1999).

The effects of stress on physical health appear to be caused by a disruption of the balance between different organs of the body, or *homeostasis*. According to this model, stress results in long-term wear and tear, which is manifested in these parameters and is related to poor long-term function. Theresa Seeman, Bruce McEwen, and colleagues (1997) looked at a broad range of stress-sensitive physical parameters, related to endocrine, metabolic, neurological, cognitive, and cardiovascular systems. This group of physical health measures included memory function and cognition, cardiovascular parameters [blood pressure, weight–hip ratio, high-density lipoprotein cholesterol (HDL-C), low-density lipoprotein cholesterol (LDL-C)], factors related to long-term metabolism [glycosilated hemoglobin (HbA1c)—a measure of long-term plasma glucose levels—and plasma insulin levels], and stress hormones and transmitters [cortisol, norepinephrine, and epinephrine, and plasma dehydroepiandrosterone sulfate (DHEA-S)]. Using this data, an index of "allostatic load"—hypothesized to be related to the long-term effects of stress on physiology—was constructed. In a study of elderly individuals, the allostatic load index was associated with poorer long-term cognitive and physical function, as well as increased risk for cardiovascular disease.

Effects of Stress on Cardiovascular Disease

The heart in particular has long been felt to be vulnerable to the effects of stress (Musselman et al., 1998; Rozanski et al., 1999). Studies have shown that factors such as low socioeconomic status, lack of social support, lack of education, and psychological factors such as depression, anxiety, or personality increase one's risk of mortality from heart disease. The few studies that have looked specifically at stress have assessed minor stressors, such as work stress. Studies looking at "daily hassles" or other minor stressors may not be sensitive enough to detect the effects of stress on cardiovascular disease.

Studies in animals found direct evidence for the damaging effects of stress on blood vessels in the heart. Studies in monkeys using social stress (in which dominance hierarchies are changed over time) discerned a relationship between stress and accelerated cardiovascular disease. Monkeys undergoing stressors had increased activation of cortisol and norepinephrine systems, which led to the accelerated development of arteriosclerosis. Stressed monkeys had increased injury to the inner lining of the blood vessels in the heart, which led to greater clumping of platelets and blood clot formation, which increased the risk for heart attack (Kaplan et al., 1982).

Stress can also exert influences on cardiovascular disease through intervening psychiatric disorders such as anxiety and depression. Studies have shown a four-to-five-fold increase in risk for mortality in patients with depression following a cardiac event compared to similar patients without depression (Mendes de Leon et al., 1998). Stress has been closely linked with the onset of depression, and it is not known whether stress has a direct effect on cardiovascular disease in patients who also develop depression, or whether the effects are mediated directly through the depressive disorder. For example, there are several findings in depression that may influence cardiovascular function. Patients with depression have increased levels of cortisol and adrenaline, which can affect cardiovascular function in several ways, including increasing heart rate and blood pressure, damaging the inner surface or causing constriction of the blood vessels in the heart, increasing endothelial injury, or affecting the function of platelets that are involved in forming blood clots. Both stress and depression may also decrease the variability of the rhythm of the heart, which is known to be associated with an increased risk for sudden death (Carney et al., 1995; Fuller, 1992; Hordsten et al., 1999; Kleiger, Miller, Bigger, & Moss, 1987; Krittayaphong et al., 1997; Pagani et al., 1991).

Studies that directly examine the effects of stress on cardiovascular function in human subjects have been more limited. Some studies have shown a relationship between cardiovascular disease and job stress. An increase in stressors, such as divorce or loss of job, was seen in the six-month interval preceding a heart attack. Several factors—including stress, psychological health (depression and anxiety), social support, socioeconomic status, and behavioral factors like smoking and diet—probably work together to increase risk of cardiovascular disease. "Clusters" of psychosocial factors can contribute a risk for heart disease equal to traditional risk factors such as diabetes and high blood pressure.

In addition to there being a link between stress and a variety of physical disorders, there is new evidence that PTSD may increase the risk of physical disorders even more. This evidence suggests that PTSD, above and beyond the influence of stress per se, may increase the risk of several physical disorders, including heart disease, diabetes, ulcers, asthma, and possibly cancer. Treating PTSD may improve more than just the misery associated with living with this disorder; it may also lead to an improvement in physical health symptoms.

Breaking Down the False Dichotomy among Mind, Brain, and Body

The conclusion that can be drawn from this research is that up until now there has been a false dichotomy between physical and mental disease that is not helpful to treating patients with disease. The same processes stimulated by stress responses that may lead to depression and behavioral changes are mediated by stress responsive systems like cortisol and catecholamines that also have effects on physical health, such as heart disease and infection. An important theme of this book is that it is artificial to separate mind and brain, physical and mental, and that the effects of psychological trauma on the individual need to be considered in neurological terms. We need to think about the things an individual sees, hears, smells, and feels during a traumatic event; how this information travels through the system of perceptions and is modified by prior memories, emotions, and beliefs; how it is processed by the nervous system; and how it is ultimately translated into a neurological response and a new set of memories and cognitions. These events also have effects on cardiovascular, immunological, and metabolic function. This unified approach to disease also needs to take into account the spiritual beliefs and cultural contexts of the individual that may have the potential to promote or obstruct the path to recovery. Thinking about the effects of stress on the individual in a unified mental and physical way will benefit individuals and promote greater happiness and a sense of well being. This type of approach will also foster physical health and promote a more rapid recovery.

We need to start thinking about all aspects of an individual's health. As doctors, we have been trained to think in compartmentalized terms. If we are trained in cardiology (i.e., the treatment of heart disease), we think only in terms of the heart; or if we are neurologists, we think about the brain. Anything that has to do with behavior or the "messy" area of psychiatric disorders and mental health we tend to exclude as being "outside of our domain." However, the field of medicine is becoming increasingly cross-fertilized, so that the most competitive doctors are being cross-trained in very different disciplines, allowing them to bring a different perspective to their approach to medicine.

Thinking across disciplines will also be better for the health of our patients. Currently, patients will go to their neurologist for a headache, to their cardiologist for chest pain, and to their psychiatrist or social worker if they have family or marital problems or suffer from depression. However, the headaches and depression may be caused by the marital problems, so that the neurologist is treating a symptom without even considering other aspects that play a critical role in contributing to the headaches. Conversely, a psychiatrist or social worker may not appreciate that headaches are having an impact on the patient's family or marital relationships. Cardiologists may not realize that their patient's chest pain could be caused by psychological factors or stress. Not only does the doctor or clinician suffer from the lack of an integrated viewpoint of a patient's disease, the patient suffers even more. He or she is left ricocheting from one specialist to another, none of whom can really address the patient's needs in their entirety.

Both doctors and their patients will clearly benefit from a more holistic approach to the effects of psychological trauma on the individual. Doctors will benefit from a more advanced and comprehensive view of what is really troubling their patients, rather than treating a laundry list of symptoms. Patients will benefit from having a clinician who understands their needs and is ready to treat all aspects of what they are seeking help for. Both doctor and patient will feel less frustrated and more fulfilled in what they are doing. Medical treatments will benefit as a whole and, because less inefficient and unnecessary trips to specialists and emergency room visits will be utilized, there will be an overall reduction in costs to our society.

In order for a comprehensive approach to the individual patient to be effective, doctors must spend more time talking to their patients. Doctors need to understand how patients' psychological concerns are affecting their physical well being, and vice versa. They need to spend enough time to find out what events are happening in patients' lives, how events have affected them in past, their system of beliefs, viewpoints about both mental and physical health and disease, and the expectations they have about treatments for their complaints. It takes a great deal of time and effort for doctors to spend this amount of time with patients, and with the current system of insurance reimbursement doctors are typically not allotted more than 10 minutes to speak with each patient. This is obviously not enough time to get a full idea of all of the patients' concerns and take a holistic approach to their disorders. However, if we added up all of the little time segments that complicated trauma victims utilize with different medical specialists, psychiatrists, social workers, and other clinicians, we might be able to make a case to insurance companies that the current system actually costs more than a more unified approach would.

Not only do doctors need to spend more time talking to their patients, but patients also need to take responsibility for getting to know themselves. As the famous philosopher Socrates said, "Know thyself." This is an adage that applies to everyone: Know yourself, listen to the signals that your own body is sending you, get to know the relationship between what is happening in your life and the mental states you are experiencing as well as the physical changes you are going through. Be ready to communicate these observations in an honest way to your clinician. Be a scientist, make notes in an impartial and logical way, even if it is painful and not flattering to yourself.

A central theme of this book has been that the effects of stress are not solely psychological, but instead need to be thought of in a comprehensive way, as affecting neurological and other physical systems. This book has tried to present a unifying theory to explain the extensive range of symptoms that affect individuals exposed to traumatic stress. According to this theory, stress results in lasting neurological consequences as well as effects on physical and mental processes. Thinking in this way, we can begin to free ourselves from the constrictions of thinking only in terms of psychology and psychiatric disorders. We can start to consider traumatic stress as having an effect on all aspects of physical, mental, and spiritual health, which may be a more useful approach than traditional thinking about traumatic stress.

If the effects of traumatic stress are thought of as a unitary disorder, there are implications for how we view approaches to the effects of traumatic stress. Such a perspective takes us away from thinking in exclusive terms of psychiatry, cardiology, or neurology, and toward a more unitary approach in which all aspects of physical health must be considered. It also implies that doctors should be cross-trained in areas such as psychiatry and neurology, or psychiatry and cardiology, and that cardiologists should think about the effects of mental processes on heart function, while psychiatrists should consider the effects of heart disease on mental processes and behavior. This is a new framework in which cardiologists are expected to talk to psychiatrists and social workers, and vice versa.

It is this unitary vision of the health of the individual and how we can maintain and promote it that is where we should be moving toward in the 21st century. We no longer can afford to have restrictive ideas about disease that involve separations into the physical and the mental. One of the most important determinants of disease is the lasting consequences of traumatic stress. In this important area, we can begin to take a comprehensive approach to understanding the strange phenomenon that is the individual human being.

REFERENCES

Abercrombie, E. D., Keller, R. W., Jr., & Zigmond, M. J. (1988). Characterization of hippocampal norepinephrine release as measured by microdialysis perfusion: Pharmacological and behavioral studies. *Neuroscience, 27,* 897–904.

Acierno, R., Kilpatrick, D. G., & Resnick, H. S. (1999). Posttraumatic stress disorder in adults relative to criminal victimization: Prevalence, risk factors, and comorbidity. In P. A. Saigh & J. D. Bremner (Eds.), *Posttraumatic stress disorder: A comprehensive text* (pp. 44–68). Needham Heights, MA: Allyn & Bacon.

Anderson, M. C., Bjork, R. A., & Bjork, E. L. (1994). Remembering can cause forgetting: Retrieval dynamics in long-term memory. *Journal of Experimental Psychology: Learning, Memory, and Cognition, 20,* 1063–1087.

Anderson, M. C., & Spellman, B. A. (1995). On the status of inhibitory mechanisms in cognition: Memory retrieval as a model case. *Psychological Review, 102,* 68–100.

Andreasen, N. J. C. (1985). Posttraumatic Stress Disorder. In H. I. Kaplan & B. J. Sadock (Eds.), *Comprehensive textbook of psychiatry, vol. IV* (pp. 918–924). Baltimore: Williams & Wilkins.

Andreasen, N. C. (1995). Posttraumatic stress disorder: Psychology, biology, and the Manichean warfare between false dichotomies. *American Journal of Psychiatry, 152,* 963–965.

Arbel, I., Kadar, T., Silberman, M., & Levy, A. (1994). The effects of long-term corticosterone administration on hippocampal morphology and cognitive performance of middle-aged rats. *Brain Research, 657,* 227–235.

Aston-Jones, G., Chiang, C., & Alexinsky, T. (1991). Discharge of noradrenergic locus coeruleus neurons in behaving rats and monkeys suggests a role in vigilance. In C. D. Barnes & O. Pompeiano (Eds.), *Progress in Brain Research* (pp. 501–519). New York: Elsevier Science Publishers.

Berkman, L. F., Vaccarino, V., & Seeman, T. (1993). Gender differences in cardiovascular morbidity and mortality: The contribution of social networks and support. *Annals of Behavioral Medicine, 15,* 112–118.

Bernstein, D. P., Fink, L., Handelsman, L., Foote, J., Lovejoy, M., Wenzel, K., Sapareto, E., & Ruggiero, J. (1994). Initial reliability and validity of a new retrospective measure of child abuse and neglect. *American Journal of Psychiatry, 151,* 1132–1136.

Bernstein, E., & Putnam, T. (1986). Development, reliability, and validity of a dissociation scale. *Journal of Nervous and Mental Disease, 174,* 727–735.

Blake, D. D., Weathers, F. W., Nagy, L. M., Kaloupek, D. G., Gusman, F. D., & Charney, D. S. (1995). The development of a clinician-administered PTSD scale. *Journal of Traumatic Stress, 8,* 75–90.

Blanchard, E. B., Kolb, L. C., Prins, A., Gates, S., & McCoy, G. C. (1991). Changes in plasma norepinephrine to combat-related stimuli among Vietnam veterans with posttraumatic stress disorder. *Journal of Nervous and Mental Disease, 179,* 371–373.

Bourne, P. G, Rose, R. M., & Mason, J. W. (1967). Urinary 17-OCHS levels in combat: Data on seven helicopter ambulance medics in combat. *Archives of General Psychiatry, 19,* 104–110.

Bourne, P. G., Rose, R. M., & Mason, J. W. (1968). 17-OCHS levels in combat: Special Forces "A" Team under threat of attack. *Archives of General Psychiatry, 19,* 135–140.

Bouton, M. E., & Swartzentruber, D. (1991). Sources of relapse after extinction in Pavlovian and instrumental learning. *Clinical Psychology Reviews, 11,* 123–140.

Bower, G. H. (1981). Mood and memory. *American Psychologist, 36,* 129–148.

Brady, K., Pearlstein, T., Asnis, G. M., Baker, D., Rothbaum, B., Sikes, C. R., & Farfel, G. M. (2000). Efficacy and safety of sertraline treatment of posttraumatic stress disorder: A randomized controlled trial. *Journal of the American Medical Association, 283(14),* 1837–1844.

Brass, L., & Page, W. (1996). Stroke in former prisoners of war (POW). *Journal of Stroke and Cerebrovascular Disease, 6,* 72–78.

Bremner, J. D. (1998a). Traumatic memories lost and found: Can lost memories of abuse be found in the brain? In L. M. Williams & V. L. Banyard (Eds.), *Trauma and memory,* (pp. 217–228). New Delhi: Sage Publications.

Bremner, J. D. (1988b). *A history of the Bremner family.* Published privately.

Bremner, J. D. (1999a). Acute and chronic responses to stress: Where do we go from here? (Editorial) *American Journal of Psychiatry, 156,* 349–351.

Bremner, J. D. (1999b). Does stress damage the brain? *Biological Psychiatry, 45,* 797–805.

Bremner, J. D., & Brett, E. (1997). Trauma-related dissociative states and long-term psychopathology in posttraumatic stress disorder. *Journal of Traumatic Stress, 10,* 37–50.

Bremner, J. D., Innis, R. B., Ng, C. K., Staib, L., Duncan, J., Bronen, R., Zubal, G., Rich, D., Krystal, J. H., Dey, H., Soufer, R., & Charney, D. S. (1997). PET measurement of central metabolic correlates of yohimbine administration in posttraumatic stress disorder. *Archives of General Psychiatry, 54,* 146–156.

Bremner, J. D., Innis, R. B., Southwick, S. M., Staib, L. H., Zoghbi, S., & Charney, D. S. (2000). Decreased benzodiazepine receptor binding in frontal cortex in combat-related posttraumatic stress disorder. *American Journal of Psychiatry, 157,* 1120–1126.

Bremner, J. D., Krystal, J. H., Charney, D. S., & Southwick, S. M. (1996). Neural mechanisms in dissociative amnesia for childhood abuse: Relevance to the current controversy surrounding the "False Memory Syndrome." *American Journal of Psychiatry, 153,* 71–82.

Bremner, J. D., Krystal, J. H., Putnam, F., Marmar, C., Southwick, S. M., Lubin, H., Charney, D. S., & Mazure, C. M. (1998). Measurement of dissociative states with the Clinician Administered Dissociative States Scale (CADSS). *Journal of Traumatic Stress, 11,* 125–136.

Bremner, J. D., Krystal, J. H., Southwick, S. M., & Charney, D. S. (1996a). Noradrenergic mechanisms in stress and anxiety: I. Preclinical studies. *Synapse, 23,* 28–38.

Bremner, J. D., Krystal, J. H., Southwick, S. M., & Charney, D. S. (1996b). Noradrenergic mechanisms in stress and anxiety: II. Clinical studies. *Synapse, 23,* 39–51.

Bremner, J. D., Licinio, J., Darnell, A., Krystal, J. H., Nemeroff, C. B., Owens, M., & Charney, D. S. (1997). Elevated CSF corticotropin-releasing factor concentrations in posttraumatic stress disorder. *American Journal of Psychiatry, 154,* 624–629.

Bremner, J. D., & Marmar, C. (Eds.). (1998). *Trauma, memory and dissociation.* Washington, DC: APA Press.

Bremner, J. D., Narayan, M., Anderson, E. R., Staib, L. H., Miller, H., & Charney, D. S. (2000). Hippocampal volume reduction in major depression. *American Journal of Psychiatry, 157,* 115–117.

Bremner, J. D., Narayan, M., Staib, L. H., Southwick, S. M., McGlashan, T., & Charney, D. S. (1999). Neural correlates of memories of childhood sexual abuse in women with and without posttraumatic stress disorder. *American Journal of Psychiatry, 156,* 1787–1795.

Bremner, J. D., Randall, P. R., Capelli, S., Scott, T., McCarthy, G., & Charney, D. S. (1995). Deficits in short-term memory in adult survivors of childhood abuse. *Psychiatry Research, 59,* 97–107.

Bremner, J. D., Randall, P., Scott, T. M., Bronen, R. A., Seibyl, J. P., Southwick, S. M., Delaney, R. C., McCarthy, G., Charney, D. S., & Innis, R. B. (1995). MRI-based measurement of hippocampal volume in posttraumatic stress disorder. *American Journal of Psychiatry, 152,* 973–981.

Bremner, J. D., Randall, P., Vermetten, E., Staib, L., Bronen, R. A., Capelli, S., Mazure, C. M., McCarthy, G., Innis, R. B., & Charney, D. S. (1997). MRI-based measurement of hippocampal volume in posttraumatic stress disorder related to childhood physical and sexual abuse: A preliminary report. *Biological Psychiatry, 41,* 23–32.

Bremner, J. D., Scott, T. M., Delaney, R. C., Southwick, S. M., Mason, J. W., Johnson, D. R., Innis, R. B., McCarthy, G., & Charney, D. S. (1993). Deficits in short-term memory in post-traumatic stress disorder. *American Journal of Psychiatry, 150,* 1015–1019.

Bremner, J. D., Shobe, K. K., & Kihlstrom, J. F. (2000). False memories in women with self-reported childhood sexual abuse: An empirical study. *Psychological Sciences, 11,* 333–337.

Bremner, J. D., Southwick, S. M., Brett, E., Fontana, A., Rosenheck, R., & Charney, D. S. (1992). Dissociation and posttraumatic stress disorder in Vietnam combat veterans. *American Journal of Psychiatry, 149,* 328–333.

Bremner, J. D., Southwick, S. M., & Charney, D. S. (1994). Etiologic factors in the development of posttraumatic stress disorder. In C. M. Mazure (Ed.), *Does stress cause psychiatric disease?* (pp. 149–186). Washington, DC: American Psychiatric Press.

Bremner, J. D., Southwick, S. M., & Charney, D. S. (1999). The neurobiology of posttraumatic stress disorder: An integration of animal and human research. In P. A. Saigh & J. D. Bremner (Eds.), *Posttraumatic stress disorder: A comprehensive text* (pp. 103–143). Needham Heights, MA: Allyn & Bacon.

Bremner, J. D., Southwick, S. M., Darnell, A., & Charney, D. S. (1996). Chronic PTSD in Vietnam combat veterans: Course of illness and substance abuse. *American Journal of Psychiatry, 153,* 369–375.

Bremner, J. D., Southwick, S. M., Johnson, D. R., Yehuda, R., & Charney, D. S. (1993). Childhood physical abuse in combat-related posttraumatic stress disorder. *American Journal of Psychiatry, 150,* 235–239.

Bremner, J. D., Staib, L., Kaloupek, D., Southwick, S. M., Soufer, R., & Charney, D. S. (1999). Neural correlates of exposure to traumatic pictures and sound in Vietnam combat veterans with and without posttraumatic stress disorder (PTSD): A positron emission tomography study. *Biological Psychiatry, 45,* 806–816.

Bremner, J. D., Steinberg, M., Southwick, S. M., Johnson, D. R., & Charney, D. S. (1993). Use of the Structured Clinical Interview for DSMIV-Dissociative Disorders for systematic assessment of dissociative symptoms in posttraumatic stress disorder. *American Journal of Psychiatry, 150,* 1011–1014.

Bremner, J. D., Vermetten, E., & Mazure, C. M. (2000). Development and preliminary psychometric properties of an instrument for the measurement of childhood trauma: The Early Trauma Inventory. *Depression and Anxiety, 12,* 1–12.

Breslau, N., Davis, G. C., & Andreski, P. (1991). Traumatic events and posttraumatic stress disorder in an urban population of young adults. *Archives of General Psychiatry, 48,* 216–222.

Breuer, J., & Freud, S. (1955). Studies on hysteria (1893–1895) In J. Strachey (Ed.), *The standard edition of the complete psychological works of Sigmund Freud, Vol. 2* (Trans. J. Strachey; pp 1–319). London: Hogarth Press.

Brewin, C. R. (1996). Scientific status of recovered memories. *British Journal of Psychiatry, 169,* 131–134.

Brewin, C. R., Andrews, B., Rose, S., & Kirk, M. (1999). Acute stress disorder and posttraumatic stress disorder in victims of violent crime. *American Journal of Psychiatry, 156,* 360–366.

Brewin, C. R., Dalgleish, T., & Joseph, S. (1996). A dual representation theory of posttraumatic stress disorder. *Psychology Reviews, 103,* 670–686.

Brindley, D., & Rolland, Y. (1989). Possible connections between stress, diabetes, obesity, hypertension and altered lipoprotein metabolism that may result in atherosclerosis. *Clinical Science, 77,* 453–461.

Brown, R., & Kulik, J. (1977). Flashbulb memories. *Cognition, 5,* 73–99.

Cahill, L., Prins, B., Weber, M., & McGaugh, J. L. (1994). Alpha-adrenergic activation and memory for emotional events. *Nature, 371,* 702–703.

Cameron, H. A., McEwen, B. S., & Gould, E. (1995). Regulation of adult neurogenesis by excitatory input and NMDA receptor activation in the dentate gyrus. *Journal of Neuroscience, 15,* 4687–4692.

Cannon, W. B. (1927). The James-Lange theory of emotions: A critical reappraisal and an alternative theory. *American Journal of Psychology, 39,* 106–124.

Carmichael, S. T., & Price, J. L. (1994). Architectonic subdivision of the orbital and medial prefrontal cortex in the macaque monkey. *Journal of Comparative Neurology, 346,* 366–402.

Carmichael, S. T., & Price, J. L. (1995). Limbic connections of the orbital and medial prefrontal cortex in macaque monkeys. *Journal of Comparative Neurology, 363,* 615–641.

Carney, R., Saunders, R., Freedland, K., Stein, P., Rich, M., & Jaffe, A. (1995). Association of depression with reduced heart rate variability in coronary artery disease. *American Journal of Cardiology, 76,* 562–564.

Chalmers, D. T., Kwak, S. P., Mansour, A., & Watson, S. J. (1993). Corticosteroids regulate brain hippocampal 5HT-1A receptor mRNA expression. *Journal of Neuroscience, 13,* 914–923.

Chapman, W. P., Schroeder, H. R., Guyer, G., Brazier, M. A. B., Fager, C., Poppen, J. L., Solomon, H. C., & Yakolev, P. I. (1954). Physiological evidence concerning the importance of the amygdaloid nuclear region in the integration of circulating functions and emotion in man. *Science, 129,* 949–950.

Charney, D. S., Deutch, A. Y., Krystal, J. H., Southwick, S. M., & Davis, M. (1993). Psychobiologic mechanisms of posttraumatic stress disorder. *Archives of General Psychiatry, 50*(4), 295–305.

Christianson, S. A., Loftus, E. F., Hoffman, H., & Loftus, G. R. (1991). Eye fixation and memory for emotional events. *Journal of Experimental Psychology: Learning, Memory and Cognition, 17,* 693–701.

Clancy, S. A., Schacter, D. L., McNally, R. J., & Pitman, R. K. (2000). False recognition in women reporting recovered memories of sexual abuse. *Psychological Sciences, 11,* 26–31.

Coplan, J. D., Andrews, M. W., Rosenblum, L. A., Owens, M. J., Friedman, S., Gorman, J. M., & Nemeroff, C. B. (1996). Persistent elevations of cerebrospinal fluid concentrations of corticotropin-releasing factor in adult nonhuman primates exposed to early-life stressors: Implications for the pathophysiology of mood and anxiety disorders. *Proceedings of the National Academy of Sciences, 93,* 1619–1623.

DaCosta, J. M. (1871). On irritable heart: A clinical study of a form of functional cardiac disorder and its consequences. *American Journal of Medical Science, 161,* 17–52.

Damasio, H., Grabowski, T., Frank, R., Galaburda, A. M., & Damasio, A. R. (1994). The return of Phineas Gage: Clues about the brain from the skull of a famous patient. *Science, 264,* 1102–1105.

Davidson, J., Kudler, H., Smith, R., Mahorney, S. L., Lipper, S., Hammett, E., Saunders, W. B., & Cavenar, J. O. (1990). Treatment of posttraumatic stress disorder with amitriptyline and placebo. *Archives of General Psychiatry, 47*(3), 259–266.

Davidson, J., Smith, R., & Kudler, H. (1989). Familial psychiatric illness in chronic posttraumatic stress disorder. *Comprehensive Psychiatry, 30,* 339–345.

Davis, M. (1992). The role of the amygdala in fear and anxiety. *Annual Reviews of Neuroscience, 15,* 353–375.

DeBellis, M. D., Baum, A. S., Birmaher, B., Keshavan, M. S., Eccard, C. H., Boring, A. M., Jenkins, F. J., & Ryan, N. D. (1999). A.E. Bennett Research Award: Developmental traumatology: Part I: Biological stress systems. *Biological Psychiatry, 45,* 1259–1270.

DeBellis, M. D., Keshavan, M. S., Clark, D. B., et al. (1999). A. E. Bennett Research Award: Developmental traumatology: Part II. Brain development. *Biological Psychiatry, 45,* 1271–1284.

Devinsky, O., Morrell, M. J., & Vogt, B. A. (1995). Contributions of anterior cingulate to behavior. *Brain, 118,* 279–306.

De Wied, D., & Croiset, G. (1991). Stress modulation of learning and memory processes. *Methods and Achievements in Experimental Pathology, 15,* 167–199.

Diamond, D. M., Branch, B. J., Fleshner, M., & Rose, G. M. (1995). Effects of dehydroepiandosterone and stress on hippocampal electrophysiological plasticity. *Annals of the New York Academy of Sciences, 774,* 304–307.

Diamond, D. M., Fleshner, M., Ingersoll, N., & Rose, G. M. (1996). Psychological stress impairs spatial working memory: Relevance to electrophysiological studies of hippocampal function. *Behavioral Neurosciences, 110,* 661–672.

Duman, R. S., Heninger, G. R., & Nestler, E. J. (1997). A molecular and cellular theory of depression. *Archives of General Psychiatry, 54,* 597–606.

Eriksson, P. S., Perfilieva, E., Bjork-Eriksson, T., Alborn, A.-M., Nordborg, C., Peterson, D. A., & Gage, F. H. (1998). Neurogenesis in the adult human hippocampus. *Nature Medicine, 4,* 1313–1317.

Fichtner, C. G., O'Connor, F. L., Yeoh, H. C., Arora, R. C., & Crayton, J. W. (1995). Hypodensity of platelet serotonin uptake sites in posttraumatic stress disorder: Associated clinical features. *Life Sciences, 57,* 37–44.

Figley, C. (Ed.). (1978). *Stress disorders among Vietnam veterans.* New York: Brunner/Mazel.

Finkelhor, D. (Ed.). (1986). *A sourcebook on child sexual abuse.* Newbury Park, CA: Sage Publications.

Fivush, R., Haden, C., & Adam, S. (1995). Structure and coherence of preschoolers' personal narratives over time: Implications for childhood amnesia. *Journal of Experimental Child Psychology, 60,* 32–56.

Foa, E. B., Davidson, J. R. T., Frances, A., Culpepper, L., Ross, R., & Ross, D. (Eds.). (1999). The expert consensus guideline series: Treatment of posttraumatic stress disorder. *Journal of Clinical Psychiatry, 60*[Suppl. 16], 4–76.

Frank, J. B., Kosten, T. R., Giller, E. L., & Dan, E. (1988). A randomized clinical trial of phenelzine and imipramine for posttraumatic stress disorder. *American Journal of Psychiatry, 145,* 1289–1291.

Freud, S. (1896/1962). The etiology of hysteria. In J. Strachey (Ed.), *The standard edition of the complete psychological works of Sigmund Freud, Vol. 3* (Trans. J. Strachey; pp. 189–221). London: Hogarth Press.

Freyd, J. J. (1997). *Betrayal trauma: The logic of forgetting childhood abuse.* Cambridge, MA: Harvard University Press.

Freyd, J. J., & Gleaves, D. H. (1996). "Remembering" words not presented in lists: Relevance to the current recovered memory/false memory controversy. *Journal of Experimental Psychology: Learning, Memory, and Cognition, 22,* 811–813.

Friedman, M. J., Charney, D. S., & Deutch, A. Y. (Eds.). (1995). *Neurobiological and clinical consequences of stress: From normal adaptation to PTSD.* New York: Raven Press.

Fuller, B. F. (1992). The effects of stress-anxiety and coping styles on heart rate variability. *International Journal of Psychophysiology, 12,* 81–86.

Gabriel, R. A. (1987). *No more heroes: Madness and psychiatry in war.* New York: Hill & Wang.

Gage, F. H. (1998). Cell therapy. *Nature, 392,* 18–24.

Gold, P. E., & van Buskirk, R. (1975). Facilitation of time-dependent memory processes with posttrial epinephrine injections. *Behavioral Biology, 13,* 145–153.

Goldberg, J., True, W. R., Eisen, S. A., & Henderson, W. G. (1990). A twin study of the effects of the Vietnam war on posttraumatic stress disorder. *Journal of the American Medical Association, 263,* 1227–1232.

Gould, E., Cameron, H. A., Daniels, D. C., Woolley, C. S., & McEwen, B. S. (1992). Adrenal hormones suppress cell division in the adult rat dentate gyrus. *Journal of Neuroscience, 12,* 3642–3650.

Gould, E., McEwen, B. S., Tanapat, P., Galea, L. A. M., & Fuchs, E. (1997). Neurogenesis in the dentate gyrus of the adult tree shrew is regulated by psychosocial stress and NMDA receptor activation. *Journal of Neuroscience, 17,* 2492–2498.

Gould, E., Tanapat, P., McEwen, B. S., Flugge, G., & Fuchs, E. (1998). Proliferation of granule cell precursors in the dentate gyrus of adult monkeys is diminished by stress. *Proceedings of the National Academy of Sciences USA, 95,* 3168–3171.

Grillon, C., Ameli, R. Woods, S. W., Merikangas, K., & Davis, M. (1991). Fear-potentiated startle in humans: Effects of anticipatory anxiety on the acoustic blink reflex. *Psychophysiology, 28,* 588–595.

Grinker, R. R., & Spiegel, J. P. (1945). *Men under stress.* Philadelphia: Blakiston.

Guerra, S., & Dibrell, W. H. (1995). Studies of adrenal function in combat and wounded soldiers. *Annals of Surgery, 141,* 314–320.

Gunne, L. M., & Reis, D. J. (1963). Changes in brain catecholamines associated with electrical stimulation of amygdaloid nucleus. *Life Sciences, 11,* 804–809.

Gurvits, T. G., Shenton, M. R., Hokama, H., Ohta, H., Lasko, N. B., Gilberson, M. W., Orr, S. P., Kikinis, R., Lolesz, F. A., McCarley, R. W., & Pitman, R. K. (1996). Magnetic resonance imaging study of hippocampal volume in chronic combat-related posttraumatic stress disorder. *Biological Psychiatry, 40,* 192–199.

Hamner, M. B., Lorberbaum, J. P., & George, M. S. (1999). Potential role of the anterior cingulate cortex in PTSD: review and hypothesis. *Depression and Anxiety, 9,* 1–14.

Heller, H. (1972). *Sourdough Sagas.* New York: Ballantine.

Herman, J. P., Schafer, M. K. H., Young, E. A., Thompson, R., Douglass, J., Akil, H., & Watson, S. J. (1984). Evidence for hippocampal regulation of neuroendocrine neurons of the hypothalamus-pituitary-adrenocortical axis. *Neuroscience, 9,* 3072–3082.

Hilton, S. M., & Zbrozyna, A. W. (1963). Amygdaloid region for defense reactions and it efferent pathway to the brain stem. *Journal of Physiology, 165,* 160–173.

Hitchcock, J. M., & Davis, M. (1986). Lesions of the amygdala, but not of the cerebellum or red nucleus, block conditioned fear as measured with the potentiated startle paradigm. *Behavioral Neurosciences, 100,* 11–22.

Hitchcock, J. M., Sananes, C. B., & Davis, M. (1989). Sensitization of the startle reflex by footshock: Blockade by lesions of the central nucleus of the amygdala or its efferent pathway to the brainstem. *Behavioral Neurosciences, 103,* 509–518.

Hordsten, M., Ericson, M., Perski, A, Wamala, S., Schenk-Gustafsson, K., & Orth-Gomer, K. (1999). Psychosocial factors and heart rate variability in healthy women. *Psychosomatic Medicine, 61,* 49–57.

Horowitz, M. D. (1976). *Stress response syndromes.* Northvale, NJ: Jason Aronson.

Hyman, I. E., Husband, T. H., & Billings, F. J. (1995). False memories of childhood experiences. *Applied Cognitive Psychology, 9,* 181–197.

Jacobson, L., & Sapolsky, R. (1991). The role of the hippocampus in feedback regulation of the hypothalamic-pituitary-adrenocortical axis. *Endocrinology Reviews, 12,* 118–134.

Kaplan, J. R., Manuck, S. B., Adams, M. R., Weingand, K. W., & Clarkson, T. B. (1987). Inhibition of coronary atherosclerosis by propanolol in behaviorally predisposed monkeys fed an atherogenic diet. *Circulation, 76,* 1365–1372.

Kaplan, J. R., Manuck, S. B., Clarkson, T. B., Lusso, F. M., & Taub, D. M. (1982). Social status, environment, and atherosclerosis in cynomolgus monkeys. *Arteriosclerosis, 2,* 359–368.

Keane, T. M., Caddell, J. M., & Taylor, K. L. (1988). Mississippi scale for combat-related post-traumatic stress disorder: Three studies in reliability and validity. *Journal of Consulting & Clinical Psychology, 56,* 85–90.

Keenan, P. A., Jacobson, M. W., Soleyman, R. M., & Newcomer, J. W. (1995). Commonly used therapeutic doses of glucocorticoids impair explicit memory. *Annals of the New York Academy of Sciences, 761,* 400–402.

Kempermann, G., Kuhn, H. G., & Gage, F. H. (1997). More hippocampal neurons in adult mice living in an enriched environment. *Nature, 386,* 493–495.

Kempermann, G., Kuhn, H. G., & Gage, F. H. (1998). Experience-induced neurogenesis in the senescent dentate gyrus. *Journal of Neuroscience, 18,* 3206–3212.

Kessler, R. C., Sonnega, A., Bromet, E., Hughes, M., & Nelson, C. B. (1995). Posttraumatic stress disorder in the national comorbidity survey. *Archives of General Psychiatry, 52,* 1048–1060.

Kihlstrom, J. (1987). The cognitive unconscious. *Science, 237,* 1445–1451.

Kihlstrom, J. F. (1995). The trauma-memory argument. *Consciousness and Cognition, 4,* 63–67.

Kirschbaum, C., Wolf, O. T., May, M., Wippich, W., & Hellhammer, D. H. (1996). Stress- and treatment-induced elevations of cortisol levels associated with impaired declarative memory in healthy adults. *Life Sciences, 58,* 1475–1483.

Kleiger, R. E., Miller, J. P., Bigger, J. T., & Moss, A. J. (1987). The Multicenter Post-Infarction Research Group. Decreased heart rate variability and its association with increased mortality after acute myocardial infarction. *American Journal of Cardiology, 59,* 256–262.

Kluft, R. P. (1984). Treatment of multiple personality disorder: A study of 33 cases. *Psychiatric Clinics of North America, 7,* 9–29.

Kluft, R. P. (Ed.). (1990). *Childhood antecedents of multiple personality disorder.* Washington, DC: American Psychiatric Press.

Kluver, H., & Bucy, P. C. (1937). "Psychic blindness" and other symptoms following bilateral temporal lobectomy in rhesus monkeys. *American Journal of Physiology, 119,* 352–353.

Kluver, H., & Bucy, P. C. (1939). Preliminary analysis of functions of the temporal lobes in monkeys. *Archives of Neurology and Psychiatry, 42,* 979–1000.

Koopman, C., Classen, C., & Spiegel, D. (1994). Predictors of posttraumatic stress symptoms among survivors of the Oakland/Berkeley, Calif., firestorm. *American Journal of Psychiatry, 151,* 888–894.

Koss, M. P., Figueredo, A. J., Bell, I., Tharan, M., & Tromp, S. (1996). Traumatic memory characteristics: A cross-validated mediational model of response to rape among employed women. *Journal of Abnormal Psychology, 105,* 421–432.

Kraepelin, E. (1896/1985). *Psychiatrie Vol. 5: Auflage* (Transl. Jablensky). Leipzig: Barth.

Kraepelin, E. (1919/1971). *Dementia praecox and paraphrenia.* Huntington, NY: Krieger.

Krittayaphong, R., Cascio, W., Light, K., Sheffield, D., Golden, R., Finkel, J., Glekas, G., Koch, G., & Sheps, D. (1997). Heart rate variability in patients with coronary artery disease: differences in patients with higher and lower depression scores. *Psychosomatic Medicine, 59,* 231–235.

Krumholz, H. M., Butler, J., Miller, J., Vaccarino, V., Williams, C. S., Mendes de Leon, C. F., Seeman, T. E., Kasl, S. V., & Berkman, L. F. (1998). Prognostic importance of emotional support for elderly patients hospitalized with heart failure. *Circulation, 97,* 958–964.

Krystal, J. H., Karper, L. P., Seibyl, J. P., Freeman, G. K., Delaney, R., Bremner, J. D., Heninger, G. R., Bowers, M. B., & Charney, D. S. (1994). Subanesthetic effects of the non-competitive NMDA antagonist, ketamine, in humans: Psychotomimetic, perceptual, cognitive, and neuroendocrine responses. *Archives of General Psychiatry, 51,* 199–214.

Kuhn, H. G., Dickinson-Anson, H., & Gage, F. H. (1996). Neurogenesis in the dentate gyrus of the adult rat: Age-related decrease of neuronal progenitor proliferation. *Journal of Neuroscience, 16,* 2027–2033.

Kulka, R. A., Schlenger, W. E., Fairbank, J. A., Hough, R. L., Jordan, B. K., Marmar, C. R., & Weiss, D. S. (1990). *Trauma and the Vietnam war generation: Report of findings from the national Vietnam veterans readjustment study.* New York: Brunner/Mazel.

Ladd, C. O., Owens, M. J., & Nemeroff, C. B. (1996). Persistent changes in CRF neuronal systems produced by maternal separation. *Endocrinology, 137,* 1212–1218.

LeDoux, J. E. (1993). Emotional memory systems in the brain. *Behavioral and Brain Research, 58,* 69–79.

Lemieux, A. M., & Coe, C. L. (1995). Abuse-related posttraumatic stress disorder: Evidence for chronic neuroendocrine activation in women. *Psychosomatic Medicine, 57,* 105–115.

Lencz, T., McCarthy, G., Bronen, R. A., Scott, T. M., Inserni, J. A., Sass, K. J., Novelly, R. A., Kim, J. H., Spencer, D. D. (1992). Quantitative magnetic resonance imaging studies in temporal lobe epilepsy: Relationship to neuropathology and neuropsychological function. *Annals of Neurology, 31,* 629–637.

Leverenz, J. B., Wilkinson, C. W., Wamble, M., Corbin, S., Grabber, J. E., Raskind, M. A., & Peskind, E. R. (1999). Effect of chronic high-dose exogenous cortisol on hippocampal neuronal number in aged non-human primate. *Journal of Neuroscience, 19*, 2356–2361.

Levi, P. (1988). *Collected Poems*. London: Faber & Faber.

Levine, S. (1962). Plasma-free corticosteroid response to electric shock in rats stimulated in infancy. *Science, 135*, 795–596.

Levine, S., Weiner, S. G., & Coe, C. L. (1993). Temporal and social factors influencing behavioral and hormonal responses to separation in mother and infant squirrel monkeys. *Psychoneuroendocrinology, 4*, 297–306.

Lewis, C. D. (Ed.). (1963). *The Collected Poems of Wilfred Owen*. New York: New Directions Publishing.

Lewis, D. O. (1998). *Guilty by reason of insanity: A psychiatrist explores the minds of killers*. New York: Fawcett Columbine.

Lewis, D. O., & Putnam, F. W. (Eds.). (1996). *Dissociative identity disorder/multiple personality disorder*. In D. O. Lewis & F. W. Putnam (Eds.), *Child and adolescent psychiatric clinics of North America*. Philadelphia: Saunders.

Liang, K. C., Juler, R. G., & McGaugh, J. L. (1986). Modulating effects of posttraining epinephrine on memory: involvement of the amygdala noradrenergic system. *Brain Research, 368*, 125–133.

Liang, K. C., McGaugh, J. L., & Yao, H. Y. (1990). Involvement of amygdala pathways in the influence of post-training intra-amygdala norepinephrine and peripheral epinephrine on memory storage. *Brain Research, 508*, 225–233.

Lindsey, D. S., & Read, J. D. (1994). Psychotherapy and memories of childhood sexual abuse: A cognitive perspective. *Applied Cognitive Psychology, 8*, 281–338.

Liu, D., Diorio, J., Tannenbaum, B., Caldji, C., Rancis, D., Freedman, A., Sharma, S., Pearson, D., Plotsky, P. M., & Meaney, M. J. (1997). Maternal care, hippocampal glucocorticoid receptors, and hypothalamic-pituitary-adrenal responses to stress. *Science, 277*, 1659–1662.

Loewenstein, R. J. (1995). Psychogenic amnesia and psychogenic fugue: A comprehensive review. In A. Tasmann & S. M. Goldfinger (Eds.), *American Psychiatric Press review of psychiatry* (pp. 189–221). Washington, DC: American Psychiatric Press.

Loftus, E. F. (1993). The reality of repressed memories. *American Psychologist, 48*, 518–537.

Loftus, E. F., Garry, M., & Feldman, J. (1994) Forgetting sexual trauma: What does it mean when 38% forget? *Journal of Consulting and Clinical Psychology, 62,* 1177–1181.

Loftus, E. F., & Loftus, G. R. (1980). On the permanence of stored information in the human brain. *American Psychologist, 35,* 409–420.

Loftus, E. F., Miller, D. B., & Burns, H. J. (1978). Semantic integration of verbal information into a visual memory. *Journal of Experimental Psychology: Human Learning and Memory, 4,* 19–31.

Luine, V., Villages, M., Martinex, C., & McEwen, B. S. (1994). Repeated stress causes reversible impairments of spatial memory performance. *Brain Research, 639,* 167–170.

MacLean, P. D. (1949). Psychosomatic disease and the visceral brain. Recent developments bearing on the Papez Theory of Emotion. *Psychosomatic Medicine, 11,* 338–353.

Madison, D. V., & Nicoll, R. A. (1982). Noradrenaline blocks accommodation of pyramidal cell discharge in the hippocampus. *Nature, 299,* 636–638.

Magarinos, A. M., Verdugo, J. M., & McEwen, B. S. (1997). Chronic stress alters synaptic terminal structure in hippocampus. *Proceedings of the National Academy of Sciences, 94,* 14002–14008.

Marmar, C. R., Weiss, D. S., Schlenger, D. S., Fairbank, J. A., Jordan, B. K., Kulka, R. A., & Hough, R. L. (1994). Peritraumatic dissociation and posttraumatic stress in male Vietnam theater veterans. *American Journal of Psychiatry, 151,* 902–907.

Mason, J. W., Giller, E. L., Kosten, T. R., & Harkness, L. (1988). Elevation of urinary norepinephrine/cortisol ratio in posttraumatic stress disorder. *Journal of Nervous and Mental Disease, 176,* 498–502.

Mason, J. W., Giller, E. L., Kosten, T. R., Ostroff, R. B., & Podd, L. (1986). Urinary free cortisol levels in post-traumatic stress disorder patients. *Journal of Nervous and Mental Disease, 174,* 145–149.

McAllister, W. R., & McAllister, D. E. (1988). Reconditioning of extinguished fear after a one-year delay. *Bulletin of the Psychonomic Society, 26,* 463–466.

McCauley, J., Kern, D. E., Kolodner, K., Dill, L., Schroeder, A. F., DeChant, H. K., Ryden, J., Derogatis, L. R., & Bass, E. G. (1997). Clinical characteristics of women with a history of childhood abuse: Unhealed wounds. *Journal of the American Medical Association, 277,* 1362–1368.

McEwen, B. S., Angulo, J., Cameron, H., Chao, H. M., Daniels, D., Gannon, M. N., Gould, E., Mendelson, S., Sakai, R., Spencer, R., & Woolley, C. (1992). Paradoxical effects of adrenal steroids on the brain: Protection versus degeneration. *Biological Psychiatry, 31,* 177–199.

McEwen, B. S., Conrad, C. D., Kuroda, Y., Frankfurt, M., Magarinos, A. M., & McKittrick, C. (1997). Prevention of stress-induced morphological and cognitive consequences. *European Neuropsychopharmacology, 7*(3), 322–328.

McEwen, B. S., & Stellar, E. (1993). Stress and the individual: mechanisms leading to disease. *Archives of Internal Medicine, 153,* 2093–2101.

McFall, M. E., Murburg, M. M., Ko, G. N, & Veith, R. C. (1990). Autonomic responses to stress in Vietnam combat veterans with posttraumatic stress disorder. *Biological Psychiatry, 27,* 1165–1175.

McFall, M. E., Veith, R. C., & Murburg, M. M. (1992). Basal sympathoadrenal function in posttraumatic stress disorder. *Biological Psychiatry, 31,* 1050–1056.

McFarlane, A. C. (2000). Posttraumatic stress disorder: A model of the longitudinal course and the role of risk factors. *Journal of Clinical Psychiatry, 61*(S5), 15–20.

McGaugh, J. L. (1989). Involvement of hormonal and neuromodulatory systems in the regulation of memory storage: Endogenous modulation of memory storage. *Annual Reviews of Neuroscience, 12,* 255–287.

McGaugh, J. L., Castellano, C., & Brioni, J. (1990). Picrotoxin enhances latent extinction of conditioned fear. *Behavioral Neuroscience, 104,* 264–267.

McNally, R. J., & Shin, L. M. (1995). Association of intelligence with severity of posttraumatic stress disorders symptoms in Vietnam combat veterans. *American Journal of Psychiatry, 152,* 936–938.

Meadows, E. A., & Foa, E. B. (1999). Cognitive-behavioral treatment of traumatized adults. In P. A. Saigh & J. D. Bremner (Eds.), *Posttraumatic stress disorder: A comprehensive text* (pp. 376–390). Needham Heights, MA: Allyn & Bacon.

Meaney, M., Aitken, D., Bhatnager, S., van Berkel, C., & Sapolsky, R. (1988). Effect of neonatal handling on age-related impairments associated with the hippocampus. *Science, 239,* 766–769.

Meaney, M. J., Aitken, D. H., Sharma, S., & Sarrieau, A. (1989). Neonatal handling alters adrenocortical negative feedback sensitivity and hippocampal type II glucocorticoid receptor binding in the rat. *Neuroendocrinology, 50,* 597–604.

Mendes de Leon, C. F., Krumholz, H. M., Seeman, T. S., Vaccarino, V., Williams, C. S., Kasl, S. V., & Berkman, L. F. (1998). Depression and risk of coronary heart disease in elderly men and women: Prospective evidence from the New Haven E.P. E.S.E. *Archives of Internal Medicine, 158,* 2341–2348.

Miller, R. G. (1968). Secretion of 17-hydroxycorticosteroids (17-OHCS) in military aviators as an index of response to stress: A review. *Aerospace Medicine, 39,* 498–501.

Miller, R. G., Rubin, R. T., Clark, B. R., Crawford, W. R., & Arthur, R. J. (1970). The stress of aircraft carrier landings: I. Corticosteroid responses in naval aviators. Psychosomatic Medicine, 32, 581–588.

Morgan, C. A., Grillon, C., Southwick, S. M., Davis, M., & Charney, D. S. (1995). Fear-potentiated startle in posttraumatic stress disorder. *Biological Psychiatry, 38,* 378–385.

Morgan, M. A., & LeDoux, J. E. (1995). Differential contribution of dorsal and ventral medial prefrontal cortex to the acquisition and extinction of conditioned fear in rats. *Behavioral Neuroscience, 109,* 681–688.

Morgan, M. A., Romanski, L. M., & LeDoux, J. E. (1993). Extinction of emotional learning: Contribution of medial prefrontal cortex. *Neuroscience Letters, 163,* 109–113.

Mott, F. W. (1919). *War neuroses and shell shock.* London: Oxford University Press.

Murburg, M. M. (Ed.). (1994). *Catecholamine function in posttraumatic stress disorder: Emerging concepts.* Washington, DC: American Psychiatric Press.

Musselman, D. L., Evans, D. L., & Nemeroff, C. B. (1998). The relationship of depression to cardiovascular disease. *Archives of General Psychiatry, 55,* 580–592.

Nadel, L. & Bohbot, V. (2001). Consolidation of memory. *Hippocampus, 11,* 56–60.

Nemiah, J. C. (1998). Early concepts of trauma, dissociation, and the unconscious: Their history and current implications. In J. D. Bremner & C. R. Marmar (Eds.), *Trauma, memory, and dissociation: Progress in psychiatry* (pp. 1–26). Washington, DC: American Psychiatric Press.

Nibuya, M., Morinobu, S., & Duman, R. S. (1995). Regulation of BDNF and trkB mRNA in rat brain by chronic electroconvulsive seizure and antidepressant drug treatments. *Journal of Neuroscience, 15,* 7539–7547.

Nibuya, M., Nestler, E. J., & Duman, R. S. (1995). Chronic antidepressant administration increased the expression of cAMP response element binding protein (CREB) in rat hippocampus. *Journal of Neuroscience, 16,* 2365–2372.

Pagani, M., Mazzuero, G., Ferrare, A., Liberati, D., Cerutti, S., Vaitl, D., Tavazzi, L., & Malliani, A. (1991). Sympathovagal interaction during mental stress: A study using spectral analysis of heart rate variability in healthy control subjects and patients with a prior myocardial infarction. *Circulation, 83,* II-43–II-51.

Papez, J. W. (1937). A proposed mechanism of emotion. *American Medical Association Archives of Neurology and Psychiatry, 38,* 725–743.

Petty, F., Kramer, G., & Wilson, L. (1992). Prevention of learned helplessness: In vivo correlation with serotonin. *Pharmacology, Biochemistry and Behavior, 43,* 361–367.

Pezdek, K., & Banks, W. P. (Eds.). (1996). *The recovered memory/false memory debate.* San Diego, CA: Academic Press.

Phillips, R. G., & LeDoux, J. E. (1992). Differential contribution of amygdala and hippocampus to cued and contextual fear conditioning. *Behavioral Neuroscience, 106,* 274–285.

Pitman, R., & Orr, S. (1990). Twenty-four hour urinary cortisol and catecholamine excretion in combat-related posttraumatic stress disorder. *Biological Psychiatry, 27,* 245–247.

Pitman, R. K., Orr, S. P., Forgue, D. F., de Jong, J. B., & Claiborn, J. M. (1987). Psychophysiologic assessment of posttraumatic stress disorder imagery in Vietnam combat veterans. *Archives of General Psychiatry, 44,* 970–975.

Plotsky, P. M., & Meaney, M. J. (1993). Early, postnatal experience alters hypothalamic corticotropin-releasing factor (CRF) mRNA, median eminence CRF content and stress-induced release in adult rats. *Molecular Brain Research, 18,* 195–200.

Prigerson, H. G., Shear, M. K., Jacobs, S. C., Reynolds, C. F., Maciejewski, P. K., Davidson, J. R. T., Pilkonis, P. A., Wortman, C. B., Williams, J. B. W., Widiger, T. A., Frank, E., Kupfer, D. J., & Zisook, S. (1998). Consensus criteria for traumatic grief. *British Journal of Psychiatry, 174,* 1–7.

Putnam, F. W., Guroff, J. J., Silberman, E. K., Barban, L., & Post, R. M. (1986). The clinical phenomenology of multiple personality disorder: A review of 100 recent cases. *Journal of Clinical Psychiatry, 47,* 285–293.

Rauch, S. L., van der Kolk, B. A., Fisler, R. E., Alpert, N. A., Orr, S. P., Savage, C. R., Fischman, A. J., Jenike, M. A., & Pitman, R. K. (1996). A symptom provocation study of posttraumatic stress disorder using positron emission tomography and script-driven imagery. *Archives of General Psychiatry, 53,* 380–387.

Resnick, H. S., Yehuda, R., Pitman, R. K., & Foy, D. W. (1995). Effect of previous trauma on acute plasma cortisol level following rape. *American Journal of Psychiatry, 152,* 1675–1677.

Roediger, H. L., & McDermott, K. B. (1995). Creating false memories: Remembering words not presented in lists. *Journal of Experimental Psychology: Learning, Memory & Cognition, 21,* 803–814.

Romanski, L. M., & LeDoux, J. E. (1993). Information cascade from primary auditory cortex to the amygdala: Corticocortical and corticoamygdaloid projections of temporal cortex in the rat. *Cerebral Cortex, 3,* 515–532.

Rose, R. M., Poe, R. O., & Mason, J. W. (1968). Psychological state and body size as determinants of 17-OHCS excretion. *Archives of Internal Medicine, 121,* 406–413.

Rosen, J. B., & Davis, M. (1988). Enhancement of acoustic startle by electrical stimulation of the amygdala. *Behavioral Neurosciences, 102,* 195–202.

Ross, C. A. (2000). *The trauma model: A solution to the problem of co-morbidity in psychiatry.* Richardson, TX: Manitou Publications.

Ross, C. A., Joshi, S., & Currie, R. (1990). Dissociative experiences in the general population. *American Journal of Psychiatry, 147,* 1547–1552.

Rozanski, A., Blumenthal, J. A., & Kaplan, J. (1999). Impact of psychological factors on the pathogenesis of cardiovascular disease and implications for therapy. *Circulation, 99,* 2192–2217.

Rubin, R. T., Rahe, R. H., Arthur, R. J., & Clark, B. R. (1969). Adrenal cortical activity changes during underwater demolition team training. *Psychosomatic Medicine, 31,* 553–564.

Saigh, P. A., & Bremner, J. D. (1999a). The history of posttraumatic stress disorder. In P. A. Saigh & J. D. Bremner (Eds.), *Posttraumatic stress disorder: A comprehensive text* (pp. 1–17). Needham Heights, MA: Allyn & Bacon.

Saigh, P. A., & Bremner, J. D. (Eds.). (1999b). *Posttraumatic stress disorder: A comprehensive text.* Needham Heights, MA: Allyn & Bacon.

Sapolsky, R. M. (1996). Why stress is bad for your brain. *Science, 273,* 749–750.

Sapolsky, R. M., Packan, D. R., & Vale, W. W. (1988). Glucocorticoid toxicity in the hippocampus: In vitro demonstration. *Brain Research, 453,* 367–371.

Sapolsky, R. M., & Pulsinelli, W. (1985). Glucocorticoids potentiate ischemic injury to neurons: Therapeutic implications. *Science, 229,* 1397–1400.

Sapolsky, R. M., Uno, H., Rebert, C. S., & Finch, C. E. (1990). Hippocampal damage associated with prolonged glucocorticoid exposure in primates. *Journal of Neuroscience, 10,* 2897–2902.

Sargent, W., & Slater, E. (1941). Amnesic syndromes in war. *Proceedings of the Royal Society of Medicine, 34,* 757–674.

Sass, K. J., Sass, A., Westerveld, M., Lencz, T., Novelly, R. A., Kim, J. H., & Spencer, D. D. (1992). Specificity in the correlation of verbal memory and hippocampal neuron loss: Dissociation of memory, language, and verbal intellectual ability. *Journal of Clinical and Experimental Neuropsychology, 14,* 662–672.

Sass, K. J., Spencer, D. D., Kim, J. H., Westerveld, M., Novelly, R. A., & Lencz, T. (1990). Verbal memory impairment correlates with hippocampal pyramidal cell density. *Neurology, 40,* 1694–1697.

Schacter, D. L., Coyle, J. T., Fischbach, G. D., Mesulam, M. M., & Sullivan, L. E. (Eds.). (1995). *Memory distortion: The brain, the mind, and the past.* Cambridge, MA: Harvard University Press.

Schlenger, W. E., Fairbank, J. A., Jordan, B. K., & Caddell, J. M. (1999). Combat-related posttraumatic stress disorder: Prevalence, risk factors, and comorbidity. In P. A. Saigh & J. D. Bremner (Eds.), *Posttraumatic stress disorder: A comprehensive text* (pp. 69–91). Needham Heights, MA: Allyn & Bacon.

Schooler, J. W. (1994). Seeking the core: The issues and evidence surrounding recovered memories of sexual trauma. *Consciousness and Cognition, 3,* 452–469.

Scoville, W. B., & Milner, B. (1957). Loss of recent memory after bilateral hippocampal lesions. *Journal of Neurology Neurosurgery and Psychiatry, 20,* 11–21.

Seeman, T. E., Berkman, L. F., Gulanski, B. I., Robbins, R. J., Greenspan, S. L., Charpentier, P., & Rowe, J. W. (1995). Self esteem and neuroendocrine response to challenge: Macarthur studies of successful aging. *Journal of Psychosomatic Research, 39,* 69–84.

Seeman, T. E., Singer, B. H., Rowe, J. W., Horwitz, R. I., & McEwen, B. S. (1997). Price of adaptation—allostatic load and its health consequences. MacArthur studies of successful aging. *Archives of Internal Medicine, 157*(19), 2259–2268.

Shalev, A. Y., Peri, T., Canetti, L., & Schreiber, S. (1996). Predictors of PTSD in injured trauma survivors: A prospective study. *American Journal of Psychiatry, 153,* 219–225.

Shay, J. (1994). *Achilles and Vietnam: Combat trauma and the undoing of character.* New York: Atheneum.

Shay, J., & Munroe, J. (1999). Group and milieu therapy for veterans with complex posttraumatic stress disorder. In P. A. Saigh & J. D. Bremner (Eds.), *Posttraumatic stress disorder: A comprehensive text* (pp. 391–413). Needham Heights, MA: Allyn & Bacon.

Sheline, Y., Wang, P., Gado, M., Csernansky, J., & Vannier, M. (1996). Hippocampal atrophy in major depression. *Proceedings of the National Academy of Sciences: USA, 93,* 3908–3913.

Sherman, A. D., & Petty, F. (1982). Additivity of neurochemical changes in learned helplessness and imipramine. *Behavioral Neurology and Biology, 35,* 344–353.

Shin, L. M., Kosslyn, S. M., McNally, R. J., Alpert, N. M., Thompson, W. L., Rauch, S. L., Macklin, M. L., & Pitman, R. K. (1997). Visual imagery and perception in posttraumatic stress disorder: A positron emission tomographic investigation. *Archives of General Psychiatry, 54,* 233–237.

Smith, M. A., Davidson, J., Ritchie, J. C., Kudler, H., Lipper, S., Chappell, P., & Nemeroff, C. B. (1989). The corticotropin-releasing hormone test in patients with posttraumatic stress disorder. *Biological Psychiatry, 26,* 349–355.

Smith, M. A., Makino, S., Kvetnansky, R., & Post, R. M. (1995). Stress and glucocorticoids affect the expression of brain-derived neurotrophic factor and neurotrophin-3 mRNA in the hippocampus. *Journal of Neuroscience, 15,* 1768–1777.

Solomon, Z., Garb, K., Bleich, A., & Grupper, D. (1987). Reactivation of combat related posttraumatic stress disorder. *American Journal of Psychiatry, 144,* 51–55.

Soufer, R., Bremner, J. D., Arrighi, J. A., Cohen, I., Zaret, B. L., Burg, M. M., & Goldman-Rakic, P. (1998). Cerebral cortical hyperactivation in response to mental stress in patients with coronary artery disease. *Proceedings of the National Academy of Sciences, 95,* 6454–6459.

Southwick, S. M., Krystal, J. H., Bremner, J. D., Morgan, C. A., Nicolaou, A., Nagy, L. M., Johnson, D. R., Heninger, G. R., & Charney, D. S. (1997). Noradrenergic and serotonergic function in posttraumatic stress disorder. *Archives of General Psychiatry, 54,* 749–758.

Southwick, S. M., Krystal, J. H., Morgan, C. A., Johnson, D., Nagy, L. M., Nicolaou, A., Heninger, G. R., & Charney, D. S. (1993). Abnormal noradrenergic function in posttraumatic stress disorder. *Archives of General Psychiatry, 50,* 266–274.

Spiegel, D. (Ed.) (1994). *Dissociation: Culture, mind, and body.* Washington, DC: American Psychiatric Press.

Spiegel, D., & Cardena, E. (1991). Disintegrated experience: The dissociative disorders revisited. *Journal of Abnormal Psychology, 100,* 366–378.

Spiegel, D., Hunt, T., & Dondershine, H. E. (1988). Dissociation and hypnotizability in posttraumatic stress disorder. *American Journal of Psychiatry, 145,* 301–305.

Squire, L. R., & Zola-Morgan, S. (1991). The medial temporal lobe memory system. *Science, 253,* 1380–1386.

Stein, M. B., Koverola, C., Hanna, C., Torchia, M.G., & McClarty, B. (1997). Hippocampal volume in women victimized by childhood sexual abuse. *Psychological Medicine, 27,* 951–959.

Steinberg, M. J., Rounsaville, B., & Cicchetti, D. V. (1990). The structured clinical interview for DSM-III-R dissociative disorders: Preliminary report on a new diagnostic instrument. *American Journal of Psychiatry, 147,* 76–82.

Sutherland, S. M., & Davidson, J. R. T. (1999). Pharmacological treatment of posttraumatic stress disorder. In P. A. Saigh & J. D. Bremner (Eds.), *Posttraumatic stress disorder: A comprehensive text* (pp. 327–353). Needham Heights, MA: Allyn & Bacon.

Thygesen, P., Hermann, K., & Willanger, R. (1970). Concentration camp survivors in Denmark: Persecution, disease, compensation. *Danish Medical Bulletin, 17,* 65–108.

Torrie, A. (1944). Psychosomatic casualties in the Middle East. *Lancet, 29,* 139–143.

True, W. R., Rice, J., Eisen, S. A., Heath, A. C., Goldberg, J., Lyons, M. J., & Nowak, J. (1993). A twin study of genetic and environmental contributions to liability for posttraumatic stress disorder symptoms. *Archives of General Psychiatry, 50,* 257–264.

Uno, H., Tarara, R., Else, J. G., Suleman, M. A., & Sapolsky, R. M. (1989). Hippocampal damage associated with prolonged and fatal stress in primates. *Journal of Neuroscience, 9,* 1705–1711.

Vaidya, V. A., Marek, G. J., Aghajanian, G. K., & Duman, R. S. (1997). 5HT-2A receptor-mediated regulation of brain-derived neurotrophic factor mRNA in the hippocampus and the neocortex. *Journal of Neuroscience, 17,* 2785–2795.

van der Kolk, B. A., Dreyfuss, D., Michaels, M., Shera, D., Berkowitz, R., Fisher, R., & Saxe, G. (1994). Fluoxetine in posttraumatic stress disorder. *Journal of Clinical Psychiatry, 146,* 517–222.

van der Kolk, B. A., Greenberg, M. S., Orr, S. P., & Pitman, R. K. (1989). Endogenous opiates, stress induced analgesia, and posttraumatic stress disorder. *Psychopharmacology Bulletin, 25,* 417–421.

Virgin, C. E., Taryn, P. T. H., Packan, D. R., Tombaugh, G. C., Yang, S. H., Horner, H. C., & Sapolsky, R. M. (1991). Glucocorticoids inhibit glucose transport and glutamate uptake in hippocampal astrocytes: Implications for glucocorticoid neurotoxicity. *Journal of Neurochemistry, 57,* 1422–1428.

Vogt, B. A., Finch, D. M., & Olson, C. R. (1992). Functional heterogeneity in cingulate cortex: The anterior executive and posterior evaluative regions. *Cerebral Cortex, 2,* 435–443.

Watanabe, Y. E., Gould, H., Cameron, D., Daniels, D., & McEwen, B. S. (1992). Phenytoin prevents stress and corticosterone induced atrophy of CA3 pyramidal neurons. *Hippocampus, 2,* 431–436.

Watanabe, Y., Sakai, R. R., McEwen, B. S., & Mendelson, S. (1993). Stress and antidepressant effects on hippocampal and cortical 5HT1A and 5HT2 receptors and transport sites for serotonin. *Brain Research, 615,* 87–94.

Weiss, J. M., Simson, P. G., Ambrose, M. J., Webster, A., & Hoffman, L. J. (1985). Neurochemical basis of behavioral depression. *Advances in Behavioral Medicine, 1,* 233–275.

Williams, L. M. (1994). Recall of childhood trauma: A prospective study of women's memories of child sexual abuse. *Journal of Consulting and Clinical Psychology, 62,* 1167–1176.

Williams, L. M., & Banyard, V. L. (Eds.) (1999). *Trauma and memory.* Thousand Oaks, CA: Sage Publications.

Williamson, G. A. (transl.). (1981). *Josephus: The Jewish war.* London: Penguin Books.

Winnicott, D. W. (1988). *Human nature.* New York: Shocken Books.

Winograd, E., & Neisser, U. (1992). Affect and accuracy in recall: Studies of *"flashbulb memories."* New York: Cambridge University Press.

Woolley, C. S., Gould, E., & McEwen, B. S. (1990). Exposure to excess glucocorticoids alters dendritic morphology of adult hippocampal pyramidal neurons. *Brain Research, 531,* 225–231.

Yehuda, R., Keefer, R. S. E., Harvey, P. D., Levengood, R. A., Gerber, D. K., Geni, J., & Siever, L. J. (1995). Learning and memory in combat veterans with posttraumatic stress disorder. *American Journal of Psychiatry, 152,* 137–139.

Yehuda, R., Lowy, M. T., Southwick, S. M., Shaffer, S., & Giller, E. L. (1991). Increased number of glucocorticoid receptor number in posttraumatic stress disorder. *American Journal of Psychiatry, 149,* 499–504.

Yehuda, R., Resnick, H. S., Schmeidler, J., Yang, R.-K., & Pitman, R. K. (1998). Predictors of cortisol and 3-methoxy-4-hydroxyphenylglycol responses in the acute aftermath of rape. *Biological Psychiatry, 43,* 855–859.

Yehuda, R., Southwick, S. M., Krystal, J. H., Bremner, J. D., Charney, D. S., & Mason, J. W. (1993). Enhanced suppression of cortisol with low dose dexamethasone in posttraumatic stress disorder. *American Journal of Psychiatry, 150,* 83–86.

Yehuda, R., Southwick, S. M., Nussbaum, E. L., Giller, E. L., & Mason, J. W. (1991). Low urinary cortisol in PTSD. *Journal of Nervous and Mental Disease, 178,* 366–369.

Zola-Morgan, S. M., & Squire, L. R. (1990). The primate hippocampal formation: Evidence for a time-limited role in memory storage. *Science, 250,* 288–290.

INDEX

Italic numbers denote illustrations.

norepinephrine (*continued*)
and long-term dysregulation, 107
and memory, 104
as neurotransmitter, 41
PET studies, 105–6
and PTSD, 88–90
repeated exposure, 87
and startle response, 81

obsessive-compulsive disorder, 161
O'Conner, F. L., 93
Olson, C. R., 49
opiates, endogenous, 7, 93
orbitofrontal cortex, *44*, 45, 48, 70
orientation, 46–47, 49
Orr, S. P., 88, 93, 125
Ostroff, R. B., 92
Owen, Wilfred, 3
Owens, M. J., 91

Packan, D. R., 109
Pagani, M., 272
Page, W., 269
pain, 7, 93
panic attacks, 35, 161
Papez, J. W., 75–76
paroxetine (Paxil), 41, 93, 119,
251–54
pathological conditioned responding,
189–90
Peri, T., 205
personality disorders, 201, 261
Petty, F., 93
Pezdek, K., 236
phenylzine, 251
phenytoin (Dilantin), 119–20, 254
Phillips, R. G., 61
physicians, 274–76
Pitman, R., 88, 93, 103, 124, 125,
128, 264
pituitary gland, 49, 91
planning, 49
platelets, 9, 11, 271
Plotsky, P. M., 91
pneumoencephalography, 59–60
Podd, L., 92
Poe, R. O., 91
positron emission tomography (PET),
51, 52, 57–59, 62–63
and norepinephrine, 105–6
and PTSD patients, *89–90*
Post, R. M., 110, 202

powerlessness, 146–47, 217
prefrontal cortex, *44, 133*
actions, 48, 131–34
and evolution, 45
medial, 131–34
neuron growth, 43
and trauma disorders, 37
see also medial prefrontal cortex
Price, J. L., 48, 240
Prigerson, H. G., 179
Prins, A., 88
Prins, B., 49–50
propanolol, 106
psychoanalysis, 15–16, 27, 29–30,
217
PTSD
brain sites, 60–62, 63
chronicity, 244
and cortisol, 91–92
diagnosis, 20–21, 81, 84
and genetics, 64–66, 152
and heart disease, 11–13
and hyperarousal, 178
incidence, 19, 128, 145–46, 180
and memory, 20, 32, 73, 103–14, x
nature *versus* nurture, 97–100
neural circuitry, *133*
and norepinephrine, 88–90
PET visualization, 89–90
prevention, 173
risk factors, 126, 128–29, 147–55,
203–5
severity, 153–54, 181–82
and smoking, 9–10
symptoms, 10, 20–21, 189–98
Pulsinelli, W., 109
Putnam, F. W., 202, 203
Putnam, T., 203

radioactivity, 52–53, 57
Rahe, R. H., 91
Randall, P. R., 61, 115, 116, 117
rape victims, 124–25, 262–63
Rauch, S. L., 134
Read, J. D., 235
reexperiencing, 178, 191–93
Reis, D. J., 94
relationships, 224–25
residual stress theory, 83, 150
resiliency, 84, 155–57
Resnick, H. S., 124, 125
rhinencephalon, 76–77

J. DOUGLAS BREMNER, M.D., is Associate Professor of Psychiatry and Radiology and Director of the Emory Center for Positron Emission Tomography at Emory University School of Medicine in Atlanta, Georgia, and Director of Mental Health Research at the Atlanta VAMC in Decatur, Georgia. He has authored over 150 publications, and written or edited three books, most recently *Brain Imaging Handbook*.